50¢

Ten things you can do TO STAY ALIVE when your brain is trying to kill you:

RELEASE **A**NGER SAFELY

CALL 1-800-**S**UICIDE

SIMPLE TAS**K**S & ACTIVITIES

PRAY **F**OR RELIEF

KEEP Y**O**URSELF SAFE

FOLLOW A C**R**ISIS PLAN

HOLD ON TO **H**OPE

GO TO THE **E**MERGENCY ROOM

CAL**L** A FRIEND

FIND COM**P**ANIONSHIP

See inside for more insight, guidance, advice, and hope. Read on, and know you can *stay alive when your brain is trying to kill you.*

Robert L. Blauner

About the Author

SUSAN ROSE BLAUNER lives on Cape Cod. She is active with national suicide prevention organizations, speaks at high schools and colleges, presents at mental health conferences, and is developing a multimedia prevention program. Susan survived eighteen years of suicidal ideation; she has been diagnosed with borderline personality disorder, posttraumatic stress disorder, and major depression. She creates sanctuary in her life through art, music, people, nature, spirituality, service, and inner vision, all supported by boundless faith, determination, and resilience.

How I Stayed Alive
When My Brain Was
Trying to Kill Me

Quill

An Imprint of HarperCollins*Publishers*

How I Stayed Alive

When My Brain Was

Trying to Kill Me

ONE PERSON'S GUIDE TO
SUICIDE PREVENTION

SUSAN ROSE BLAUNER

A percentage of all royalties from the sale of this book will be donated to The National Hope-line Network (1-800-SUICIDE) in support of their work toward suicide prevention.

The contents of this book are based on the author's own experiences with suicidal thoughts, and her research into avenues of help available to the suicidal thinker. The information given herein is intended to help the suicidal thinker and his/her loved ones, and is not intended as a substitute for professional treatment. If you are experiencing suicidal thoughts, we urge you to seek help from a psychiatric professional and/or call 1-800-SUICIDE.

Discussion of medication in this book is based solely on the personal experiences of the author, who is not a medical professional. There are many medications available, and each has its benefits and side effects. Never take any medication without a prescription from a medical professional.

Page 303 constitutes a continuation of this copyright page.

A hardcover edition of this book was published in 2002 by William Morrow, an imprint of HarperCollins Publishers.

HOW I STAYED ALIVE WHEN MY BRAIN WAS TRYING TO KILL ME. Copyright © 2002 by Susan Rose Blauner. Foreword copyright © 2002 by Bernard S. Siegel. All rights reserved. Printed in the United States of America. No part of this book may be used or reproduced in any manner whatsoever without written permission except in the case of brief quotations embodied in critical articles and reviews. For information address HarperCollins Publishers Inc., 10 East 53rd Street, New York, NY 10022.

HarperCollins books may be purchased for educational, business, or sales promotional use. For information please write: Special Markets Department, HarperCollins Publishers Inc., 10 East 53rd Street, New York, NY 10022.

First Quill edition published 2003.

Designed by Gretchen Achilles

The Library of Congress has catalogued the hardcover edition as follows:

Blauner, Susan Rose.
   How I stayed alive when my brain was trying to kill me : one person's guide to suicide
prevention / Susan Rose Blauner.—1st ed.
       p. cm.
   Includes bibliographical references and index.
   ISBN 0-06-621121-2
       1. Suicide—Prevention. 2. Suicidal behavior—Prevention. I. Title.
   RC569 .B585 2002
   362.28'7—dc21

                                                                            2001051388

ISBN 0-06-093621-5 (pbk.)

03 04 05 06 07 ❖/RRD 10 9 8 7 6 5 4 3 2 1

To you

I thank all who have been my legs when I could not walk and my eyes

when I could not see, but most of all I thank Sylvia,

for teaching me how to be a person on this planet

Then a woman said,

Speak to us of Joy and Sorrow.

And he answered:

Your joy is your sorrow unmasked.

And the selfsame well from which your laughter rises
was oftentimes filled with your tears.

And how else can it be?

The deeper that sorrow carves into your being,
the more joy you can contain.

Is not the cup that holds your wine the
very cup that was burned in the potter's oven?

—KAHLIL GIBRAN, *The Prophet*

Welcome

I welcome you into this moment, where change is at your fingertips. Change, one of the most challenging things for humankind to embrace. Yet when we embrace it, great reward can be found.

I welcome your sorrow and your pain. I welcome your humor, imagination, and joy. I welcome your mind. I welcome you as you are, for only when we accept our present can we begin to change our future.

How I Stayed Alive When My Brain Was Trying to Kill Me is meant to be read slowly, with intention. There is a lot of information between the covers of this book. If you try to take it in all at once, you'll be wallpapering your living room with all the lists and charts I give you to post. Pick and choose. Take what you like and leave the rest.

If you feel overwhelmed or pushed while reading, take a break, take a breath, and find something nice to do. If you feel like throwing the book across the room, throw it. I won't mind. I only hope that you return to it, for I am here for you, just as others were there for me. I care about you and how you are.

I welcome you into this moment of life. Like any moment, it contains endless possibilities and limitless choices—regardless of how we feel or what we think. I can honestly say that because of the choices I made, the depth of my pain has been filled with contentment. I live, feeling everything—difficult and easy—but I live in peace. I no longer wish to die.

I welcome you into this moment of *my* life. In a short while you will know more about me than most of the people I see every day. I know for certain that part of my destiny was to write this book. Perhaps part of yours is to read it. I wish you well as you do.

—SUSAN BLAUNER, *June 2001*

Foreword

My personal experience with death comes from my family and years as a physician. As the years have gone by I consider living difficult and dying easy. I see many people use their disease as a convenient way to commit suicide, and perhaps that is why so many young people today consider suicide as their treatment of choice. Yet I wonder if they ever consider the fact that they are choosing to kill someone while wounding many others. One of our sons is an FBI agent and he was asked if he could kill someone as part of his training. Perhaps to protect the lives of my loved ones I could, but even then I find it a difficult question to answer. A teenager I know was contemplating suicide after being physically, psychologically, and sexually abused by his parents. He was HIV-positive and ready to jump in front of a subway train. I wondered why he chose to kill himself rather than the people who were destroying his life. When I asked him, he responded, "I never wanted to be like them."

I think that when you don't know what to do with your pain and are feeling unloved, suicide seems like a better choice than life. As one of our sons e-mailed to me one day, "Life sucks, most people suck, and if you wake up one day and everyone loves you and the weather is beautiful, you're dead." That gets a laugh when I read it, but I'm afraid there is a lot of truth in it.

We are born beautiful creations and then run into parents, teachers, and religious leaders, all of whom have the potential to make us feel unworthy and defective. We have to remember that, as authority figures, we can kill with words when they become wordswordswords . . . swords. It is an exceptional child who grows up loved and feeling like a child of God. When you do, you care for yourself in a way the unloved do not. Their addictions and destructive behavior are searches for the feeling of being loved, a feeling they never had.

Because of this childhood experience stored within us we think we are the problem and suicide is a way of ending our problem. At workshops I ask people to tell me their favorite animal and why it is their favorite. What would your answer be? One woman said, "I hate pets and killed my canary," and I knew she was talking about herself and might destroy herself as well. Another young woman said, "I am here to decide whether to commit suicide or not. My favorite animal is an eagle." By the time she had finished describing the beauty of an eagle soaring through the sky, she said, "I have decided not to commit suicide."

We need to understand that he who seeks to save his life will lose it. We give up our lives to please others and we die inside. When you develop a life-threatening illness or just accept your mortality, you may come to realize that he who is willing to lose his life will save it. You give up the life that was killing you and start living your true life. Then you will outlive any expectations related to your disease, and often you will heal physically and psychologically. What this teaches me is that the suicidal need to learn to eliminate what is killing them from their lives and not kill themselves. My New York friend Carmine says if something is killing you—your job, marriage, or anything else—eliminate it from your life. But if it isn't a threat to your health, then ask how love could change the situation and solve the problem.

The pain of depression and despair can build enough heat to melt the lead walls surrounding you. The darkness of charcoal, under pressure, can turn into a diamond. We need to realize blessings come in many strange shapes and sizes, and if we are willing to learn from our pain, then suicide is not on the list of options. The son I quoted above once said to me, "If you write another book about how to deal with life's difficulties call it *Holy Shit*." I agree with him and think that when we learn to use the compost of life to fertilize new growth we do not kill ourselves but are reborn to life and its labor pains. I know how easy it is to get high school students to write suicide notes and how hard it is for them to write notes about why they are lovable. I never considered suicide because of how I was parented, but I know the majority of people have—including many self-help experts and authors. For me it seemed a better idea to just go out and have fun. Be a clown and embarrass everyone rather than destroy myself. But that's me and my upbringing.

I was born an ugly duckling, but had a grandmother who had no problem loving me while my mother was trying to hide me from the neighbors. It is not an easy thing to do to find your own beauty as the ugly duckling did, but if everyone had a loving grandparent available, the suicide rate would plummet. I received a phone call one day asking me for Jack Kevorkian's phone number; the young lady on the line had been abused, had a brain tumor, and wanted to die. I told her she was a child of God and I wanted her to send me some drawings of herself. Nine years later she is still alive and feeling loved. Remember that we can all be a CD or CM for those in pain—a Chosen Dad or a Chosen Mom—someone who loves them even if we don't like what they are doing or thinking.

When you realize that those who admit they are suicidal really get our attention, you begin to see it is their way of filling the space devoid of love. The opposite of love is not hate but indifference. So keep on loving until the person you are loving feels that he or she is worth loving thanks to your persistent love and attention.

You can help by maintaining connections. Get a pet who will teach you about love and the meaning of life. Accept the darkness but also see the light around it that is a part of your life. Start to change by acting as if you are the person you want to be. When you are in a dark place, ask yourself: What would Lassie do now? Or, What would Lucille Ball do now? I know several lives that were saved by people doing that simple thing. Become a child again and live.

When a policeman I know called to tell me he was going to commit suicide, I said, "Jimmy, if you kill yourself I'll never talk to you again." He showed up in my office twenty minutes later, mad at me for being so insensitive. He said he had a gun in his mouth and I said something stupid. I pointed out that he hadn't killed himself and he is still alive today because the child in me responded to his pain.

So be a survivor. Ask for help. Get your baby pictures out and look at them. Realize we are all here for a limited time, so use it and live your chocolate ice cream. Remember that we need not information but inspiration to survive. If you don't inspire, you expire. So find meaning and inspiration and a way to serve the world and contribute love to it. We are not here to be served but to serve and to offer our bodies for the benefit of others in the way we choose to contribute.

I know a woman who learned she had cancer, was fired from her job, and had her husband tell her he wanted a divorce all in one day. She sipped a glass of wine and planned a leap from her tenth-story window. A friend had given her one of my tapes, which she put on. She said, "It made me laugh and it made me cry and so I decided to live." That is what life is about, and when others are crying, show them compassion and you will heal your life too. Love and laughter are the bricks we build our lives out of and the mortar that cements them together.

Remember that life is not a problem to be solved but a mystery to be lived. Read on and learn how to live the mystery from the experience and wisdom expressed in this book. We love you. Learn from our pain in a way that only natives can understand and because of their experience help each other in a way that tourists never could.

To summarize, "Be what you is and not what you ain't, 'cause if you is what you ain't, you ain't what you is." Let Susan's book and experience help you to become what you is.

BERNIE S. SIEGEL, M.D., author of *Love, Medicine & Miracles* and *Prescriptions for Living*

Editor's Note:
Why This Book Matters to *Me*

Before the proposal for *How I Stayed Alive When My Brain Was Trying to Kill Me* landed on my desk, I received a phone call from Sue's agent. She said something like, "Hello, Jennifer, you don't know me, but I think I have a project that might be right for you." *Now*, I thought, *how many times have I heard* that?

She said somewhat tentatively, "I've heard that you lost a brother to, um, suicide." Well, yes, I had. My brother Christopher killed himself in June 1993.

My brother's suicide is no secret. Although it has had a profound effect on my daily existence and I think about it often, it does not *define* me, nor does it impede my living. That distinction is important, because many suicidal thinkers romanticize the aftereffects of their suicide, envisioning how their survivors will go on—in guilt or anguish or love. My family and I *have* gone on, and we are fine, and I wish to God my brother was here to share the joys and sorrows of everyday life as I experience it—as *he* could have experienced it.

A day later the proposal was sitting on my desk. Eighteen neatly typed pages of what could be, I thought, one of the most powerful, hard-hitting, and *hopeful* books that I'd ever read on the subject of suicide. Something spoke to me in Sue's short yet eloquent proposal. That declaration: "It's a feeling, and feelings pass, and if you talk to me, I'll help you get through it, just like I did." And so today we have this book.

Why this note? Well, Sue and I have shared a lot of our feelings about suicide over the past year or so, albeit from different sides of the fence; we both agreed that my perspective is an important one to include. Through this book, Sue has helped me come to terms with

many of the unresolved emotional conflicts I harbor about Chris's suicide. As I've said to her, I wish I'd had this book a decade ago.

In anticipation of writing this note, I dug out my "Chris" file for
the first time since his death. This is what I found:

- Numerous letters from our family that Chris had kept, including
  one that our brother Ben wrote to him in 1983, saying in part: "It
  may sound corny, but you're all a brother could ever want in an
  older brother."

- Computer disks with Chris's poetry and various writings.

- The suicide notes—one to our parents and one to his siblings.

- The order of service leaflet from his funeral.

- A letter from the funeral home thanking us for our "patronage."

- Correspondence with insurance companies, doctors, the ceme-
  tery, the IRS. (*They* don't forget you when you're gone.)

- The deed to Chris's burial plot.

- The death certificate.

And so what do I have? Paper, photos, mementos, words—artifacts, carefully preserved, of a wonderful life, beautifully, painfully
lived. I'm thankful to have these artifacts, but they aren't enough.
Chris is still dead. Thirty years old with a bullet through his head.

On the morning of the funeral my siblings and I went to the
funeral home. We asked if we could see our brother to say good-bye,
and a soft-spoken woman said no, we couldn't—wouldn't want to—see
his face. But wait, she said, and went into the room where his coffin lay
waiting to be taken to the church. When she returned, she allowed us
to approach the casket; she'd very kindly opened the bottom half. Each

of us was able to touch his hands. I often try to recall the last time I saw my brother's face. I hate to admit it, but I can't. It was probably one of those innocuous occasions we all take for granted. But whenever it was, I didn't know it was the last time.

I ask myself often, could I have done anything to prevent Chris's death? Maybe *I* couldn't have, but *Chris* could have—if he had had knowledge and straight-talking affirmation from someone like Sue who has endured the agony that he suffered. I could not understand what he meant when he told me, "It hurts me to live." I did not know what to say. But Sue does. That's why this book means so much to me: Sue gives me a voice, an understanding I wish I had had years ago, a voice I wish my brother Chris had heard eight years ago.

A wise man who knew and admired Chris said he thought my brother had suffered a "brain attack" at the moment he pulled the trigger—that Chris wouldn't have done it if he'd thought it through. At the time I thought this man (who later became my father-in-law) was being simplistic. But now I think he was right. If Chris had had a Crisis Plan, if he had really considered the realities of suicide and its aftermath—if he had waited *five damn minutes*—I don't think he would have pulled the trigger. Therein lies the tragedy.

And herein lies the hope. Whoever you are—a suicidal thinker, a family member or friend of someone who is considering suicide—please read this book and take it to heart, and know that you *can* stay alive when your brain is trying to kill you.

—JENNIFER BREHL, *August 2001*

Contents

If you need immediate assistance, please call
1-800-784-2433 • 1-800-SUICIDE

THREE

TRICKS OF THE TRADE

PART ONE

So You Think You Want To Die?

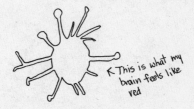

Journal drawing, 1994

Change often occurs when we are ready to give up.

—ANONYMOUS

Hello

Congratulations. Your lungs are breathing, your fingers are touching these pages, and your eyes are reading these words. At this very moment the part of you wanting life is stronger than the part of you that thinks it doesn't—otherwise you wouldn't be reading this book. Let me repeat that: *At this very moment the part of you wanting life is stronger than the part of you that thinks it doesn't—otherwise you wouldn't be reading this book.* Every word, belief, and idea it contains is dedicated to you.

I wish I could make your suicidal thoughts disappear, but I can't. What I *can* do is teach you how to get through those excruciating moments when every cell in your brain and body is screaming, "I want to die!" By surviving those moments unharmed and learning new ways of coping, you will gradually create a set of tools that can make life more manageable. Suicidal thoughts will occur less frequently and with less severity.

The thing to remember is change takes time and practice. Fortunately, you'll have plenty of time to practice. The good news is that practice and repetition can make these skills a part of you, and that increases your chances of getting rid of suicidal thoughts altogether.

How I Stayed Alive When My Brain Was Trying to Kill Me is based on the following beliefs:

1. Most suicidal thinkers don't want to die; they just want their feelings to change or go away.

2. Every single feeling we experience eventually *does* change—with or without any help from us. They never stay the same or at the same intensity.

3. Feelings and thoughts are just electrochemical impulses in the brain.

4. It is possible to *outthink* the brain, actively change feelings and eventually eliminate suicidal thoughts.

5. The reality of suicide is far different from the fantasy. Most suicidal thinkers romanticize their death by suicide, failing to realize that any suicide gesture or attempt can result in permanent brain, kidney, or liver damage, loss of limbs, blindness, or even death.

When I was fourteen, I never thought I'd live to be twenty-one. Ironically, I didn't make my first major suicide gesture until I was twenty-five, one year *after* I found Sylvia, the therapist who helped me save my life. In the years following the 1991 overdose, I was locked in a psychiatric ward three times; wound up in the intensive-care unit twice; and made two more big suicide gestures—an overdose in 1992 and another in 1998. During the eighteen years I had suicidal thoughts, I experienced the excruciating "I want to die" moment thousand of times and did my best to destroy my life. Fortunately, I did not succeed.

The brain has a mind of its own, particularly when it's trying to kill you. It can say nasty things, based not in reality but in old patterns, fears, and intensified emotion. Since most suicidal thinkers don't want to die—what they want is relief from emotional pain—it's important to stay alive and healthy *long enough* to find the relief that's out there (and inside of you). To stay alive and healthy I had to develop new coping skills and philosophies. These tools I affectionately named "Tricks of the Trade." They've saved my butt countless times. I hope to teach you these tricks in part 3, leaving room for your own creative imagination.

Even if a person calls for help after making a suicide gesture (like I did) or leaves a clue so that he or she will be found before the suicide is complete, what most of us fail to realize is that we might *not* be found. We might wind up losing a limb or the use of a limb. We might wind up with brain damage, paralysis, or internal injury. We might even wind up dead.

One thing I finally got after ten years of therapy was it's okay to have suicidal thoughts, just don't act on them. They are *just thoughts*. Instead of feeling isolated or ashamed for having them, I had to acknowledge my suicidal thoughts, look beneath them at the feelings, and find a healthy way to address the feelings in order to diminish the thoughts. I had to grasp the notion that *all* thoughts are temporary— even suicidal ones—just as *all* feelings are temporary.

Letting go of suicide was the hardest thing I've ever had to do. It took hard work and determination, but if I can do it, anyone can. If you don't believe me, simply borrow some of my strength and belief in you. I had to borrow other people's strength and belief in me for years. Now I have plenty for myself with extra to lend.

That's not to say my road to healing was smooth and straight. I battled for years, ripped with despair and loneliness. Often my brain held me hostage and tried to convince me that I was pathetic, useless, and unloved, and that ending my life was the only solution. It was wrong.

If you feel resistance while reading this book, that's a good sign, and it's perfectly natural. It means something good and new is sinking into your brain. When I am starting to change a part of my psyche, my brain sometimes feels threatened. Resistance can take the form of fatigue, headaches, shallow breathing, distraction, a sense of being overwhelmed, tight shoulders, a swimmy head, a squirmy stomach, a "what's the use" message from the brain. If any of this happens to you, take a deep breath and read on, or take a break and do something nice for yourself.

IF RESISTANCE GETS TOO STRONG:

1. Find some way to get it out of your body:

   - Take a look at the Tasks and Activities List on p. 143 and find a few things to do.

   - Write or draw about the resistance—let it out, even if what you create makes no immediate sense, even if it's lines on paper, boxes, circles, or splotches of color.

   - Tell your brain to leave you alone: "Leave me alone! I can do this."

   - Exercise or call a friend.

2. Then return to the book in about twenty minutes.

Remember, the fact that you feel resistance is a good sign. It means your brain is starting to squirm, because you're taking steps to out-think it.

I continued to romanticize my death by suicide long after I discovered how to outthink suicidal thoughts. The fantasy of killing myself remained strong because it was a habit, an addiction. I spent hundreds of hours planning my funeral and imagining the remorse of my family and friends. I stood under trees with a noose in my hand. I stuffed my head into trash bags. I overdosed. I poked at my wrists with razor blades. I begged God to stop my heart from beating. I wrote good-bye letters, composed wills, and disrupted the lives of everyone close to me. Then reality hit.

The Reality of Suicidal Fantasy

My worst suicide gesture began on May 27, 1992, when I swallowed handfuls of lithium and the antidepressants Prozac and nortriptyline. When the meds kicked in, I got scared—as usual—and called someone to tell him what I'd done—as usual. He demanded I hang up the phone so he could call back and alert my dad and stepmother, who were downstairs watching TV in the den. My father found me in the bathroom, kneeling in front of the toilet with my fingers down my throat. He and my stepmom helped me down the stairs, through the kitchen, out the front door, and into the back of the Cadillac. I passed out on the way to Cape Cod Hospital and wound up unconscious in the intensive-care unit.

I woke to consciousness in the ICU because I couldn't breathe and began gasping. Something was blocking my airway. The lights above me were bright, and the room was a blur. I heard muffled voices and felt the presence of bodies standing nearby. I swung my head back and forth, groaning for help. When I tried to reach up and remove the blockage, I found that my wrists were tied to the bed rails. I felt totally helpless to save my own life, and I was terrified.

I remember opening my eyes in terror, looking straight ahead and seeing only the beige hospital curtain separating me from the rest of the world. In my head swam the thoughts "Oh, my God, I'm really going to die. I really did it this time. I'm going to die, but I don't *want* to die! *Somebody help me. I don't want to die!*" Isn't that ironic, seeing as I had just overdosed? That's what I mean by suicidal thinkers not really wanting to be dead. I only wanted relief from the emotional pain.

Amid all this confusion I heard someone tell me to swallow. The nurses were trying to slide a tube down my throat to fill my stomach with a charcoal solution and deactivate the overdose. (If you're *really* lucky and you're not unconscious, you have to drink this stuff out of a cup. It has the consistency of thick molasses mixed equally with fine beach sand. You have to drink the whole thing, every last drop. It's disgusting.)

When I swallowed, the tube glided past my windpipe and I could breathe again. I fell back to sleep. Moments later the entire contents of my stomach were purged all over the bed, the nurses, and me. I heard it splash when it hit the floor. I fell back to sleep as the nurses cleaned me and changed the bed with me in it. After spending three days in the ICU, I was transferred to the psych ward for the third and final time.

During my last stay in the psych unit, I met a young woman who had tried to hang herself; she was left brain-damaged. I met a young man who slit open his arm; he lost the use of his hand. I had made the level of medication in my body five times greater than it should have been. I could have wound up blind, deaf, or with permanent kidney damage.

That is the reality of suicidal fantasy. It's not fun and it's not romantic. It's messy, scary, and embarrassing. People lost trust in me. I was treated like fine china. My relationships revolved around suicide prevention, not common bonding. Once I had made the first suicide gesture, it was easier to make the second and the third. It took one moment, one choice, to act on a suicidal thought. It took *years* to get beyond the aftermath and the self-imposed image of instability. And I never *really* wanted to die.

For the last five or ten minutes your brain has been focused on my words, ideas, and images. Hopefully your suicidal thoughts and difficult feelings were put on hold. This is outthinking suicide in action. It is what this book is all about. Without knowing it, you've already begun. Congratulations.

SOME THINGS TO THINK ABOUT

• Once I felt the overdose kick in, I called for help.

• My father found me kneeling in front of the toilet with my fingers down my throat, trying to get the pills out of my system.

• When I thought I was going to suffocate, I fought to breathe.

• This is a true story: A woman jumped out of a seven-story window and wound up paralyzed from the waist down. She lived the rest of her life in a long-term care facility, rolling herself around on a hospital stretcher because sitting in a wheelchair gave her too many sores.

• This is another true story: A young man was found hanging in his basement with deep gouges around his neck from where he tried to remove the noose but could not. He died trying to save his own life.

• And finally: In a book entitled *The Suicidal Mind*, Dr. Edwin S. Shneidman tells of a young man who "must have placed the gun [a .45 fully automatic pistol loaded with jacketed hollow-point bullets] to the right side of his face and squeezed the trigger. . . . The bullets tore through his face, blew away many of his teeth, most of his tongue, parts of his nose and cheekbone, and destroyed his right eye. It was all over in a nanosecond." He survived the gunshot blast, by the way, and lived with "irreparable memories of new kinds of pain."[1]

Moderation and Time Limits

It took your whole life to reach this moment; significant change takes time and patience. If you're anything like I was, you're clutching to suicide like it's the only water on a barren desert. Because of this, you might feel threatened or trapped if you try to change too fast. Your brain might shut down, screaming, "Forget it!" This usually leads to fatigue, stomachaches, confusion, headaches, or a feeling of separateness or disconnection, all of which can contribute to feelings of helplessness.

Take it slow, little by little. Remember, every small step you take now is adding to bigger change later. Change builds exponentially, with increasing momentum, multiplying on itself. I encourage you to keep your expectations realistic and your patience high.

When my mind is crammed with new information or I try to do too much, I get tired. Sometimes I feel overwhelmed and give up. Not good. What's the point in doing something productive if I end up feeling worse because of it? Moderation is the key. It provides a sense of accomplishment and reinforces self-trust.

Before I turn on my computer, I set a goal for that particular writing session. For example, "I'm going to work on the book until noon." When I reach my goal, I turn off the computer, get out of my office, and do something nice for myself. I may choose to extend work time, but already I feel a sense of accomplishment. This reinforces self-confidence, builds self-esteem, and makes it easier to work on the book next time, because I didn't get overwhelmed *this* time.

I encourage readers to set time limits while working with this book, particularly in the beginning. Start with short spurts—fifteen minutes at a time, twenty-five minutes, whatever feels comfortable for you. I also encourage you to be aware of how you feel emotionally and physically while reading.

EXERCISE: MODERATION

1. Set yourself the goal of a reasonable amount of time to work with this book—say, fifteen minutes.

2. Use a clock, watch, or kitchen timer to keep track of the time. When the fifteen minutes are up, close the book.

3. Do something nice for yourself: get up and stretch, call a friend, send an e-mail, draw, go outside, listen to music, wash the dishes. Physical exercise is good.

4. If you feel up to it, try another fifteen minutes.

5. Schedule another time to work with the book and stick to it. Remember to reward yourself each time you meet your goal.

6. Optional: You might choose to keep a record of how much time you spend with the book. Writing things down helps to reinforce the inner, lingering quality of people and events.

Me

For eighteen years I lived with suicidal thoughts; there is no one reason why. Like any life story, mine is a collage of events, instincts, and memories. Clinically speaking, I've been diagnosed with major depression, borderline personality disorder, and post-traumatic stress disorder, owing to a combination of genetics and significant life trauma. Bear with me as I define these three diagnoses for you. (For more information on depression, see part 5.)

The National Alliance for the Mentally Ill (www.nami.org) states:

Unlike normal emotional experiences of sadness, loss, or pass-
ing mood states, *major depression* is persistent. . . . Symptoms
of major depression include: profoundly sad or irritable mood;
pronounced changes in sleep, appetite and energy; difficulty
thinking, concentrating, and remembering; . . . lack of interest
in or pleasure from activities that were once enjoyed; feelings
of guilt, worthlessness, hopelessness, and emptiness; recurrent
thoughts of death or suicide; persistent physical symptoms
that do not respond to treatment—headaches, digestive disorders and chronic pain. Major depression can occur at any age
including childhood, the teenage years and adulthood. . . .
Between 80 and 90 percent of those suffering from major
depression can be effectively treated and return to their normal daily activities and feelings. . . . If untreated, episodes
commonly last anywhere from six months to a year. Left
untreated, depression can lead to suicide.

My depression started when I was fourteen and was left untreated
until I took myself to therapy when I was nineteen. Not until I was
twenty-four did anyone suggest antidepressant medication.

Originally thought to "border on" schizophrenia, *borderline
personality disorder* now appears to be more related to serious
depressive illness. . . . It is characterized by impulsivity and
instability in mood, self-image, and personal relationships. . . .
Among the symptoms of BPD are: uncontrolled anger; recur-
ring suicidal threats or self-injurious behavior; unstable,
intense personal relationships with extreme black and white
views of people and experiences; chronic boredom or feelings
of emptiness; frantic efforts to avoid abandonment, either real
or imagined.

In the psych unit the doctors described one of my BPD symptoms as a tendency to "get in my own way," meaning that I repeatedly did things to sabotage myself. An interesting side note from NAMI definitely applies to my case history:

Symptoms of the disorder are not easily changed and often interfere with therapy. Periods of improvement may alternate with periods of worsening. *Post-traumatic stress disorder* (PTSD) is an anxiety disorder that can occur after someone experiences a traumatic event that caused intense fear, helplessness, or horror.

In my case the traumatic events were childhood sexual abuse and the death of my mother when I was fourteen.

While it is common to experience a brief state of anxiety or depression after such occurrences, people with PTSD continually re-experience the traumatic event; avoid individuals, thoughts or situations associated with the event; and have symptoms of excessive emotions.

Like all evolution, mine involves countless elements, some good, some not so good. In addition to my present state of contentment and gratitude, there were many stretches of happiness during the thirty-four years leading to this moment. My life has been, and continues to be, rewarding. It has also been riddled with profound hopelessness and despair. The purpose of this chapter is to paint the picture of my suicidal mind, not to cast blame. Those who harmed me did so out of their *own* internal unrest; their dysfunction was a product of *their* history.

I encourage you to read through this chapter quickly, focusing on the hope. After this chapter, we dive straight into outthinking suicide and Tricks of the Trade. I know from experience how easy it is to fall into someone else's drama when the brain is bent on despair, but it's far more important for you to learn how to outthink suicide than it is to dwell on my past.

I was born on October 15, 1965, into an upper-middle-class family in Westchester County, New York. The youngest of five, a doctor's daughter, I was a resilient, creative, and resourceful child. I had friends, rode horses, played the piano and violin, built forts, and climbed trees. With prosperity came a sense of freedom and faith in the world; my imagination blossomed. But prosperity did nothing to shield me from trauma. In fact, it created an illusion of happiness that ultimately masked the truth and compounded the injury.

Yes, my family had some of the finer things, but we also dealt with tremendous loss and strain. My father's first wife died abruptly, leaving him with three children under the age of twenty. He married my mother one year later, moved the whole family to a new house in Westchester, and tried to start again, adding another brother and me to the mix.

All brothers and sisters squabble to some degree, but I learned in therapy that what I thought was normal sibling rivalry between my brother and me was in fact excessive. I recognize that we are each a product of our environment; nonetheless, the relentless name-calling and teasing, and the physical fighting contributed to the erosion of my self and left me feeling unprotected and on guard.

After *our* mother died and we grew older, a lot of the tension between us fell away. Grief can do that to people. As adults, we became close compatriots and shared a lot of laughter until I started exploring my childhood in therapy and realized how angry I felt about it. In 1997, after several years of personal reconstruction, I asked to meet with my brother to discuss our past.

We met on neutral territory—a Papa Gino's restaurant. Before I could say anything, he apologized for his past behavior, and I believed him when he said, "I don't know why I did it. I would never do it again." We sat and talked for a long while, speaking the truth, no holds barred. Our masks were off, our hearts open. It was such a liberating experience. A seed began to grow that day, rejoining the brother and sister who had once been good friends. Our relationship continues to grow, and I rejoice in knowing that our bond remains strong. I love him and feel proud that he's my brother.

A bit less bruising but no less significant was the death of Rose Harrig—my mother's mother and my last surviving grandparent. Her idyllic Vermont farm and grandmotherly love provided great sanctuary from the stress I felt as a child. She was more structured and disciplined than either of my parents, but that provided a sense of reliable order. In her presence I felt safe and protected, and my free spirit could flourish. I was ten years old and alone with her the day she left for the hospital; the next time I saw her she was asleep in a casket. With Grandma Rose's death, I lost my sanctuary, the magic of the farm, and the comfort of her love. I felt lonely, stranded, and unprotected.

The memory of my mother has grown from a patchy, catch-me-if-you-can series of pictures, feelings, and events to a whole sense of her. She was a cheerful spirit who loved to paint, fish, and play the piano. I've been told we could communicate without words; we shared a gentle understanding.

In 1979 my father retired from medicine, we moved from West-chester to Cape Cod, Massachusetts, and my mother found ovarian cancer rotting in her body. She died one year later, May 5, 1980, at the age of fifty-five. I was fourteen and on the threshold of teenage rebellion, just beginning to stretch my wings in search of an identity and alienating my parents in typical teenage fashion. She died before I had a chance to sweat through my teens and reembrace her on the flip side.

The night she left for her final hospital stay, she looked me square in the eye and said, "Don't worry, I'll be home soon." That statement eventually contributed to my sense of worthlessness until I examined the whole situation in therapy and processed my anger toward her for "abandoning" me.

As a result of her death, aspects of my personality were stalled in their development, just as they had been at ages three and nine and other points of trauma. The building blocks that were already unsteady were squeezed further out of alignment. Suicidal thoughts crept into my mind to control a life that was collapsing around and within me.

Dad married for the third time one year after my mother died, to a woman forty-one years younger; she was twenty-nine, he was seventy. She walked out three months later. I lost another hoped-for ally but was not entirely crushed by her departure.

While he was an excellent provider, my father's anger was unpredictable, and his emotional inadequacy after my mother's death reinforced the false notion that I was alone in the world. When I was sixteen and dared to voice my sadness about her death, his frustrated reply was "Can't you just sweep it under the rug?" I quickly felt ashamed about my feelings. I learned not to talk about anything difficult and instead would retreat to my room, put on my headphones, and get lost in music. Because he could not deal with his own grief, he could not support me in mine. The general stress of our relationship was grossly magnified after my mother's death. From my point of view, our father-daughter connection was based in fear and control rather than love, trust, and understanding.

During this three-year period, 1980 to 1983, my best friend was back in New York, there were no siblings living at home, and I was semi-drafted as a housewife. Typical adolescent anger was spread all over the place, and although I was a hockey cheerleader, had a close group of friends, and was voted "most individualistic" of my senior high school class, I was lost. Suicide loomed large and began consuming my thoughts. It was my mental escape from my soulful confusion.

I could make no sense of my mother's death and had very little adult support to do so.

While he was far from perfect—as am I—my father was a remarkable man. Besides the fact that he married for a *fourth* time in 1986, when he was seventy-five, he more than anyone stretched his limits and grew by tremendous bounds when I began to rock the Blauner boat in 1991. We created an amazing, gracefully imperfect new father-daughter relationship despite our fifty-five-year age gap. By the time he died in 1999, he was my friend, confidant, cribbage partner, and I loved him. His courage and willingness to change remain profound blessings in my life.

As I mentioned earlier, I was sexually abused as a child. This occurred with at least one extended family member, much older than me. It began when I was three and probably continued on and off until I was eleven.

I didn't learn to respect myself as a woman until I started therapy with Sylvia in 1990, when I was twenty-five. Like most sexual abuse survivors, I sometimes doubt the reality of the memories—which are inherently sketchy—but the aftershock certainly validates the experience. Because of the abuse, I sought acceptance through sex, lost my virginity at fifteen, and was very promiscuous throughout high school and college. I saw myself as an object. Sex made me feel powerful because I could "get" or "keep" the guy; it also left me feeling guilty, confused, and dirty. For most of my sexual life I feared the other person's rejection if I refused. I would participate but mentally split from my body—a typical reaction for a survivor. This splitting intensified the feelings of aloneness and often led to suicidal thoughts.

Sexual abuse distorted my self-trust and my trust in the world. It devalued me, warped my impression of intimacy, and wrapped layers of confusion around the issue of sexuality—which is *supposed* to be a wonderful gift. In therapy I retrieved several abuse memories, processed the feelings, and worked through the aftermath. I am still affected by the abuse but now understand it and know how to work with it. At thirty-five, I'm finally beginning to learn the truth about sex. Lovemaking is magical when done in a mutual, healthy way.

I excelled in college, graduated cum laude in 1988, held interesting jobs, fell in love several times, traveled to Eastern Europe, and made a solo drive across the country, but internal conflict remained strong despite my external achievements. After a high, I would often crash to an incredible low. I went from straight As at Bridgewater State College one semester—a perfect 4.0—to a 1.81 at the University of Vermont (UVM) the next. In complete and undiagnosed depression, I stopped attending classes, took up knitting, and blew off all my finals. The following semester I returned to Bridgewater and got another 4.0. I can't say exactly why there was such a dramatic shift, other than that my life itself was dramatic, I was back in familiar surroundings, with my friends, and I was doing something I enjoyed. Also, after I arrived at UVM, I found out that Burlington, Vermont, is one of the top ten overcast cities in the country owing to its proximity to Lake Champlain (not the greatest weather for someone who is depressed).

Suicidal thoughts continued to sharpen throughout college and into my twenties. During that time internal strife was compounded by the words of frustrated well-wishers: "You know what your trouble is? You don't stick with one thing long enough." "Why do you keep doing this to yourself?" "Honestly, Susan, I don't see why you can't move on." "Can't you find something to be happy about?"

These statements were effective, yes, but only in reinforcing my experience of abandonment and despair. I felt unheard, judged, criticized. Anger boiled and seeped through me without a healthy outlet.

After such a comment, I would shut down emotionally, cut that person off from any internal connection, and crank up the volume on suicidal thoughts. This became a habit that was extremely hard to break.

I'm still not sure why I waited until 1991 to make my first big gesture. One theory is that I finally found someone to trust—Sylvia—and I was testing her. Test her I did. Once I actively stepped into the suicide ring, I was caught in the madness for seven years. Suicide gestures remained at my fingertips because the outcome was so predictable: immediate attention, control of those around me, temporary relief, decreased personal responsibility.

During my third hospitalization—after my second overdose—the staff psychologist said, "What I see before me is a very angry young woman who is using herself as a pawn." The anger wasn't *clean* anger, though. Like most difficult feelings—sadness, fear, and loneliness—the anger was snarled with suicidal thoughts. It took *years* of therapy, Twelve Step practice, spiritual exploration, and courageous risk-taking to learn how to untangle these feelings and address them properly.

Fortunately, my family was willing to change as I did over the next six or seven years. Most of them came to therapy with me once or twice. But like any boat-rocker, I was breaking the mold. As I began to outgrow my old Blauner role, it was hard to change their vision of me, particularly because I often kept myself in crisis. Not only did I have to alter my entire mental factory, I had to rebuild people's trust in me through consistent, self-affirming behavior. I know I made it tremendously hard for everyone, especially from 1991 to 1993, and I'm both embarrassed and sorry.

In the fall of 1998 I made my final suicide gesture, an overdose of Valium and the antidepressant Serzone. Once again I called for help once the meds kicked in (this time I used 911) and wound up in the emergency room drinking that charcoal stuff.

I should have been admitted to the psych ward for stabilization, but instead I asked to be released—and was, the next morning, to the care of my therapist with a promise not to hurt myself again. This was highly unusual. It's also a prime example of how people can fall through the cracks. I overdosed on a Sunday and returned to work that Tuesday. The hospital did no follow-up whatsoever. Not that I returned to work bouncing for joy. I was extremely fragile, getting by one moment at a time until my constitution was strong again.

Ironically, all this followed several years of tremendous psychological healing and personal advancement, which included dealing with issues of sexual abuse. I had long since been told my diagnosis, and I certainly had all the tools I needed to stay safe. I had established a close-knit circle of friends, knew how to outthink my brain, and had a strong, trusted bond with Sylvia. The relationship with my father had improved beyond belief; I had approached my brother and was mending that relationship. I loved my family and enjoyed my job.

By then I totally believed in creating my own reality and had begun to make dreams come true. I was writing this book and knew in my heart it would be published. I was well versed in Twelve Step philosophy and principles and had a deep spiritual understanding.

My suicide gesture may have been triggered in part by a significant loss. That spring I left an emotionally strained four-year relationship. I moved out of the house we had shared, put most of my stuff in storage, and found a home-sharing situation. Two months later I learned that my ex-boyfriend was in a new relationship almost immediately after our breakup. I felt deeply betrayed.

Another factor may have contributed to the mix. Several months prior to the breakup, under medical supervision, I changed antidepressants in the hopes of regaining sexual libido. I switched from Prozac to Remeron to Serzone. I am guessing that the repeated stress of chemical disturbance, combined with my hopes for regaining libido and subsequent disappointment, added to my fragility, though I had stabilized on Serzone by November 1998.

Regardless of the triggers, I chose to ignore the tools that had worked so well in the past. Why? Why did I deny myself relief? Why did I hold on to the pain? It remains a mystery. One thing is certain: it was a conscious choice, a last-gasp effort to hang on to the familiar. I chose to do something to "get in my own way." In thinking about it now, I see that I was like a baby, unwilling to leave the comfort of the womb, the comfort of suicidal thoughts. I fought, kicking and screaming, until finally I let go and arrived.

There were significant differences with the 1998 overdose. First of all, I was lucid enough to feel embarrassed and experience immediate regret (which is a *good* thing). In the past I had bragged about my suicidal behavior. This time I stayed quiet; I didn't want or need that kind of attention. Instead of craving victimhood, I wanted to take responsibility for my actions and move forward with the life I'd been creating.

Suicidal thoughts may be with me for the rest of my life. They're an addiction, like alcohol to an alcoholic or heroin to a junkie. But since the fall of 1998, I've had just one tiny glimmer of a semi-serious suicidal thought. It came and went for about a week and a half.

Today there is abundant joy in my life, and *usually* I feel grateful for it. In addition to giving and receiving love with a great circle of friends and feeling a strong connection to my community, I have developed working relationships with all of my family members, though some are closer than others. I have a highly responsible job and work with fun, supportive people. This book is being published, and I recently purchased my own home. I live with two great cats, Prozy and Ember, am in a healthy, authentic relationship with a truly exceptional man, and find great solace in the Divine.

Low points still occur—as they do for everyone on the planet—but I'm generally comfortable in my own skin, fully capable of meeting my own needs. When I can't meet my needs, I *ask for help* (see chapter 1 of part 3). When I do hit a slump, I ride it out, nurture myself to the best of my ability, and remind myself that it will pass. It always does, 100 percent guaranteed.

Like any work in progress, I am as complete as I can be in the present moment, still changing all the while. Vulnerability, fear, and weakness sit right beside strength, bravery, and insight. Perhaps I'm lucky: natural death does not frighten me. I sometimes think I've lived a full life—and I'm only thirty-five. I have felt the depths of despair, risen from the fire, and many of my dreams have and are still coming true. Maybe my work is done. Then again, I have no idea what the universe has in store for me . . . and it's far greater than anything I could ever imagine. I think I'll stick around a while.

Finding Life Essence

Merriam-Webster's Collegiate Dictionary defines life as "the sequence of physical and mental experiences that make up the existence of an individual."

Essence is defined as "the permanent as contrasted with the accidental elements of being; the individual, real or ultimate nature of a thing especially as opposed to its existence."

Confused? Sorry. "Life essence" is hard to describe because it's the unseen feeling-experience of self, the sacred, other people, and life events. It's a lot like having memories, but instead of recalling information, you recall a feeling connection. Finding life essence is the ability to hold on to the experience of a person, place, or thing even when they're out of sight. This is easy for most people because they have a built-in reservoir in which to dip their cup, but for suicidal thinkers with tunnel vision, it's not that simple.

"Out of sight, out of mind" was the syndrome I often faced at the conclusion of an event or following a visit with a friend. To a large degree the essence of my life would dissolve because my ability to integrate it into my self was so limited. Instead of feeling closer to a person after he or she left, I would feel abandoned, rejected, and lonely. Depending on my overall state of mind, these feelings sometimes intensified into suicidal thoughts.

In a sense my brain would mock me: "So you think you have friends, do you? You don't have *anyone,* you can't *feel* them, right? They don't love you because you can't *feel* their love. Face it, you're all alone and always will be." And I would believe this rubbish! Back then I didn't have the strength to fight back or stand up for myself. Instead, I caved in under the pressure of such negativity and focused on the holes in my life rather than the joys. Perhaps because of the borderline personality disorder, much of life skimmed off of me and ricocheted into space, leaving gaps instead of ties.

The first time I consciously recognized this phenomenon in action was April 1993. I was leaving the Esplanade in Boston after an AIDS fund-raiser walk and rally. It was a warm, sunny afternoon. Along with thousands of other people, I had just completed the walk, eaten lunch, and listened to a concert. In the end we all joined hands and swayed together, singing.

When I started to leave the scene, the whole experience started slipping away. And I had just had it! I can remember dropping my head in frustration and walking back to the crowd to try to rekindle the experience, but when I got back to the Esplanade, I felt separate and alone, like I didn't fit in.

By the time I reached my car, most of the experience had slid off like water after a swim. There were lingering droplets, sure, but they were clouded with anger, frustration, and loneliness. I couldn't remember what it *felt* like to walk and talk with the other participants, to witness their joy and sorrow, to be a part of their community. I couldn't bring back the essence of them or the event. Later, with conscious effort, I could recite a synopsis to tell other people, and I could feel—to a degree—what it was like, but even then the memory was more external; it didn't spring from within. In recounting the event, I felt more like a commentator than a participant.

I felt angry and cheated that I had extended myself with all those people for a great cause, and then the essence of the experience was taken away because of a malfunction in my brain. The whole thing made me profoundly sad (a good sign). Feeling sad about feeling disconnected meant I knew there was an alternative and I wanted it.

I went to my next therapy session with a mission. I said I wanted to change this part of me. I wanted to be able to incorporate life experiences into my self, into my being, so they wouldn't dissolve like soap in dishwater. I wanted to be able to feel a long-lasting connection to things. This was a pivotal moment: not only did I have a conscious recognition of a deeply rooted subconscious process, but I wanted to change it and was willing to do the work to get there. I'm sure Sylvia was thrilled with the news.

Over the last eleven years, Sylvia has guided me through the fire and helped me find and hold on to my life essence. The end result has been my new ability to build on a firm foundation instead of waffling on a high wire with no safety net. I rarely feel an aching hole at my center. Instead, that center is full, sometimes overflowing. In fact, I periodically need downtime to regroup and mentally file my life experiences or I get overloaded—a condition that, interestingly, can trigger feelings of abandonment because I lose my center.

Much of this book deals with integration and reinforcing life essence. A lot of what I share in parts 2 and 3 may sound over the top, but I just do what works for me, whether or not other people think it's strange. It works for me, so why not give it a try? It may work for you, too. The only thing you've got to lose is another moment of misery.

Change (Arghhh) and Choices

> Although my life was filled with chaos, it was familiar
> chaos, which gave me the feeling that I had some
> control over it. This was an illusion.
>
> —ANONYMOUS

I had to go through what I went through in order to get to where I am today, but I'm not so sure my rutty road had to be quite so long. There were plenty of opportunities to change my path, but I held on to self-destruction for as long as I could. When I finally began to let go, I started to find relief, though none of it was a straight line toward freedom.

You may ask, "What's going to take the place of the *old* stuff if I start to let it go? What will fill the hole?" It is scary to have one foot on the ground and the other one in the air, reaching for something different and unfamiliar. Even scarier is when both feet are off the ground before the first one has a chance to land on new territory. Rest assured, you will definitely land, though perhaps on wobbly legs until you get familiar with your surroundings. I stumbled and fell hundreds of times, maybe thousands, as I scratched my way into life. The cool part is, once you embrace change, you start to see—and *feel*—the result of your hard work, even though it might feel strange and uncomfortable.

Even after I started making big changes, I still had to deal with a suicidal brain. Inevitably, before or after a period of significant growth, I would become subconsciously afraid that no one would ever meet my needs again (for companionship, love, nurturance, food, shelter, money). Old behavior patterns and thoughts would return and intensify because I was too afraid of being self-sufficient. Thus, I learned that shakiness is a good sign—it usually means a big change is about to occur. I ride it out, wait, and let my growth unfold.

That's why I mentioned moderation earlier. By remembering to practice moderation, you can better tolerate the upheavals of change. And change *does* cause upheavals, not only in us but in those around us. It can be tough being a boat-rocker.

When you choose to change, your brain will probably try to derail your efforts. Be strong and *do* in spite of how you *feel*. Remember: if your brain has been trying to kill you and you've made it thus far, you certainly have the strength and courage of a warrior. I am honored to be in your presence and stand firmly by your side. We are warriors together.

I encourage you to draw a warrior—you—in the space below. Give yourself sturdy legs and feet and hands that reach for the sky. Draw a heart in the center of your chest. This warrior lives within you every moment.

PART TWO

Outthinking

Suicide

—Journal drawing, 1994

Thank God, you decided to stick around a little longer than
you ever thought you would.
Thank God, you decided to stick around a little longer than
you ever thought you could.

—JENNIFER STRATTON, "Sue's Song"

Breathing

Breathing quiets the mind, slows the heart rate, lowers blood pressure, and releases toxins from the body. Deep breathing eases stress and lessens suicidal thoughts by soothing the brain when it feels overwhelmed. Your mind becomes focused on the air going into and out of your body while your brain gets a healthy supply of oxygen.

To get the most out of this book, it's important to listen to your mind and body and honor their needs. Breath awareness is a good barometer for both. As you work with this book, check in with your breath every so often. Is it shallow and fast? Slow and deep? If my breathing gets shallow and short, it usually means I'm afraid, tense, or angry. If my breathing is slow and deep, I am usually relaxed or in a more peaceful state. Take a moment to notice your breath.

EXERCISE: HOW DO WE BREATHE NATURALLY?

1. Lie down on your back with a pillow under your head.

2. Rest your hands on your stomach.

3. Focus your eyes on your hands.

4. Breathe normally through your nose for a minute or two, watching your hands.

5. Do this until you can see your hands rise and fall with the breath. Try to keep your shoulders still.

The breath comes from the belly area. Often when people are asked to breathe deeply, they lift their shoulders instead of extending their belly. This actually makes it harder to get a full breath. Your abdomen needs to expand as you inhale, contract as you exhale. Beneath your lungs lies the diaphragm, a powerful muscle separating the chest and abdomen. When you inhale, the diaphragm pulls down, sucking air into your lungs. When you exhale, the diaphragm relaxes, rises, and pushes air out through your nose or mouth.

EXERCISE: DEEP BREATHING

(First try this while lying on your back. After you've practiced a few times, try it sitting up. It can be done either way. It can also be done while you're walking, listening to music, even when you're standing in line at the supermarket. If you begin to feel light-headed or dizzy, simply return to regular breathing.)

1. Lie down on your back with a pillow under your head.

2. Picture a deflated orange balloon in your belly.

3. Keeping your shoulders still and your back flat, slowly inhale through your nose.

4. Imagine the orange balloon filling with air, getting bigger and bigger as your stomach area expands, rising toward the ceiling.

5. When the balloon is as big as it's going to get, take in a bit more air and hold your breath for two seconds.

6. Now pretend you're about to whistle and then slowly let the air pass out through your lips. This is called "pursed-lips breathing."

7. Watch as your stomach drops slowly and the balloon deflates.

8. When the balloon is totally deflated, push a little more air out and hold your breath for two seconds.

9. Repeat steps 1 through 8 three times, trying to make the inhalation and exhalation last eight seconds each. Remember to pause for two seconds between the inhale and exhale.

10. Notice the quality of the air as it goes into and out of your body. It is cooler and dryer when you inhale, and warmer and moister when you exhale.

11. Take a minute and check in with your body and mind. Do you notice a change? Do you feel more relaxed? Warmer? Do you feel cold, tense, or shaky? How are your thoughts? Quieter, calmer, or still going as fast as a runaway train? Try not to judge your responses; just be an observer. If you'd like, write about the experience in a journal or notebook.

I'll talk more about breathing in the "Spirituality, Nature, and Meditation" chapter in part 3. For the moment, be aware of your breath and use it as an indicator. If during your day you begin to feel overwhelmed, tense, anxious, afraid, or wound up, think of that balloon and practice making it expand and contract. Your breath is always there to comfort you as long as you're alive to breathe.

IF YOU FEEL STRESSED OR AFRAID WHILE READING THIS BOOK

1. Take several deep breaths.

2. Remember that change is happening in this moment.

3. Try to focus on what's in front of you.

4. Look at your surroundings. Describe them out loud. What do you see?

5. Feel the texture of this paper. See the shapes of these letters.

6. Look at your feet. Wiggle your toes. Swivel your neck. Let out a sigh. This is where you are, right here, right now.

SOMETHING TO THINK ABOUT

- Breathing is essential to all life. If you've read this far, you *definitely* want to be alive.

- It was my breath—or the lack of it—that shook me from unconsciousness in the ICU and made me realize I wanted to live.

- Whenever I tried to suffocate myself, I always ripped off the contraption once I could no longer get a good breath.

- The woman who tried to hang herself is now brain-damaged because she denied her brain the oxygen it needed.

- When the young man hanged himself, he changed his mind when he could no longer breathe, but it was too late.

The Language of Suicide

From an outsider's point of view, suicidal behavior may appear straightforward, but when you're living it, it's very complex. It's a whole other reality. I had to examine and dissect the suicide cycle before I could step out of it. I had to change my perception of the self-destruction merry-go-round and make it an independent being, with its own personality and characteristics.

The first and easiest thing to look at is the language of suicide. Language is powerful; it helps create our reality. While depression or mental illness might not be within your direct control, language is. You can practice changing it at any time, and it's the least threatening of all the elements you'll need to change in order to break the suicide cycle.

There are five important points to consider when looking at the language of suicide:

1. "Suicidal" is not a feeling.

2. There is a huge difference between "having a suicidal thought" and "being suicidal."

3. A suicide "gesture" differs greatly from a suicide "attempt."

4. There is no such thing as a "successful" suicide attempt.

5. Beware of "always," "never," and other all-or-nothing terms.

"Suicidal" is not a feeling. A person focused on suicide will often use the phrase "I feel suicidal" to describe his or her state of being. This statement isn't exactly accurate, however, because "suicidal" is not a feeling, it is a state of being. Anger is a feeling. Sadness and loneliness are feelings. The mystery began to unravel for me when I realized that feelings groaned beneath my suicidal thoughts. I began to use other words, like "angry," "sad," "afraid," "frustrated," or "lonely," to express my state of mind instead of voicing them as the singular expression "suicidal."

This practice in language awareness gave me positive power because I was no longer bound by the suicide box. Suicidal thoughts, I learned, were an indication that some deep feeling or need was being triggered or stirred. I had to figure out what the feeling or need was and address it.

Instead of saying, "I feel suicidal," say, "I'm having a suicidal thought and I feel (angry, lonely, sad, terrified, abandoned, etc.)." Once you start separating your feelings from your thoughts *verbally,* you can start doing it emotionally.

LANGUAGE EXERCISE

1. The next time your thoughts focus on suicide, take a few deep breaths and say to yourself, "I'm having a suicidal thought and I feel _____." Check out the Feelings Galore List and the Feelings, Chart on pages 86 and 84 for ideas.

2. If there is someone safe you can share your feelings with, do so.

3. Even if you have to practice this a hundred times a day, try it. It works.

The skill of identifying feelings takes a lot of practice, but it's certainly possible to learn. I encourage you to make this change in language and see what a difference it makes in your perception of reality.

There is a huge difference between "having a suicidal thought" and "being suicidal." "I can't take this anymore; I want to kill myself." "Why don't I just hang myself?" "I'd be better off dead." These are all suicidal thoughts. Swallowing razor blades is being suicidal. So, unless you're doing something drastic like eating a Breakfast of Gillettes instead of the Breakfast of Champions, the phrase "I'm suicidal" is also inaccurate. Once again, I encourage you to say, "I'm having a suicidal thought, and I'm feeling _____."

The American Association of Suicidology (www.suicidology.org) offers these words to suicidal thinkers: "Although it might seem as if your unhappiness will never end, it is important to realize that crises are usually time-limited. Solutions are found, feelings change, unexpected positive events occur. Suicide is sometimes referred to as 'a permanent solution to a temporary problem.' "

The next time a suicidal thought surfaces, try this exercise.

EXERCISE: TAKING ACTION

1. Say aloud, "Hey, brain!" (or "Fuck you, brain!") "I want to be alive! Leave me alone!" Repeat this as often as you need to in the moment. Get mad if you need to. Scream it. But be gentle with yourself, too.

2. Say aloud or to yourself: "I'm having a suicidal thought, and I feel _____; I don't have to act on this suicidal thought. All feelings pass."

3. Find simple activities to divert your thoughts: make your bed, take a walk, play with the cat, call a friend, take a shower. See the Tasks and Activities List on page 142.

4. Practice the Tricks of the Trade I teach you in part 3.

A suicide "gesture" differs greatly from a suicide "attempt." Every time I overdosed, I made a suicide "gesture" rather than an attempt. I always called for help once the medication began to take effect. I always wound up with my fingers down my throat.

Both a gesture and an attempt are clear messages that something must be done. Usually a gesture is less severe and the person finds help before he or she gets too far. Keep in mind, however, that even though a gesture may be less severe, it is no less significant. Never take a suicide gesture lightly—your own or someone else's. This is serious business. Particularly because once you make your first suicide gesture, it's easier to make the second, the third, and so on.

According to Focus Adolescent Services (www.focusas.com), half of all children who have made one suicide attempt will make another, sometimes as many as two a year, until they "succeed."

There is no such thing as a "successful" suicide attempt. Traditional language defines a suicide attempt as "successful" if the person dies. I disagree. You either die, which is *not* a success, or you don't die, which, if anything, *is* a success.

Beware of "always," "never," and other all-or-nothing terms. As I've said, language helps create our reality. These days I try to avoid the words "always," "never," "can't," "won't," and "ever," unless I'm saying something positive, like "Feelings always change," "God is always with me," or "I'm never alone."

If my brain tries to sneak in a "never" ("You're *never* going to be able to finish writing this book. Why don't you give up?") I have to reply to that voice ("Leave me alone. I am finishing this book. I can do it.").

In my opinion, "always" and "never," when used in their negative sense, are usually a sign of fear. When people say, "I'll never change," it's not that they can't change, but that they *think* they can't, or just plain won't. When someone says, "I'll always feel this way," well, that's simply not true. All feelings change, with or without any help from us. They never stay the same at the same intensity 100 percent of the time.

There are some other words and phrases to watch out for: "impossible," "should," "shouldn't," "hate," and statements that start with "You . . ." when you're trying to express a feeling and put it on someone else. For example, "You make me feel so angry." No one can *make* us feel anything. It's up to us to feel whatever we feel. Try something like this instead: "I feel angry when you ignore me. And I need to know you care about me."

Instead of saying, "I *should* have done this or that," say, "It *would have been better* if I had done this or that." Can you feel the difference in those statements?

And as you'll learn in the chapter on feelings in part 3, there is a *huge* difference between the words "I am" and "I feel." Read these sentences aloud: "I am lonely." "I feel lonely." "I am angry." "I feel angry."

Remember, feelings are temporary. By stating a feeling as "I feel," you allow more movement into the picture. By stating the feeling as "I am," you're telling your brain that it is part of your identity. It sounds more permanent. Feelings are not who we are, they're just feelings—electrochemical impulses that slosh around between our ears on the neuron superhighway.

The Neuron Superhighway

To shed my suicidal skin, I had to develop an understanding of how things work upstairs. Once I could see my mental landscape, it was easier to navigate. This did not require a Ph.D. in neuropsychology, just some basic information from my therapist. The following explanation is far from scientific and drastically simplified. I just want to give you a visual picture so that you can see suicidal thoughts for what they really are.

To my understanding, thoughts and feelings are electrical impulses that travel along a complex web of specialized nerve cells in the brain called neurons, with the help of chemicals called neurotransmitters. Feelings and thoughts are certainly very real. They mold our perception of the world and our place in it, and they can get so intense that it feels like a meat grinder is churning through your body. But the fact remains that, biologically speaking, feelings and thoughts are just energy particles born of life experience and genetics.

In *Human Anatomy and Physiology*, Elaine N. Marieb describes the nervous system as "the master controlling and communicating system of the body. It is responsible for all behavior—indeed, every thought, action and emotion reflects its activity. Cells of the nervous system communicate by means of electrical signals which are rapid, specific and usually cause almost immediate responses."[1]

Pretend for a moment that you're flying above a busy highway at rush hour. Below you, cars and trucks on the road are streaming toward their various destinations. If you apply that image to how your brain works, the cars and trucks are your thoughts and feelings, and neurons are the highway they're traveling on.

Now you're driving a Federal Express truck along that highway. Suddenly the highway ends at a river. No bridge is in sight, but there's a ferry that can take you across the river. What do you do? You drive your truck onto the ferry, pay a toll, and float across the river to the other side, where you are reconnected with the highway and go on your way again.

A similar thing happens in the brain. In the brain, an electrochemical signal (the FedEx truck) travels along the neuron (the highway), carrying important packages and letters (your thoughts and feelings), until it reaches a gap called a synapse (the river). Synapses are, "for the most part, non-contact, chemical transmissions between one part of the neuron and another. Synapses permit the conduct of electrochemical impulses among a [vast number] of neurons almost instantly."[2]

Take a look at the diagram opposite. See the little circular molecules floating in the gap? Those are neurotransmitters, and they are the "ferries" that float the message across the synapse to the next neuron. Technically speaking, a neurotransmitter "transmits nerve impulses across a synapse."

Just as faulty construction or improper maintenance can cause a highway to deteriorate, so brain function is compromised by severe trauma, stress, or chemical imbalance. My own mental landscape was full of accidents waiting to happen.

I believe I was born predisposed to major depression, which is biochemical in nature. In other words, I was brought into the world with creaky bridges. This chemical imbalance, combined with the death of

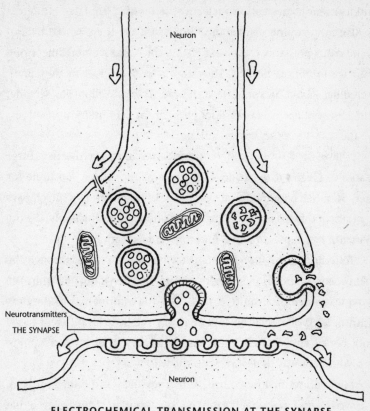

ELECTROCHEMICAL TRANSMISSION AT THE SYNAPSE

my mom, sexual abuse, and the other factors I described earlier, weakened my bridge construction to the point where I had potholes the size of Rhode Island in my thought processes. Two things happened: my body stopped making enough of the critical neurotransmitter serotonin, and what *did* get produced was used up too quickly. Instead of traveling safely over a waterway, my feelings and thoughts either crashed on the rocks or stalled at the tollbooth. And guess what, folks? I had no change.

Prozac is my "change." In addition to easing the symptoms of depression, Prozac is also thought to help with borderline personality disorder and post-traumatic stress disorder. There are many types of antidepressant medication—selective serotonin reuptake inhibitors (SSRIs), monoamine oxidase inhibitors (MAOIs), tricyclic and hetero-cyclic antidepressants (TCAs and HCAs), and selective norepinephrine reuptake inhibitors (SNRIs). They are prescribed under many names, including: Paxil, Effexor, Celexa, Prozac, Zoloft, Wellbutrin, Serzone, and Remeron. For a detailed description of antidepressant medications, see the NAMI website, www.nami.org.

I have tried several different antidepressants; for the past three years I've taken Prozac. It does not cure me, nor is it a substitute for therapy or behavior modification. Prozac keeps my bridges intact, pays my tolls, and helps my brain get its work done more efficiently. See the "Vitamin P" chapter in part 3 for more on medication.

To recap: Information (thought/feeling energy) passes through the brain along neurons, traveling over gaps called synapses. Within the synapse are neurotransmitters that carry the information to the next neuron. Everyone's neuron superhighway is a little bit different based on genetics, environment, and personal history. Therefore, each brain has a different way of dealing with the world.

My brain wanted me to believe that my life was destined for pain, sorrow, and disappointment. Until my late twenties, I truly believed that some people were born to be happy and some were born to be sad, and I was one of the sad ones. Rubbish. By chosing to repeat self-destructive behavior patterns, I just reinforced the false belief that I was meant for misery. Suicide crept into my mind as a "solution" to the problem. A Grim Reaper took up residence under my skin and in my breath. He waited in the corners of my brain and became an angry tenant.

We are good people, you and I. We never asked for any of this pain and confusion. We didn't ask to be born with a tendency toward depression. We didn't ask to be sexually abused, to lose a parent pre-maturely, or to feel on guard growing up. We didn't ask for it, but alas, we wound up with a Grim Reaper hitchhiking on our mental highway. It's time to leave him in the dust.

EXERCISE: NEURON SUPERHIGHWAY VISUALIZATION

This is a visualization exercise. You will need a quiet place to sit. If you like to draw, you will also need a pencil and paper.

1. Take a few deep breaths and sit comfortably.

2. Close your eyes and imagine your neuron superhighway. Picture the scene as clearly as you can. It can be cars and trucks on asphalt, or neurons, synapses, and neurotransmitters. What does it look like? How is the traffic flow?

3. Now imagine a warm glow pouring over the scene, surrounding it with soft brightness. Let the glow touch every part of the image.

4. Keeping the scene surrounded with the glow, imagine every element of the highway running the way it's supposed to: traffic jams are released; cars and trucks are moving smoothly; electrical impulses are traveling effortlessly over synapses. Everything is flowing exactly the way it needs to be.

5. Sit with that image for a couple of minutes as you continue to breathe deeply.

6. Now expand that glow to surround your body. Feel the warmth of the glow.

7. As you breathe in, breathe in the glow; as you breathe out, breathe out the glow.

8. After several minutes, wiggle your toes and fingers, slowly open your eyes, and become aware of your surroundings.

9. If you'd like, take a few minutes and draw the image from your mind.

This exercise is nice to do before falling asleep, or if your brain is really ranting and you need to quiet it down. The comforting glow is yours whenever you want it to be.

The Grim Reaper

Tortured. That's the only way to describe life inside a suicidal mind: both hostage and terrorist was I. Whatever I did, wherever I went, the Grim Reaper tiptoed in the shadows. He waited for a weak moment to scream, pounce, and rocket these messages through me: "You're totally useless. Why even bother?" "Nothing's *ever* going to get better." "You're *never* going to be happy, why even try?" "Life's so fucking hard, why don't you just kill yourself?" Like fingernails on chalkboard, he grated at my spirit until finally I would act out to silence his nagging voice, but upon facing death I *always* ran back to life. I thought I could control or improve my life by ending it, but I didn't want death either! Therein lay the torture.

Planning and thinking about suicide provided a twisted sense of control, but in reality my life was completely *out* of control. Overdose was my primary method of choice, but being a creative thinker, I also fantasized about hanging, hiring a hit man, or driving to Roxbury—a notoriously violent neighborhood of Boston—to make myself a target for a drive-by shooting. Aside from overdosing or occasionally putting a noose around my neck, I was too scared to do any of it.

What I really craved—as do you, I assume—was relief, love, understanding, and connection. It took me years to realize I could find all that and more right here on earth, in this lifetime, if I just became willing to make different choices.

This book was originally titled "Outthinking Suicide." I chose the word "outthink" because surviving suicidal thoughts is like facing an opponent in a game of strategy:

1. I recognized that I had an opponent (a "Grim Reaper"), who traveled along the neuron superhighway.

2. I developed a strategic plan of action ("Tricks of the Trade").

3. I examined the way my brain responds to the world and why ("Brain Style").

4. I became willing to make new choices ("Recognizing and Avoiding Triggers").

5. I learned to put the brakes on emotional spirals ("Stopping the Snowball").

The bottom line to all of this is safety and willingness. To experience lasting relief, we have to be *willing* to keep ourselves physically *safe* long enough to be able to learn and practice new skills while we let go of old behaviors and thought patterns. By practicing the Tricks of the Trade and reorganizing my internal structure, I eventually learned how to stand up to the Grim Reaper, refocus my thoughts, change my behavior, and make life-affirming decisions. In short, I learned how to outthink suicide.

By bending around suicidal thoughts, we form gaps in their persistent flow. We find relief. In the relief there is room for healing and growth. We step outside the suicide cycle, if only for a moment, shift our perspective a bit, and gather strength for the next round. It's a slow process, but the more we practice, the stronger we become.

After a while the distance between suicidal thoughts lengthens and recovery time quickens. Once I observed this phenomenon in action and humbly embraced its possibilities, my healing took off. I was no longer a hostage or a terrorist. Yes, there were plenty of setbacks, usually just when I thought I had turned a corner. When I started to let go of old patterns, they tried to hold on tight.

EXERCISE: RELEASING

You will need a piece of paper, a pencil, and a quiet place to sit.

1. Close your eyes. Take three slow, deep breaths.

2. Sit quietly with yourself for a few minutes, continuing to breathe slowly. Try to tune out your surroundings and focus on your inner world.

3. What messages do you hear from your brain?
   From the Grim Reaper?

4. As the messages surface, picture them on a movie screen in your mind.

5. Read them without judgment, then open your eyes and write the words down on the piece of paper.

6. Close your eyes again and picture the words flying off the screen.

7. Wait for another message and repeat steps 4, 5, and 6.

8. After a few minutes open your eyes, fold the paper in half, and take a deep breath.

9. Get up, shake your body, jump up and down, stretch a bit, maybe splash some water on your face.

10. Now tear the paper into tiny pieces and throw it away.

11. Say this affirmation while you're ripping the paper: "I am releasing these self-defeating thoughts now and forever. I am completely free."

12. Turn to page 142 and find a nice thing to do for yourself or someone else.

This exercise can be done at any time, but be careful not to dwell on the self-destructive messages. Rip them up and move on to something else—preferably something physical.

Brain Style

Just as everyone's neuron superhighway is a little bit different, so is the way each brain processes the world. Some people get depressed, some get anxious, some fly through life with hardly a care, some stay mad and resentful, some always see the bright side.

When I was fourteen, suicidal thoughts became my knee-jerk reaction to stress and conflict. It was the way I dealt with the world. I got pissed off? Focus on suicide. Went to someone's wedding and felt sad because I was lonely? Focus on suicide. Lost my wallet? Focus on suicide. Got a great new job and felt overwhelmed by the responsibilities? Focus on suicide. Like alcohol, pot, heroin, crack, food, sex, work, television, cigarettes, you name it, is for other people, suicide was my drug of choice.

The key word here is "choice": It was my conscious *choice* to focus on suicide. And like any other habit-forming drug, it became an addiction. It became an automatic reflex.

Okay. We know that most suicidal thinkers don't want to die, they want relief from emotional pain. And we know that thoughts and feelings are just electrochemical impulses in the brain—the famous neuron superhighway. We also know it is possible to outthink the brain and find relief.

To make sense of life and how I reacted to it, I had to figure out my brain style—how my brain processed information. "Brain style" may be a strange expression, but it's the best way I know to pinpoint the culprit of suicidal thoughts. It's all in the brain.

This was my brain style (see the Feelings Time Lines on pages 90 and 91 for another view):

1. An event would trigger certain feelings. These events could be as small as losing my address book or as big as having trouble in a love relationship. It didn't matter. Because of the PTSD, borderline personality disorder, and depression, nearly everything held the same weight.

2. Usually I would have a one- to two-day delayed reaction.

3. Suddenly feelings would surface, but I wouldn't know exactly what they were. I would quickly become overwhelmed, and the feelings would turn into anger.

4. Without a healthy outlet for anger, I would start to detach from myself mentally—from the feelings and/or the event (called "splitting"). Typically I would get very tired, and my mental state would become fuzzy.

5. The anger would begin to turn inward. Detachment would intensify until I lost my sense of self completely (my feelings snowballed). I felt isolated from everyone and everything. The world became good or bad, positive or negative. There was no gray area. All-or-nothing thinking would take charge.

6. Eventually I would feel so lost and angry that my thoughts would shift to suicide. It was the only way I knew to release the emotion. And in those moments it seemed to me to be the only way I could connect with myself.

It took twenty-five years or more to develop this style, so it didn't change overnight. Slowly I had to pick apart the cycle. I figured out my triggers, learned how to stop my feelings from snowballing, and became willing to make new choices and stick to them.

Most people don't have to *think* about how they deal with life. Suicidal thinkers do. Other people know it feels good to run a mile, look at their stamp collection, meditate, build a birdhouse, garden, do a crossword puzzle. They do these things instinctively. Their thought process is not: "I feel like shit. I'd better find some way to divert my attention and improve my mood before I fall deeper into despair." Their brain styles allows them to cope with stress and pain, like a car engine having enough gas and oil to keep it running smoothly. My brain was short on gas and low on oil.

By learning and practicing the Tricks of the Trade in part 3, you'll acquire plenty of choices besides suicide for easing emotional pain. You will find the strength to stop the snowball from rolling you into oblivion. If the snowball starts to roll, you'll know how to get out of the way.

Recognizing and Avoiding Triggers

A trigger is defined as "something that acts like a mechanical trigger in initiating a process or reaction."

After my 1992 suicide gesture, Sylvia was nearly fired by my father. In retrospect, I can see how frustrating it must have been for my family to watch me stay in therapy with her for several years and wind up back in the psych ward again and again. I know now that it was *me* who didn't keep up my end of the bargain, not her. My father asked me to get a second opinion from an outside psychiatrist to see whether Sylvia should be replaced or if I needed long-term care.

Sylvia prepared a summary of my history along with clinical notes and questions. I brought her report to psychiatrist number five. Ironically, after our session the psychiatrist's main recommendations were: (a) that I stay with Sylvia; and, (b) that my father join me in therapy.

Sylvia reported the following "recent triggers" as probable causes for my 1992 suicidal episode:

1. In early April [Susan] processed sexual activity at different ages.

2. Applying for a job.

3. Breaking up with boyfriend.

4. Susan's psychiatrist leaving in June.

5. My vacation in June.

6. End of chorus, therefore, a purpose.

7. Recent stability and fear of expectations/needs not getting met.

The word "trigger" is synonymous with "stressor" but holds more firepower. A trigger sets off a feeling or chain reaction of feelings; a stressor creates a state of mind. A trigger is usually a specific type of event or incident. For example, when important people leave my life— even temporarily—my feelings of abandonment are triggered: Sylvia's upcoming vacation and my psychiatrist's job transfer.

One reason it's important to practice Feelings Versus Facts (part 3) and learn how to reality-check a situation is that triggers tend to exaggerate feelings. I am not being abandoned when people leave, it just *feels* like I am.

Take trigger number 3 from Sylvia's report, "Breaking up with boyfriend." Who doesn't feel abandoned in some degree by a breakup? For me, the gravity of my mother's death and my inability to hold on to her life essence caused a severe reaction. Facing any type of loss, even ones I initiated, generated—triggered—incredible fear.

I would mentally disconnect from the person as if he or she didn't exist—out of sight, out of mind—thus triggering internal splitting and the feelings of abandonment associated with my mother's death. Then I'd start to scramble, and the situation would "snowball" in my mind, growing bigger and bigger until I felt out of control. To feel more in control I'd focus on suicide with an "I'll show you" attitude, as if killing myself would actually control other people's lives. How could I control their lives? I'd be dead! Sure, they'd come to my funeral and grieve my death, but after a while they'd get on with their lives, and I would have missed all kinds of life opportunities for nothing.

The false sense of control lay in knowing I probably *wouldn't* die, that I would call for help and cause the chaos that made everyone drop what they were doing to run to my side. That kind of control is short-lived, and the ramifications are so very great. These days I'd rather throw myself a surprise party and have people run to my side smiling than have them run to my side in the ICU.

Today I plan ahead. If I know someone is moving, retiring, going on vacation, getting really busy with life, or otherwise moving away from me for a while, I intentionally talk to him or her about it and try to integrate that person's essence into my being *before* the departure. When people leave me, I write about it in my journal, talk about it with friends, and tell them how I feel about their leaving and how I will miss them. Sometimes I ask for a picture or give them a picture of me to keep a visual connection. I remind myself that their leaving doesn't mean I am abandoned; the connection we share still exists even when they are gone. They are gone from sight, but not from spirit and love. I don't need to cut them off to avoid feeling the pain. I can embrace them now and hold on to them later. This is what Sylvia means by integration: the ability to hold on to all aspects of yourself and all of your experiences to create a whole sense of self.

Even with all the years of practice I literally forget about people if they aren't in my life on a regular basis. It's not like forgetting their name or how I met them; it's as if they never existed. So I drag out the pictures, take quiet time to remember their essence, write about them, call them, and reconstruct our connection.

Let's look at trigger number 6: "End of chorus, therefore, a purpose." Do you ever feel let down after completing something big, something you've been working toward for a long time? This letdown happens for most people, but for me it can trigger intense feelings of abandonment and loss of identity, because I'm suddenly without that *thing* I had—the thing that once helped define me. Or the goal may have required structure and routine—chorus rehearsal once a week, play rehearsal every night, writing this book every day—and now that structure is gone, and suddenly there is a gap to fill. That gap can trigger fear, loneliness, and confusion. When it did, I would eventually feel lost but not know why. I'd get depressed, then start the scramble to fill the void in any way possible.

Since I now know my brain style, I can prepare long in advance for these types of situations. If I know play rehearsal is going to end next Thursday, I either make plans with people for the following few Thursdays, to adjust gradually to the change in routine, or I find another activity to take the place of the rehearsal on a long-term basis, thus decreasing the likelihood of difficult feelings being triggered. It's all about prevention.

Number 7 is a biggie. It's the one that took the longest to decipher and was the hardest to release: "Recent stability and fear of expectations/needs not getting met." Trigger number 7 was at the core of my suicide cycle. After a crisis I would gradually get stronger and begin to reinforce my coping skills; as a result, I would become more independent, more able to meet my own needs. But with independence came the fear that no one would ever meet my needs again. (There's that word "ever.") I would act out or fantasize about suicide to make other people meet my needs and soothe the fear. It was a complicated dynamic.

Interestingly, this dynamic is now a clear signpost of growth because it means I am getting stronger and more self-sufficient. My fear of not getting needs met still surfaces in times of great stress or fatigue, but instead of acting out I ask for help, or I coach myself until the fear is quelled. I'll ask a friend to cook me dinner or drive me to an appointment. I'll ask people for support in a big decision or for reassurance that I am not alone. I'll even ask for advice about simple things like flossing, storing winter clothes, cleaning upholstery, or deciding what kind of gas to put in my car.

Or—and this sometimes works the best—I'll give someone else exactly what I need. I'll cook dinner for a friend, send someone a loving card, offer to help with chores, bring someone flowers. In Judaism this is known as a "mitzvah" (see the chapter "Service—Helping Others" in part 3). Mitzvahs are particularly effective when done in complete anonymity. When I am feeling financially insecure, I sometimes walk down the street and drop quarters on the sidewalk for strangers to find, figuring it will reinforce their sense of abundance.

————————

Like any experiment, some of my coping techniques were formed through trial and error, and others were prescribed and fit nicely into an existing plan. I should also stress that needs change as you grow; therefore, my approach has changed as I have. Though it kept a basic shape, my new way of dealing with life became less rigid, more pliable, more open to movement.

It took a long time to learn how to recognize triggers, longer still to start avoiding them, even longer than that to understand the resulting feelings, and longest of all to find the willingness to stay better once I got better. However tedious, it's what I had to do to stay alive and well.

SOMETHING TO THINK ABOUT

- Most of the triggers that used to knock me for a loop have little or no effect on me now because I practiced the Tricks of the Trade over and over again until they became as much a part of me as suicidal thoughts once were.

Stopping the Snowball

Everyone knows how to make a snowball, right? You gather up some snow and squeeze it into the shape of a ball. Then you throw it at someone or make it into a snowman. To make a snowman, you roll the snowball around the yard until it gets big enough in size to be a body part. The snow has to be just the right consistency, or your hard work yields nothing but a sore back and wet mittens.

To snowball is "to increase, accumulate, expand, or multiply at a rapidly accelerating rate." That's exactly what my brain used to do with difficult feelings and suicidal thoughts. My brain was sticky and steep enough to make the smallest snowball grow in size with just the slightest push, and I pushed a lot, until the feeling or thought was so out of proportion that I thought suicide was the only answer.

Stopping the snowball means putting the brakes on a feeling before it runs wild. It's another form of outthinking the brain. I can still remember the first time I consciously stopped suicidal thoughts from snowballing. It was probably in 1993. I had been struggling with despair for days. Then one night I thought, "Okay, I'm going to change this. I'm going to make a conscious effort to change my thoughts"—and it worked! I couldn't believe the relief. For all of you women out there, it felt like the reprieve you get between menstrual cramps, just after they peak and before they peak again. Suddenly I was without emotional pain, and having none made me realize how good it felt to feel good. I had used the key and unlocked my mind.

I remember feeling a little shocked that it actually worked. I even called Sylvia to tell her. At the time I thought I had changed suicidal thoughts for eternity. Sadly, I was mistaken. That was only the first of hundreds of times I consciously stopped the snowball and put the brakes on suicidal thoughts. But the more I did it, the better I got at it. Like I said, we get plenty of opportunity to practice.

EXERCISE: STOPPING THE SNOWBALL

All of these steps are described in detail in part 3.

1. Sense the snowball in action by using your thoughts, feelings, and body as guides. Are you in all-or-nothing mode? Are you thinking in terms of "shoulds," "nevers," and so on? Does your mind feel out of control?

2. Take a step outside the cycle to observe yourself in it. Remember to avoid self-judgment. Just be an observer.

3. Listen to the message beneath the suicidal thought or difficult feeling.

4. Identify the feeling or thought that was triggered, causing the snowball to roll.

5. Ask these questions: "Which of my needs is not getting met?" "What just happened to trigger this experience?"

6. Review recent events to see what may have triggered the thought or feeling.

7. Have a plan of action ready (Tricks of the Trade) to deal with the feeling or thought.

8. Use the plan of action.

Finding Relief

Once I became aware of all these elements of suicide prevention—brain style, feelings, triggers, limit setting, Tricks of the Trade, and willingness to stay safe—I began to find long-lasting relief *without* suicidal thoughts. Instead of giving in to my brain, I began listening to my heart. I began to see that relief can be painless and more permanent.

This kind of relief has given me more love, connection, and comfort than anything I've ever known. It is truly a joy to live in my own skin. Whatever discomfort I may feel, I know it will pass, 100 percent guaranteed. It is a blessing for which I am truly grateful. Yes, I cry and get angry and hurt, but deeper than that experience is the knowledge that life is good and I can find peace, regardless of the whirlwind around me. Every morning I can choose to step into my skin and greet the day with hope. Here is a song I often listen to first thing in the morning:

> *Take your situation, all your circumstances,*
> *Put it on you like it's made to fit you right.*
> *Take your friends and family, take the mile around you,*
> *Take the time that's left and step inside your life.*
> *Slip it like a glove around you*
> *Don't you miss this love that's found you*
> *Look at all that's real.*
>
> *Climb in, wear it like a suit around your heart.*
> *You've been thinking you could not be where you are.*
> *Every morning don't be thinking where you might have been.*
> *Every morning, shake it out and step into your skin.*
>
> *There is no mistaking, this is where you've got to.*
> *Here's the life that you have dragged around so far.*
> *'Cause you could stretch it out and make it fit you better*
> *If you put it on and start with where you are.*
> *Don't be halfway out and dreaming*
> *Don't be lost in doubt and scheming*
> *Look at all that's real . . .*
>
> *Climb in, wear it like a suit around your heart.*
> *You've been thinking you could not be where you are.*
> *Every morning don't be thinking where you might have been.*
> *Every morning, shake it out and step into your skin.*

—DAVID WILCOX, "STEP INTO YOUR SKIN"

PART THREE

Tricks of the Trade

Journal drawing, 1994

This above all: to thine own self be true.

—WILLIAM SHAKESPEARE

Trick #1
Asking for Help

I am a kind of paranoiac in reverse. I suspect people of
plotting to make me happy.

—J. D. SALINGER

I was so intent on being miserable that I often second-guessed people when they tried to help, even if I asked them to help me. This
was the process in my brain: "I don't want to feel better! But I do.
Leave me alone! But don't leave me alone. Leave me to my misery!
But don't leave me to my misery. It's mine, you can't have it, but
here, take it!"

Push-pull. When I pushed people away, I felt rejected and alone,
feelings that caused angst to escalate, which in turn caused me to crave
connection, but when offered it, I'd pull away, feel abandoned, and the
vicious cycle would start all over again. It was a cycle that was very
hard to break. But I did break it—by asking for help, practicing the
Tricks of the Trade, and being willing to let go of pain.

Here's Sue's doctrine on asking for help:

1. To get help, you have to ask for it.

2. It is both normal and necessary to ask for help.

3. Asking for help is a sign of strength.

4. Asking for help gives other people permission to ask for help.

To get help, you have to ask for it. I have friends who reach out if
they see that I need help, but for the most part it's up to me to do the
reaching. This doesn't mean they care for me any less. It just means

they are people with lives that don't revolve around mine. I am *not* the center of the universe. Are you?

It was hardest to reach out when things were really heavy for a number of reasons:

1. My brain would tell me no one really cared.

2. My brain would tell me life would never get better anyway.

3. I was afraid of people's rejection if I *did* ask for help.

4. The harder it got, the fewer help options I seemed to have.

Number 4 was probably the biggest fallacy of the bunch. In reality, if a person has fifteen help options today, he or she has that many—*or more*—tomorrow. These options *still exist* even though suicidal thoughts scream otherwise. My help options slid out the window whenever my feelings started to escalate or my brain constricted with tunnel vision. I'd find myself left with two choices (or so I thought): life or death. That is why it's important to learn how to outthink the brain, push beyond what you *think* is real, and reach out for the help that is available.

It is both normal and necessary to ask for help. I've always been an emotional person, and I now see that as a tremendous asset. I grew up with the message, "No one wants to hear it," which I discovered was absolutely untrue. The truth is that the person who says "No one wants to hear it" is the one who doesn't want to hear it. I found plenty of people willing and able to hear and accept me, feelings and all; I just had to look in the right places. Had I been afflicted with diabetes, migraine headaches, allergies, cancer, or high blood pressure, I would have been taken to a doctor immediately, examined, treated, and monitored. Because my problem was psychological in nature, my disease was virtually ignored until I took myself to therapy when I was nineteen, and by that time childhood coping mechanisms had solidified in such a way that therapy was more of a Band-Aid than real treatment.

Asking for help is a sign of strength. When I found places to share my feelings and ask for help, I let it rip. In fact, I eventually had to learn how to regulate the amount I shared instead of spilling myself all over the place. But in the beginning I needed to purge. I sometimes felt embarrassed after sharing so deeply, but people would often approach me and say, "Your sharing really helped me a lot. Because you were so willing to be honest about what you were feeling, I felt safe to be honest too. Thanks."

Asking for help gives other people permission to ask for help. I've been gifted with the ability to ask for what I need when I need it. I think it stems from being hospitalized in the psych ward and from years of therapy in which I'm often asked, "What do you need? How can I best help you?" I've been told *repeatedly* by people that when I reach out and ask for what I need, it makes it easier for them to reach out and do the same.

————

In my experience there have been three distinct sources of help: spirituality, other people, and myself. I've created a pie chart (see page 62) to give you a feel for where and how I found help. In terms of creating long-term life change, therapy was the most important, followed by spirituality. In my mind, spirituality includes animals, nature, and the Divine.

Other people. My therapist Sylvia was the main force and touchstone throughout the transformation, but certain family members were also key, as were friends and acquaintances woven through stretches or particular moments of my life. Aside from Sylvia, the most helpful people in times of acute crisis were the ones I could call and ask for direct, immediate relief: talking for a long time on the telephone, providing company, a sleep-over, a video or movie, holding me, cooking dinner for me. I gravitated toward those who were least judgmental and more open, because they felt safe.

It's funny: Most of the people who were so important in the beginning are no longer actively part of my life. Those relationships were gradually replaced by new friendships, based in mutual interests rather than self-preservation. The relationships that withstood years of crisis

SOURCES OF HELP

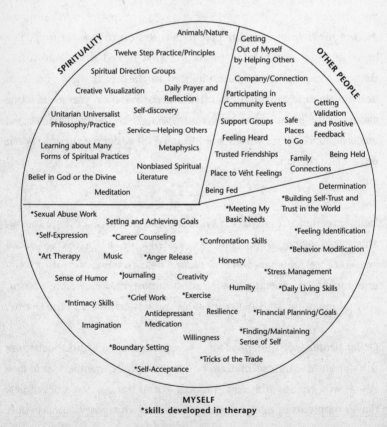

SPIRITUALITY

Animals/Nature
Twelve Step Practice/Principles
Spiritual Direction Groups
Creative Visualization
Daily Prayer and Reflection
Unitarian Universalist Philosophy/Practice
Self-discovery
Service—Helping Others
Learning about Many Forms of Spiritual Practices
Metaphysics
Nonbiased Spiritual Literature
Belief in God or the Divine
Meditation

OTHER PEOPLE

Getting Out of Myself by Helping Others
Company/Connection
Participating in Community Events
Support Groups
Feeling Heard
Safe Places to Go
Getting Validation and Positive Feedback
Trusted Friendships
Family Connections
Being Held
Place to Vent Feelings
Being Fed

MYSELF
*skills developed in therapy

Determination
*Building Self-Trust and Trust in the World
*Meeting My Basic Needs
*Sexual Abuse Work
Setting and Achieving Goals
*Feeling Identification
*Self-Expression
*Career Counseling
*Confrontation Skills
*Behavior Modification
*Art Therapy
Music
*Anger Release
Honesty
*Stress Management
Sense of Humor
*Journaling
Creativity
Humilty
*Daily Living Skills
*Intimacy Skills
*Grief Work
*Exercise
Resilience
*Financial Planning/Goals
Imagination
Antidepressant Medication
Willingness
*Finding/Maintaining Sense of Self
*Boundary Setting
*Tricks of the Trade
*Self-Acceptance

and growth were those with family, and they were the hardest to change.

Spirituality. A newly understood belief in a loving "God" provided the comfort and answers that underscored and outshone all human contribution. (God, Goddess, Universe, Nature, it's all the same to me. For lack of a better word, I will alternate between God and the Divine.) I have loved God, hated God, and loved God again. Because the God of my understanding is all-loving, I can scream my pain without fear of retribution. I can ask for suicidal thoughts to be removed from my brain. I can pray for guidance and clarity. I can pray for strength and comfort. I can pray for forgiveness and understanding. God does for me what I cannot do for myself (see the chapter on "Spirituality, Nature, and Meditation" for more).

Myself. I found a friend in me the moment I became willing to consciously change my life. As I've said, therapy has been the number-one factor in my transformation, but all the therapy in the world won't make a damn bit of difference if I refuse to pick up my feet and do the legwork. It is up to me—with the help of the Divine and other people—to do what's in my best interest and *keep* doing it. That can be hard when my brain is trying to keep me down. The next time you need help, but your brain tells you not to ask for it, I suggest you try this fake-out exercise.

EXERCISE: FAKING OUT THE BRAIN

1. Say to your brain, "Leave me alone! I'm asking for help."

2. Do exactly the opposite of what your brain tells you to do. For example, if your brain says, "Don't call Sam," pick up the phone and call Sam. If it says, "Don't tell Sam what's going on," tell Sam immediately.

3. If your brain tells you to get into bed and unplug the phone, stay out of bed and keep the phone plugged in. Better yet, put stuff on top of your bed so you *can't* get into it.

4. If the phone rings and your brain tells you not to pick it up, pick it up.

5. If you haven't eaten in twelve hours and your brain says not to eat, eat something healthy.

6. If your brain says not to call your therapist, call your therapist.

7. If your brain says not to call 1-800-SUICIDE, call 1-800-SUICIDE.

8. You get the idea.

Trick #2
Emergency Contacts

Sometimes the greatest growth comes through pain, but it's
not the pain that helps me grow, it's my response to it.
Will I suffer through the experience and continue as
before, or let the pain inspire changes that help me grow?
The choice is mine.

—ANONYMOUS

According to Befrienders International (www.befrienders.org), "An esti-mated 1 million people kill themselves every year. Many wouldn't if they only had someone to talk to. Listening saves lives. Suicide is often a permanent solution to a temporary problem. When we are depressed, we tend to see things through the very narrow perspective of the present moment. A week or a month later, things may look completely different. Most people who once thought about killing themselves are now glad to be alive. They say they didn't want to end their lives—they just wanted to stop the pain."

1-800-SUICIDE • 1-800-784-2433

National Hopeline Network

If you are in crisis right now and experiencing strong suicidal thoughts, I suggest you continue to reach out by calling 1-800-SUICIDE (1-800-784-2433), the toll-free twenty-four-hour confidential national suicide hotline. You will reach a nonjudgmental, compassionate, trained crisis-line worker who can get you help. You are definitely worth it.

IF YOUR BRAIN TELLS YOU NOT TO:

1. Ignore it and call the number anyway.

2. Say to your brain, "Leave me alone. I want to make this call."

3. If that doesn't work, tell your brain, "Fuck off! Leave me alone. I want to make this call."

4. If your brain really starts screaming, I suggest you reread these words over and over again (aloud is good) while you go to a phone, pick up the receiver, and dial 1-800-SUICIDE.

5. When your call is answered, you'll first hear a very brief recorded message, then some recorded music. Stay on the line and breathe deeply; within seconds you will be routed to a human being who will listen and help.

6. If your brain tries to trick you, remember: if you really wanted to be dead, you wouldn't be reading this book. Relief is possible without self-harm.

Each of the following hotlines is confidential and available twenty-four hours a day, seven days a week. For complete descriptions of each, see part 7.

- **National Hopeline Network:**
  1-800-SUICIDE (1-800-784-2433)
  The National Hopeline Network links callers to the nearest certified crisis hotline. After a twenty- to twenty-five-second recorded message (which the Hopeline is working to eliminate by 2002), followed by five seconds of recorded music, "you can expect to reach a trained crisis line worker who will do a lethality assessment, make appropriate referrals, and provide intervention if needed. You can also expect to reach a nonjudgmental empathetic listener." In the year 2000, the National Hopeline Network routed over 250,000 calls.

- **Covenant House Nineline: 1-800-999-9999**
  The Covenant House Nineline "provides crisis intervention, referral, and information services to troubled youth and their families throughout the United States. In the year 2000, the Nineline received over 58,000 crisis calls from youth throughout the country." There is a five- to ten-second recorded message, offering the option of English (press 1) or Spanish (press 2). I was connected with a friendly human being immediately.

- **Girls and Boys Town National Hotline: 1-800-448-3000**
  "Highly trained counselors provide free confidential services twenty-four hours a day, seven days a week. Calls range from

relationship and parental discipline to depression and suicide." In a crisis situation, the counselor will assist the caller by providing emergency intervention and information about community resources. You'll hear a fifteen-second message offering the option of English or Spanish is followed by five seconds of music before you're connected with a counselor. For more information, visit the website at hotline @boystown.org.

- **Trevor Project: 1-800-850-8078**

  This is a helpline for "gay, lesbian, bisexual, or questioning youth." If all the counselors are currently helping other people, the phone rings awhile, then you get a friendly fifteen-second message asking you to call back in ten to fifteen minutes or to leave a message with your name and phone number; they will call you back as soon as one of the counselors is free. If you get this message, call 1-800-SUICIDE (1-800-784-2433).

- **Kids Help Phone: 1-800-668-6868 (Canada)**

  "Kids Help Phone is a national bilingual and anonymous phone counseling and referral service for children and youth [of Canada]. Their professional counselors answer an average of 1,000 calls every day. Kids call about a range of concerns, including relationships, substance abuse, violence, and suicide. Any problem, big or small, they are here to help you through." There is also a Kids Help Phone Parents' Hotline (1-888-603-9100). For more information, visit the website at www.Kidshelp.sympatico.ca. *Note:* This number works only in Canada. If you are in the United States, please dial 1-800-SUICIDE (1-800-784-2433).

- **Befrienders International: www.befrienders.org**

  With a network of 361 centers (staffed by 31,000 volunteers) in 41 countries, Befrienders International provides a "free, confidential, and nonjudgmental listening service to people who are lonely, despairing, and suicidal." The service is available in ten languages. People are befriended by telephone, in face-to-face meetings, by letter, and by e-mail. Start by visiting the website. Scroll down and click on "Enter." You can then choose from several options. Click the top option, "Feeling Suicidal or Depressed?" and you will be given another list of choices, including support via e-mail, a crisis hotline near you, and more.

• **Your therapist or psychiatrist**
I hope this person has a twenty-four-hour answering service that you can call in times of crisis. Keep the telephone number posted by the phone. If you reach your therapist's answering service and you are in crisis, you need to tell the person that it is an emergency situation and that you require immediate assistance; otherwise, your therapist might not get the message for an hour or so. If you do not make voice contact with a human being, call 1-800-SUICIDE (1-800-784-2433).

• **Your local emergency room**
This number can be found in the business pages of the phone book or by calling Information (411). Look up your hospital; there should be a listing of all the departments. You can also dial the first number on that list and be connected with the emergency room.

• **Your medical doctor**
This is a good number to keep handy as a backup. If you feel safe with this person, he or she can be a link to finding specific help for your situation.

• **TTY user emergency number**
This toll-free number is usually listed on the first page of the phone book, along with other emergency numbers.

Important Note: I was recently advised by the executive director of the National Hopeline Network to *exclude* 911 as a number to call when having a suicidal crisis, particularly one involving firearms or knives. Because police officers have had limited training in deescalating a suicidal crisis, it can become a life-threatening situation for both the caller *and* the police officer who arrives on the scene. This is new information for me. In the Crisis Plans I made, 911 was always the last option, *after* "Call Sylvia" and/or "Call the Psych Center." I used 911 two or three times.

Trick #3
A Crisis Plan

I was required to make a Crisis Plan before being discharged from the psych ward, which really pissed me off. I didn't want to make any promises about keeping safe. Suicidal thoughts were my drug of choice, and I didn't want to let them go. Guess what? I didn't have to. I just had to let go of acting on them.

Nevertheless, making a Crisis Plan seemed like an enormous task. It felt like the doctors and nurses were trying to control me, and beyond that, I was deeply afraid that no one would ever meet my needs again if I could suddenly meet them on my own. In reality, the doctors were teaching me how to manage my feelings. The Crisis Plan gave me choices, my *own* choices. When my feelings got out of control or I was hit with a suicidal thought, there were simple instructions to follow:

1. Take a deep breath.

2. Pray for help.

3. Ask for suicidal thoughts to be removed from my brain.

4. Choose an activity and pay attention to it.

5. Practice Feelings Versus Facts.

6. Call someone. . . .

The Crisis Plan not only helped me figure out what my needs and feelings *were*, it taught me how to ask for help without the drama of a suicide gesture.

Despite the severe resistance I felt at first, designing my Crisis Plan became enjoyable. I actually had fun with it. I've included various Crisis Plans to show how they changed as I did. I suggest you use Crisis Plan #1 as a guide to create your own.

Take a look at the sample plan opposite and remember—none of this can be learned overnight. "Chunk it down," as my therapist would say. It's one step at a time. One moment at a time. Everything in Crisis Plan #1 is discussed in this part of the book. All the elements—the Brady Bunch Syndrome, HALT, and so on—are listed in the table of contents in *roughly* the same order as they appear in the plan.

Difficult feelings come and go for *everyone*. A lot of people talk about "feeling their feelings." I couldn't afford that luxury; it usually led me into the suicide maze. I had to find the gray area inside my gray matter—black-and-white thinking was too dangerous an option. By using a Crisis Plan, I learned how to shine light on reality and lessen the effects of tunnel vision (either-or thinking). I learned how to distract my brain, shove suicidal thoughts aside, and create a better space for

CRISIS PLAN #1

For When I'm Feeling
Overwhelmed
Angry
Helpless
Trapped
Confused
Lonely

Possible Activities
Take a warm bath.
Play word games.
Clean my bedroom.
Do a puzzle.
Go for a walk.
Knit or crochet.
Shower.
Make a gift for someone.
Reorganize my closet.
Make notecards.
Play with the cat.
Blow soap bubbles.
Draw or color.
Plan menus for the week.

1. Take a deep breath
2. Ask for suicidal thoughts to be removed from my brain.
3. HALT.
4. Take another deep breath.
5. Identify feelings.
6. Practice Feelings Versus Facts.
7. Write down feeling for later.
8. "Do in spite of how I feel."
9. Choose an activity or task.
10. Pay attention to that activity or task.
11. Choose another activity or task.
12. Call someone:
    Jeff 1-000-0000
    Julie 1-000-0000
    Jen 1-000-0000
    Jenny 1-000-0000
    Al-Anon 1-888-4AL-ANON
    Church 1-000-0000
13. Take a deep breath.
14. Choose an activity or task and pay attention to it.
15. Call an emergency contact:
    Sylvia (therapist)
    1-800-0000
    Cape Psych Center
    1-800-0000
    Cape Cod Hospital
    1-800-SUICIDE
16. Put down any weapons and keep both hands on the phone.

Remember
Feelings Versus Facts
Brady Bunch Syndrome
HALT
All feelings change
Do in spite of how I feel
Act as if

myself. It wasn't easy by any means, but when I had a plan to follow, I was more likely to do something positive rather than fall into Never-Never Land.

A Crisis Plan is an organizer, a step-by-step recipe for survival. This simple list of activities, phone numbers, and reminders keeps you safe when your brain starts flipping out. This is the one trick I would urge you to follow completely. It is the backbone from which the rest of the book flows.

A Crisis Plan provides clarity when the brain is fogged by emotions. It makes decisions for you: if number 1 doesn't work, go on to number 2; if 2 doesn't work, go to number 3; and so on until you reach step 15, "Call an emergency contact," and step 16, "Put down any weapons and keep both hands on the phone." Hurting yourself is not an option on the Crisis Plan.

I didn't usually reach the final step in my Crisis Plan. By then, suicidal thoughts and difficult feelings were either gone or shoved aside; I had followed the plan and diverted my brain with simple tasks like washing the dishes, making my bed, or making a card for someone. Or I had used other tricks: turning on all the lights, dancing in the living room, going for a walk, yelling into a pillow, calling a friend, going to a support group meeting.

If the thoughts or feelings *hadn't* subsided, then at least I was no longer physically alone. I would have invited myself to someone's house, or invited them over to mine. Another option was to stay on the phone until it was time to sleep, then plan to call someone first thing in the morning. It may sound tedious, but it worked. For that round I had kept myself safe.

A Crisis Plan helps you find and create relief. I encourage you to make and use one.

STARTING YOUR CRISIS PLAN.

You will need several sheets of notebook paper, a pencil, a phone book, and tape. Before starting your plan, let's do a stress reliever: Close your eyes or focus them on an object near you. Take several deep breaths and allow your body to sink into the chair or the floor. Then scrunch your shoulders up to your ears while scrunching your face tight, hold for three seconds, then release everything—including your breath—and let your shoulders drop. Take a deep breath. Repeat this exercise three times. Take another deep breath. Let's begin.

A Crisis Plan follows a basic format and you provide the details, such as names and phone numbers, enjoyable tasks, hobbies, and so on. I encourage you to use your imagination.

SETTING UP A PLAN. REFER TO CRISIS PLAN #1.

1. At the top of your paper, write "Crisis Plan" in the middle.

2. Under the heading "Crisis Plan," write down the first eleven items from Crisis Plan #1.

3. Write "For When I'm Feeling" in the top left corner of the page. Under that heading, write at least four or five feelings that trigger suicidal thoughts for you (anger, sadness, frustration, and so on). Look at the Feelings Galore List on page 86 and the Feelings Chart on page 84 for ideas.

4. Beneath the "For When I'm Feeling" list, write "Possible Activities." Then list eight to ten activities that you enjoy—hobbies, household chores, creative projects, sports. These activities need to be easy so that you don't get stressed out trying to do them. See the Tasks and Activities List on page 142 for ideas.

Note: drugs, alcohol, sex, cigarettes, and any mind-altering substance don't belong in your Crisis Plan.

5. Before moving on to step 6, take a little break if you need it. Get up and stretch. Go outside for a breath of fresh air, get a snack. This eases the tension in your body and brain.

6. At the top right corner of the page, write "Remember." Write down the list of tricks and reminders that appear under that heading in Crisis Plan #1.

7. On a separate sheet of paper, write the names of people you trust, who know what's going on for you emotionally. Be choosy. If you are a teenager, be sure at least one of these people is over thirty years of age. It's important to ask these people if they'll be on your Crisis Plan. Later in this chapter I tell you how to do it. For now, just write down their names. Be sure to pick people who really know how to listen. If you call them and they start offering advice or shut you out, you might feel rejected, and that could make you feel worse.

8. Under that list of names write the names of the support hotlines that apply to you: Alateen, Al-Anon, AA, NA, OA, and so on.

9. Find phone numbers to put next to all the names on your list. For Twelve Step contact information, see part 7 or look in the phone book.

10. Write "12: Call someone:" on your crisis plan, then transfer the names and numbers from steps 7, 8, and 9 above.

11. Continue your Crisis Plan by writing down items 13 and 14 from Crisis Plan #1.

12. Add item 15, "Call an emergency contact," and write down two or three emergency contact names and numbers, includ-

ing 1-800-SUICIDE (National Hopeline Network), the local hospital, your therapist, and your doctor. See the previous chapter, "Trick #2: Emergency Contacts," for a list of other options.

13. The final step in the Crisis Plan is item 16: "Put down any weapons and keep both hands on the phone."

Congratulations! This is your Crisis Plan. You did it. Now the trick is to *use it.*

ASKING PEOPLE TO BE ON YOUR PLAN

Yikes. For my first Crisis Plan, I had about five people to ask: my sisters, my niece, two friends. Since I like to get these things over with, I did it as soon as possible. I was still in the psych ward when I made the calls. It was hard. I felt embarrassed by what I'd done, angry that I had to call them, afraid of their possible rejection, and generally confused. But hearing their acceptance gave me hope and connection.

HOW TO ASK PEOPLE TO BE ON YOUR CRISIS PLAN

1. Ask one or two people each day, either over the phone or in person. If you phone, try to call when you know they're not busy; if they're in a hurry, you might feel rejected. Avoid dinnertime. If you know they're home during the day, call then.

2. Try to have people nearby when you are making the calls. If you're in therapy, try calling from your therapist's office so that you'll have support.

3. If you decide to ask in person, try to arrange a walk or some kind of activity. It's easier than asking face-to-face at a dinner

table. What you'll probably find is that once you've talked to one person, the rest will seem less frightening.

4. Plan to do something enjoyable after you finish: listen to a great CD, play with the dog, watch a movie.

WHAT TO SAY

1. "Hi. Do you have a minute to talk?" With luck, it will be a good time. If not, say, "Okay. When would be a good time for me to call you back?"

2. "I'm making a Crisis Plan to help me get through difficult moments, and I was wondering if you'd be willing to be part of my support system. Could I put your name on my phone list? I just need you to listen, rather than offer answers or advice. I just need support." If the person says yes, that's all you need do for the moment. Thank that person and either chat or say you've got other people to call.

3. If that person says no, thank him or her for being honest and take several deep breaths. You might feel rejected, which stinks, but it just means there's someone more suitable to ask. It's better for someone to say no *now* than it is for that person to say yes and then not be able to hear you later when you need help the most. Thank that person for listening to your request and say you have other people to call. Call the next person, then do something nice for yourself.

USING YOUR CRISIS PLAN

1. *Make copies of your Crisis Plan*. I even shrunk mine on the copier and kept it folded in my pocket. This way I always knew answers were at hand. Most libraries and schools have copiers.

2. *Post your plan*. Post copies of your plan wherever it will reinforce its presence in your life. Keep a copy by your bed on your nightstand. Tape a copy inside your journal or inside your locker door. Keep a copy in your desk. Keep a copy in the glove compartment, and another in your wallet. Tape one to the refrigerator and one to the bathroom mirror. Even if it feels threatening to put the plan everywhere, I encourage you to do it and simply glance at the plan when you walk by. You don't have to become a Crisis Plan wizard. Simply bring it into your life. The information will gradually sink in, and it will become a habit. Remember: I don't need one anymore. The Crisis Plan is not forever.

3. *Show the plan to someone*. If you're in therapy, definitely give a copy to your therapist. When I called my therapist in crisis—a common occurrence—it was helpful for her to walk me through the plan over the phone. If you're not in therapy, give a copy to at least one person you trust so that person can remind you to use it if you fall into crisis and are asking for help.

SOME THINGS TO THINK ABOUT

- I was an excellent martyr. I forced myself to suffer unnecessarily until the misery grew so great it was all I saw in front of me. Finally, I would let go of the misery and turn to the plan. I'd reach out for help—from myself, other people, or the Divine. Gradually the feelings would lessen, and in turn the intensity of the suicidal thought would lessen, or they would go away it altogether. Sometimes it took an hour, sometimes it took two days or

CRISIS PLAN #2

I used this plan in addition to my regular Crisis Plan when I was going through a phase of severe instability and testing (of others). I was determined to be hospitalized.

Cape Psych Center	508-000-0000
Mass Mental Health	617-000-0000
Mass General	617-000-0000
Beth Israel Hospital	617-000-0000
St. Elizabeth's Hospital	617-000-0000

A. If Dad and Bert (wife) are home:
   1. Sylvia calls hospital and finds bed.
      a. Bed available: Dad and Bert drive me to hospital.
      b. Bed not available: I go to emergency room if I don't feel safe.

B. If Dad and Bert are not home:
   1. Sylvia calls hospital and finds bed.
      a. Bed available:
         1. Calls Sally (her phone number) to drive me.
         2. If no #1, call Bob (Bob's home and work numbers).
         3. If no #1 or #2, call Dave (Dave's phone number).
      b. If I have to wait:
         1. If I feel safe, go to Sally's, or . . .
         2. Go to Sylvia's office and wait.
         3. If I don't feel safe, go to emergency room.

CRISIS PLAN #3

This is a later, more fine-tuned plan that I used after I began to understand my feelings and knew more options. You can tell I was really getting into it.

For when I'm feeling
Overwhelmed
Angry
Helpless
Trapped
Confused
Lonely

Relaxation ←
Deep breath.
Close eyes.
Smile.
Take off shoes.
Turn off TV.
Stretch, etc.
Coloring book/markers.
Stress management, etc.
Give self massage.
Listen to healthy music.
Drink herb tea.
Shower.
Take a warm bath.

1. Take a deep breath.
2. Say Serenity Prayer.
3. Pray for help.
4. Identify feelings (sad, mad, glad, scared)
5. Accept feeling.
6. Address source of feeling if I can.
7. Write down feelings (for later).
8. Relaxation
9. Give myself space.
10. Pray for help and guidance.
11. Say Serenity Prayer.
12. Set goal and complete task.
14. Pay attention to task.
15. Do in spite of how I feel.
16. Feelings do pass, they never last forever.
17. Call someone:
Jeff 508-000-0000
Julie 508-000-0000
Jen 508-000-0000
Jenny 508-000-0000
18. Call CODA people.
19. Go to a meeting.
20. Share a hug at a meeting.
21. Call Sylvia 1-000-0000
22. Stay put and keep my hands on the phone.
23. Take a deep breath.
24. Call an emergency contact:
Cape Cod Hospital
1–000–000–0000
1-800-SUICIDE
25. Stay put and keep my hands on the phone.

Remember
Feelings Versus Facts
Brady Bunch Syndrome
Doing in spite of how I feel

Give myself space
1. "I'm feeling saturated right now; it has nothing to do with you. I need a breather."
2. Stop the interaction—gradually. Set boundaries.
3. Make physical distance.
4. Go to a different room.
4. Leave building.
5. Leave house.

→ **Finding a task**
Do word games.
Do a puzzle.
Go for a walk.
Knit, crochet.
Make a gift for someone.
Make notecards.
Blow soap bubbles.
Draw or color.
Make card for someone.
Reorganize room, closet.
Play recorder/music.
Meditate.
Write affirmations in journal.

CRISIS PLANS #4 AND #5

Both of these plans illustrate how my Crisis Plan changed as I did. The one on the left was designed specifically to deal with anger once it started to surface around the sexual abuse, my mother's death, and so on. The other is an abbreviated version of the original plan that I used much later, after most of the original had become automatic.

Second-Stage Anger

1. HALT.
2. Make food (eat) if necessary.
3. Ask God what to do.
4. DO IT!
5. Talk about it:
   Karen 508-000-0000
   Sam 508-000-0000
   Linda 508-000-0000
   Marie 508-000-0000
6. Get anger out of my system:
   Throw rocks, eggs, or pillows.
   Pound pillows.
   Stomp around.
   Scream in the car or into a pillow.
   Rip up paper.
   Do something physical.
7. Go to a meeting—SHARE!
8. Pray about it. Turn anger over to God, ask God to distance me from anger.
9. Go walking on the beach or in the woods.

Crisis Plan

1. "Stop."
2. HALT.
3. Get out of self.
4. Get up and do something:
   Go to Animal Rescue League.
   Walk on the beach or in the woods.
   Color, draw.
   Straighten up.
   Take a shower.
5. Go to a meeting.
6. Call someone:
   Jeff 508-000-0000
   Julie 508-000-0000
   Jen 508-000-0000
   Jenny 508-000-0000
7. Call Sylvia 508-000-0000.
8. Call Emergency Services
   1-000-000-0000
9. Call Cape Cod Hospital
   (1-000-000-0000).
10. Call 911.

a week, but it always passed, 100 percent of the time. If I experienced the "I want to die" moment thousands of times, then suicidal thoughts have passed *just as many times*.

- When I was first out of the hospital, I turned to my Crisis Plan several times a day, every day. I carried it with me, kept a copy in my pocket, in my car, on the refrigerator, and in my journal, and gave my therapist a copy. Today I don't use a Crisis Plan at all. I stopped needing one years ago. Using it was like strengthening the muscle of life. The more I used it, the stronger I got. I got better at managing my feelings and thoughts. I fell down less and got up faster.

- One day I realized, "Why be miserable if I have a choice not to? What am I trying to prove by hanging on to misery?" I was trying to be in control, but like I said, I was completely *out* of control. When I thought I wanted to die, my brain was in control. When I chose to change, my heart and spirit were in the driver's seat.

- As I already mentioned, most suicidal thinkers don't want to die, they want their feelings to change or go away; all feelings change, with or without any help from us. You can use the Crisis Plan to get you through difficult feelings, but you don't have to wait until you're having suicidal thoughts to use it. As you'll see, the trick to all of this is to stop the domino effect *before* it reaches the suicide level.

- As when you learn any new skill, it can feel awkward when you first start using a Crisis Plan. The first time I rode a bike without training wheels I was thrilled—until I lost my balance and crashed on the pavement. I cried and didn't want to get back on the bike because I didn't think I could do it. Still, I kept trying and eventually found the balance to ride without crashing. I quickly discovered that to stay upright I had to move forward. Or if I slowed to a halt, I had to put my feet to the ground for stability. Healing from suicidal thoughts is a lot like learning how to ride a bike. We ride. We crash. We get up and ride a little farther. We have to move forward to stay upright. If we slow down we need to find support. We ride up hills, panting; we coast down the other side. Our legs and lungs get stronger, and pretty soon the hardest hill becomes a piece of cake. Eventually we learn how to ride with no hands, but it all takes practice and reinforcement.

Take a look at other Crisis Plans to see how things changed as I did.

Trick #4
Feelings

They say that pain is inevitable, but suffering is optional.
—ANONYMOUS

First things first—*feelings just are*. They are neither good nor bad. The word "bad" when referring to feelings is a misnomer because there is no such thing as a bad feeling. Difficult feelings do exist, yes, and some humans feel them more deeply than others, but remember what Kahlil Gibran said: "The deeper that sorrow carves into your being, the more joy you can contain." It's important to learn how to observe our feelings and not judge ourselves for having them. Those who struggle with emotions are equally as valuable as those who appear to breeze through life. Here's a great saying: "Don't compare your insides to other people's outsides." Sure, they might be smiling, but there could be turmoil beneath that grin. No one feels good all the time. Everyone has problems.

Feelings are powerful. Anger can put me to sleep if I "stuff it." Anger can also give me tremendous fuel if I release it; I can clean a whole house in a couple of hours if I'm angry and expressing it. I can stay stuck in resentment and low self-esteem if I ignore my fears. If I face my fears, I gain significant life momentum. Happiness gets me going so high that I sometimes wear myself thin. On the other hand, happiness fills me with love and gratitude, bringing me closer to myself and the sacred. For me, the important thing is to find the gray area, the middle ground. Identifying feelings is the first step in that direction.

EXERCISE: IDENTIFYING FEELINGS

You will need a piece of paper, a pencil and the Feelings Chart.

1. Take a deep breath.

2. After you exhale, say to yourself, "How do I feel in this moment?" Take five seconds to think about it. Do you feel sad, happy, angry, relaxed? Listen to your body. Is your breath shallow or deep? Are your hands fidgeting or still? Does your head feel heavy or light? These are all good indicators of different feelings.

3. Scan through the Feelings Chart. Can you relate to anything you see? Be as honest with yourself as possible. It's okay to feel optimistic even if you feel angry or sad, or playful even if you feel overwhelmed. Most of us have more than one feeling at any given moment. (For example, right now I feel happy, tired, relieved, a little nervous, and a little stressed out.)

4. Jot your feeling words down on the piece of paper.

FEELINGS CHART

How do I feel in this moment?

Alert   Anxious   Angry   Afraid   Ashamed   Bashful   Bored

Blissful   Calm   Cautious   Confused   Cold   Curious   Disappointed

Determined   Embarrassed   Excited   Envious   Exhausted   Enraged   Flat

Funny   Grateful   Happy   Hot   Humble   Interested   Lonely

Lovestruck   Moody   Nervous   Numb   Optimistic   Overwhelmed   Paranoid

Playful   Raw   Relaxed   Safe   Separate   Surprised   Tense

Terrific   Trapped   Undecided   Uneasy   Validated   Weepy   Withdrawn

5. Using the words you just wrote, say this sentence aloud, filling in the blank with a feeling: "In this moment I feel _____." Repeat the sentence for each feeling.

6. Take a deep breath.

7. Turn the paper facedown and keep it by your side. You'll need it in a minute.

Given that feelings are usually at the root of all suicidal thoughts, it's important to learn how to identify them. Once we start to identify them, we can start to see (and feel) them change, instead of lumping them together as "I feel suicidal." Accepting this concept was one of the first turning points in my healing process. Remember, feelings are a part of life. It's okay to feel good, just as it's okay to feel lousy. Most people have a hard time hearing about intense feelings. Either they think they have to fix the person who is having them (they don't) or they "take on" the other person's feelings and try to change them (they can't). They're uncomfortable with the responsibility (which isn't theirs in the first place), and because of their own discomfort, they try to minimize the feelings with statements like, "Don't feel that way. It's not *that* bad." When learning about feelings, it's important to find people who know how to listen, or who can at least hear your experience without trying to change it.

EXERCISE: FEELINGS CHANGE

1. Repeat steps 1 and 2 from the exercise in identifying feelings, but when you get to step 3, scan the Feelings Galore List on page 86. Can you relate to anything you see? Be as honest with yourself as possible.

2. Jot the feeling words down on the *blank side* of the piece of paper.

FEELINGS GALORE LIST

Fill in the blank: At this moment, I feel _____

accomplished	embarrassed	lazy	quiet	terrific
afraid	enraged	light		thoughtful
aggravated	envious	lonely	ragged	tired
alive	excited	loved	raw	torn
alone	exhausted	lovestruck	reflective	touched
angry		lucky	regretful	trapped
anxious	flat		rejected	
arrogant	fortunate	mad	relaxed	undecided
ashamed	frightened	manipulated	relieved	uneasy
	frustrated	marvelous	restless	upset
bashful	funny	mean	romantic	used
bewildered		mellow		useless
blissful	good	mischievous	sad	
bold	grateful	miserable	safe	validated
bored	guilty	moody	satisfied	valuable
brave			scattered	violated
	happy	naughty	sensitive	vulnerable
calm	healthy	nauseous	separate	
cautious	heavy	negative	sexy	warm
cold	hot	nervous	shocked	wasted
comfortable	humble	nice	shy	weak
concerned	hungry	numb	silly	weepy
confident	hurt		smart	willing
confused		obsessive	smothered	withdrawn
connected	indecisive	optimistic	smug	worried
content	indifferent	overwhelmed	sore	
courageous	innocent		sorry	youthful
crazy	insulted	paranoid	stressed out	
creative	intelligent	peaceful	strong	zany
curious	interested	pessimistic	supported	
	irritable	playful	surprised	
determined		pleased	suspicious	
dirty	jammed	present	sympathetic	
disappointed	jealous	proud		
doubtful	joyful	puzzled	tender	
drained	judged		tense	

3. Now turn your paper over and compare it to what you wrote in the previous exercise. Did any of your feelings change or lessen? Probably so. Maybe a new feeling came into the picture, like feeling angry at me for suggesting you do this exercise! That's okay—be as mad at me as you want. The point is: Every single feeling we experience does change, with or without any help from us. Feelings never stay the same or at the same intensity 100 percent of the time.

I often denied feeling good because I was so afraid of giving up suicidal thoughts. I'll let you in on a little secret: even if you feel good, no one can come and take away your suicidal thoughts. That's up to you, my friend.

FEELINGS CHART

The Feelings Chart on page 84 chart is a visual representation of feelings. It reminds me that there are many shades of emotion and that nothing is black or white, all or nothing. When I first started to figure out my feelings, I found it helpful to use this chart, particularly when I didn't know *how* I felt. You've probably experienced several feelings since the beginning of this book: anger, surprise, sadness, relief, hope, curiosity. Make a mental note of that.

FEELINGS CHART SUGGESTIONS

1. Make copies of the Feelings Chart.

2. Post one copy on a wall you frequently pass.

3. Whenever you walk by the chart, take a deep breath and ask yourself, "How do I feel in this moment?"

4. Choose whichever feelings pop out for you. Make a mental note of the feelings.

5. Notice how feelings come and go, or how they change in intensity, depending on what else is happening at any given moment.

FURTHER SUGGESTIONS

1. Keep copies of the chart on hand and check in with yourself once or twice a week.

2. Sit with a copy of the chart, take a few deep breaths, and scan through the faces.

3. Circle as many of the feelings as you are experiencing in the given moment.

4. Keep the marked-up copies of your Feelings Chart and refer to them whenever your brain tries to tell you nothing changes. You've got evidence that it does!

FEELINGS GALORE LIST

The Feelings Galore List is another useful tool for identifying feelings and states of being. The list will also help you see that feelings can and do change all the time. One day you might feel sad, the next happy.

FEELINGS GALORE LIST SUGGESTIONS

1. Post a copy of the list on the wall or refrigerator. Keep a copy in your car, notebook, handbag, knapsack, locker, desk.

2. Scan the list often and fill in the blank aloud. Check in with yourself as to how you're experiencing life each day, especially if you are having suicidal thoughts. What is the feeling beneath the thought? Use the phrase "I'm having a suicidal thought, and I feel _____."

3. Add feelings to the list if you don't see one that you've experienced.

4. Remember, "suicidal" is not a feeling.

TRACING FEELINGS BACK

Let's take feelings one step further. I know I'm throwing a lot of new information your way, but it will start to make sense as you practice the Tricks of the Trade and get a feel for your brain style.

Feelings stem from experience. "Tracing feelings back" means tracing an uncomfortable feeling back to the source: an argument, a disappointment, a change, an event. I still use this technique almost every day; it helps to keep my feelings in check.

There are three challenges in tracing feelings back, but each can definitely be overcome through practice. One is *pinpointing the trigger* by recalling the chain of events that led to the exact moment the feeling began. The second is *admitting to fear, insecurity, mistrust, or anger,* because so much judgment has been placed on those feelings for so long. The third is *taking a positive step* to address the feeling.

Take a look at the Feelings Time Lines to see how I used to process feelings compared with how I process them today. Maybe these time lines will help you identify some of your own patterns and see your brain style.

FEELINGS TIME LINE #1:
HOW I USED TO PROCESS FEELINGS

1	**EVENT**	1 An EVENT occurred that would cause a
2	**TRIGGER**	2 TRIGGER, which cause a
3	**DIFFICULT FEELING**	3 DIFFICULT FEELING (but I wouldn't know it at the time).
4	**DELAYED REACTION**	4 Hours (or days) later I would have a DELAYED REACTION and suddenly feel tired, overwhelmed, disconnected, or trapped, but I wouldn't know why.
5	**ROLLER COASTER**	5 The ROLLER COASTER ride would begin.
6	**INTENSIFY TO ANGER**	6 Feelings would INTENSIFY INTO ANGER.
7	**ANGER TURN INWARD**	7 The ANGER would TURN INWARD because I had no healthy release for it.
8	**SHUT DOWN**	8 I would start to SHUT DOWN, and then
9	**DISCONNECT**	9 DISCONNECT from myself and the world, a state that triggered feelings of
10	**HOPELESSNESS**	10 HOPELESSNESS and helplessness that eventually led to feeling
11	**OUT OF CONTROL**	11 OUT OF CONTROL, which led to
12	**SUICIDAL THOUGHTS**	12 SUICIDAL THOUGHTS, which gave me a false sense of control.

FEELINGS TIME LINE #2:
HOW I PROCESS FEELINGS NOW (MOST OF THE TIME)

1	EVENT	1 An EVENT occurs that causes a
2	TRIGGER	2 TRIGGER, which causes a
3	DIFFICULT FEELING	3 DIFFICULT FEELING. Most of the time I recognize the feeling in the moment.
4	SMALL DELAYED REACTION	4 Sometimes I have a SMALL DELAYED REACTION. Either way, I
5	IDENTIFY FEELING	5 IDENTIFY THE FEELING. Then I
6	STATE FEELING	6 STATE THE FEELING to myself or someone else.
7	TRACE IT BACK	7 Next I TRACE IT BACK to the original source and alleviate the confusion. Depending on the situation, I either
8	ADDRESS FEELING	8 ADDRESS THE FEELING in the moment, if I feel clear enough, or I
9	PUT IT ON HOLD	9 PUT IT ON HOLD and deal with it later, when I have some perspective or after I regroup. Either way, I usually
10	TELL SOMEONE ABOUT IT	10 TELL SOMEONE ABOUT IT, unless I feel comfortable dealing with it on my own and know what I need to do.
11	PROCESS FEELING	11 Then I PROCESS THE FEELING, and do my best to
12	LET GO AND MOVE ON	12 LET IT GO AND MOVE ON.
13	NURTURE MYSELF	13 Throughout the whole process, from the initial event to the letting go, I try to NURTURE MYSELF as best I can, by talking to myself gently, reassuring myself, and so on.

TRACING FEELINGS BACK

1. I ask myself (usually aloud), "Okay, what am I feeling right now?"

2. Once I figure that out, I ask, "When did it start?"

3. If I can't remember, I mentally retrace my steps, recalling the events of the day, until I get to the one that triggers the feeling again and I say, "Ooooooh, so *that's* what's really bothering me." Sometimes it's obvious: a fight with a friend, making a mistake at work, a death, the frustration of losing something important. Other times it's much more subtle: hearing a certain song on the radio, or seeing someone who reminds me of my mom. Hearing about someone's accomplishment can trigger jealousy or low self-esteem. Sometimes there is no reason.

4. With this new information, I can choose to let the situation go by forgiving someone or apologizing. I can pray for help in resolving the issue. I can ask someone for help in solving the problem. I can confront the situation and take care of the trigger. If I separate out the feelings from the thoughts, I can see all my options.

Tracing a feeling back lets me be an observer. I can dissect the situation objectively, do a reality check, and stop the emotional snowball from growing in size. Sometimes just naming the feeling makes me feel better because it lessens the confusion.

Finding the source helps make sense of the feeling. At least then I can say, "No wonder I feel this way." As my confusion and self-judgment ease, things stop getting blown out of proportion. I can then choose to sit with the feeling, put it on a shelf for later, or address it now. I have many choices; I'm no longer at the mercy of my brain.

SOMETHING TO THINK ABOUT

- What happened to the teenager who was found hanging with scratch marks around his neck? His feelings changed. Maybe they went from anger to fear. Maybe then they changed from fear to love (for a family member). His feelings changed, and then his thoughts changed. He decided he wanted to live, but it was too late. The feelings that had long since passed had already killed him, and that is a tragedy. Feelings and thoughts can and do change. Death can't and doesn't. It is a permanent solution to a temporary problem.

STATING A FEELING

When stating a feeling, I try to be conscious of word choice. Instead of saying, "I am angry" or "I am happy," I say, "I feel happy" or "I feel angry." I believe that the words "I am" tell my brain that I *am* anger, which I'm not; I just *feel* angry. There's a big difference.

EXERCISE: STATING FEELINGS

Read the following sentences aloud and see whether you feel a difference in either your body or your mind.

I feel so lost.	I am so lost.
I feel incredibly happy.	I am incredibly happy.
I feel sad.	I am sad.
I feel overwhelmed.	I am overwhelmed.
I feel delighted.	I am delighted.

Do the "I am" statements feel more permanent? They do to me. The "I am" defines a characteristic instead of indicating a feeling that is bound to pass.

———

It's much harder to change a state of being than it is to change a feeling. Feelings stated as "I feel . . ." have much more flexibility and movement. An awareness of how we use language for emotional expression is important. Our brain hears everything we say; even the slightest positive change can have a huge ripple effect.

Now that we've talked about feelings, it's time to learn how to check them against reality.

Trick #5
Feelings Versus Facts

As noted in the previous chapter, feelings can be complex and confusing. Moreover, they can get exaggerated by the past and have nothing to do with present reality, even though the feelings are very real.

I learned Feelings Versus Facts in the psych ward. It quickly became one of the most useful tools in my bag of tricks, always within my reach. Here's how it works. (As you read these examples, watch for either-or, all-or-nothing, black-white thinking.) I have a feeling and a related thought. Let's say I feel rejected. I state the *feeling*: "I feel rejected." Why? "Because no one ever calls me, and I don't have any friends." The *fact* is, people do call me, they just haven't called tonight. I do have friends.

Other examples:

FEELING: I feel embarrassed. I screwed up at work, and everyone thinks I'm an idiot.

FACT: Everyone makes mistakes. I am a good person and work hard. People at work think well of me.

FEELING: I feel abandoned. Jane forgot to come over. I must not mean anything to her.

FACT: Something must have come up. Jane did not abandon me. If she did forget, it has nothing to do with how much she cares about me. Her actions are not about me.

FEELING: I feel defeated. I'm never going to get anywhere. Everything is such a dead end. It's useless to try.

FACT: I *am* getting somewhere. I may *feel* defeated right now, but I am a success. I try hard, and it is paying off. I have to remember to be good to myself through this rough spot. It will pass.

See what I mean? It took practice and discipline to make Feelings Versus Facts a reflex action, but now it is. To make it a part of me, I posted "Remember Feelings Versus Facts" on the refrigerator, in my journal, on my nightstand—everywhere. It's a fairly simple idea. First you state the feeling as "I feel _____." Then you state what you *think* happened. Then you state the facts.

It's also important to point out the difference between stating a feeling and stating a belief. "I feel like such a loser" is stating a belief, because "loser" is a belief about yourself, not a feeling. You could say, "I feel embarrassed and afraid that people think I'm a loser." "Embarrassed" and "afraid" are words that express feeling. This is very important to understand, because feelings can and do change a whole lot quicker than beliefs. And remember, feelings are just feelings. A stated belief reinforces an idea that may or may not be true.

Read the following two sentences aloud:

1. I feel like I'm never going to get anywhere.

2. I feel afraid that I might never get anywhere.

Do you feel a difference in your body when you read them? Try again. This time read a bit slower and focus on your internal reaction rather than the external.

1. I feel like I'm never going to get anywhere.

2. I feel afraid that I might never get anywhere.

Feel the difference now? If not, slow it down even further and really concentrate on each word as you say it.

For me, sentence 2 has more flexibility and more room for change and is more about inner emotion than heady thought. There is a humility in sentence 2 that makes it seem more open. I feel heavier inside when I read sentence 1, like it's a message of doom. I feel more vulnerable when I read 2. It exposes a deeper layer of me.

It's hard work weeding out negativity when it's being magnified by the brain, but it can be done. Peeling off the suicidal layer to get to the feelings brings you to a place where healing can occur. Sure, it's uncomfortable to expose those inner layers, but how comfortable was it to stuff my head into a pillowcase, cover it with a trash bag, and cut off my air supply by tying a sash around my neck? At least feeling discomfort because I'm choosing to be vulnerable doesn't pop blood vessels in my cheeks like suffocation does.

Sometimes feelings aren't based in reality because they are exaggerated by the past. Old wounds deep within us are triggered by present events (see "Recognizing and Avoiding Triggers" in part 2). Because of the exaggeration, we may label ourselves falsely to make mental sense of the exaggeration. It's important to separate the past from the present and to label the feeling instead of labeling ourselves.

Feelings can also be exaggerated by conditions in the present: hunger, fatigue, stress. Other feelings such as anger and loneliness can magnify a situation and cause a runaway brain. Feelings Versus Facts puts the brakes on a brain that's working overtime to create chaos. Feelings Versus Facts helps you say, "Wait a minute, brain! I don't think so. This is what's *really* happening."

When you start to hear yourself say the words "always," "never," "ever," "should," and "shouldn't," a little bell needs to go off—a little alarm. It's time for a reality check; it's time for Feelings Versus Facts. Examples: "People *always* leave me." "I'm *never* going to have any friends." "No one *ever* calls me." "I *should* be better at _____." "I *shouldn't* be so _____." Not only are these statements false, but they contribute to feelings of helplessness, hopelessness, and general despair. They are counterproductive.

Feelings Versus Facts puts things into perspective and takes the edge off.

Trick #6
The Brady Bunch Syndrome

I first heard about an affliction called "the Donna Reed Syndrome" in the psych ward. Donna Reed is an actress who played the perfect American mom in a 1950s television show, *The Donna Reed Show*. You know the scenario: perfect house, perfect mom, perfect dad, and perfect family that solved every problem in just half an hour. This show gave a false impression of reality, and it's all too easy for highly sensitive people to compare their own lives to such false pictures. They ask, "Why can't I be like them?"

I grew up watching *The Brady Bunch* and *The Partridge Family*—same format, different generation—so I took the liberty of changing the name to "the Brady Bunch Syndrome."

I grew up believing that this white-bread American family was the ideal. Why couldn't my family be like the Brady Bunch? Comparing my life to theirs only caused feelings of inadequacy and disappointment.

If there is a crisis in a real-life family, it takes time to resolve, not just thirty minutes. Yes, real-life families often get along, but some hardly communicate. It's untrue that all family members love each other unconditionally and that no one harbors ill feelings. I suppose the other television extreme would be a soap opera. The same problem lingers from generation to generation, and grudges last lifetimes. In either case, TV doesn't give us a fair representation of the truth.

Families are imperfect because humans are imperfect. Life is imperfect. Sisters don't all get along. Brothers don't all support each other. Parents argue. Parents yell. We don't have Astroturf in the backyard, we have weeds in the garden.

Life can be difficult and life can be painful. Life can be joyous and life can be magical. *The Donna Reed Show* and *The Brady Bunch* depict the bright side of life. They don't reflect reality; any problem they do present is resolved before the last commercial break. And how painful are these problems? Jan losing her glasses and riding her bike into the family portrait that was hidden in the garage? Come on.

The Brady Bunch Syndrome is another way to check reality. When you feel overwhelmed by life and start comparing your situation with an artificial ideal, remember the Brady Bunch Syndrome. Their reality was a false one; yours is real and valid. Life is imperfect. We all face challenges daily.

Trick #7
Spirituality, Nature, Meditation

This book is about staying alive and healthy. Spirituality, nature, and meditation may be unfamiliar to some, but they are three of the most significant tools for release and relief. Had I not incorporated each into my life, my healing would have remained at a snail's pace.

Since I'm a Jewish Unitarian Zen-Quakerish, earth-loving type who believes in metaphysics and the power of creative visualization, "God" or "the Divine" are just expressions I use to name a source far greater than humankind. When I say the word "God," I am simply referring to the universal source, the higher intelligence, the all-loving spirit that lives within each of us. Some call it Higher Power, HP, Goddess, Buddha, Great Spirit, Allah, Creator, Mother Mary, the Sacred, Jesus Christ, One, Inner Light, the Universe, Mother Earth.

For me, *spirituality* is the belief in a source greater than what I can physically see or experience. When I speak of *nature*, I am referring to the symbiotic relationship of plants and animals in the natural world. Some say prayer is talking to the Divine and *meditation* is listening for answers. For our purposes here, meditation is the practice of quieting the mind. It is an excellent way to ease stress and reroute suicidal thoughts. The meditation exercises I offer in this chapter are basic but important beginnings. I am only one messenger. If you're looking for nirvana, there are many books on the subject as well as spiritual centers and self-discovery groups.

SPIRITUALITY

Being brought up without organized religion had benefits and drawbacks. Because I wasn't forced to believe in anything, my personal discovery of the sacred was that much easier—there was very little to undo.

I grew up with a religious smorgasbord: Hanukkah menorahs and Christmas trees, Passover seders and Easter baskets. There was no talk of supreme beings except every April when the Exodus story was retold. Being a Jew held little or no significance for me other than going to bar and bas mitzvahs, preparing special food for seder, and finding the matzo for a prize. When and if I prayed, it was the standard "Now I lay me down to sleep," borrowed from my Christian friends.

After my mother died, I hated God (even though I didn't believe in God). He had taken her from me with no explanation. Why did *she* have to die? Why didn't he take someone cruel instead of someone so kind? How could there be a loving God if it chose to cause this kind of pain? I still can't answer that question, but I no longer hold God in contempt for her death. I am still angry that she was taken so young, but at the same time I feel gratitude for the many miracles that are brought to me daily.

I began a determined spiritual search in my mid-twenties, through friends, relatives, PBS specials, films, and books. Something within me longed for answers. I had already begun changing my external reality with the help of Shakti Gawain's little gem, *Creative Visualization*, and was exploring higher consciousness with another handy book, *The Lazy Man's Guide to Enlightenment*, but not until I started praying to a higher being did my internal life really start to shift.

Every night in the psych ward we met for a meditation group. After leading us in meditation, the nurse would pass around a basket full of positive sayings (affirmations), and each of us was supposed to pick one and talk about it. One night, when it was my turn to share, I started crying and couldn't stop. I had to pass and let the next person go. The patient to my right reached out and gently placed his hand on my shoulder. He looked me straight in the eye and said, "It's all going to be okay."

After the group that night, he and I sat up and shared our thoughts about spirituality, nature, and God. He suggested I start to get on my knees and pray for help, "even if you don't believe in anything." I took his advice and started to pray, but my perception of the sacred was far from trusting. I can remember being on my knees and yelling, "You know I don't trust you, but I'm going to try this anyway! It seems to work for other people."

After we were both discharged from the psych unit, we remained friends, and through him I met other folks who believed in a power greater than themselves. I followed their suggestions and got on my knees to pray every morning and every night. I began asking God for guidance and courage. I began asking God to remove suicidal thoughts from my brain. I asked for clarity and forgiveness. I asked for intense fear, loneliness, and anger to be removed from my brain and transformed into positive energy. I asked for the strength to get through the next twenty-four hours. Gradually I started to believe that there was someone or something out there, watching over me, and that it was all-loving, not merciless.

Around the same time (1991) I was introduced to the Unitarian Universalist Church and found great community there. It's a simple belief system, based in love, truth, service, and the sacred in all beings. My own congregation includes Buddhists, Jews, Muslims, straight and gay people, transgendered, transsexual, Catholics, humanists, theists, agnostics, Hindus—you name it, our church has it. Prayer quickly delivered miracle upon miracle (along with lingering unanswered questions), and my faith in the sacred began to take hold. I had found another ally.

I encourage you to find your own understanding of a higher source. Explore and ask questions. My belief in a higher source is what got me to where I am today. Even if you don't believe in a higher being, I strongly urge you to practice the following exercise. The reason you are still reading this book is because you want relief without having to hurt yourself. This is one way to find it.

EXERCISE: EMOTION CLEANSING

1. Close your eyes and imagine you are in the presence of an all-loving force. This could be anything: the ocean, God, Jesus, Allah, a mountain, a forest, a warm light, the stars, magic, whatever or whoever provides a sense of comfort for you.

2. Say these words aloud: "Dear _____, please remove suicidal thoughts from my brain today and replace them with hope, courage, and clarity. Please give me the strength to let go of suicide and reach out for help. Thank you. Amen" ("Blessed Be," "Ho!" or whatever you wish).

3. Write down the prayer and keep it with you or post it by your bed. Decorate the edges to make it your unique creation.

4. Throughout the day, when suicidal thoughts rear their crabby heads, say this prayer. Say it over and over if you need to. You can even simplify it to "Please help me." God knows what you mean. Say it quietly to yourself or aloud, but speaking it aloud gives the prayer more power and intention. Demand that God remove suicidal thoughts from your brain. Scream it if you have to, but remember, it's up to you to do the footwork and follow your Crisis Plan.

5. Even if you don't believe, "fake it till you make it." You may not see immediate results, but change will come. Eventually you will find that it is easier to shift suicidal thoughts and refocus your mental energy. The prayer temporarily breaks the pattern, sending new information to your brain. In the gap you can turn to your Crisis Plan. Start at step 1 and continue down the list.

God Box. Another interesting tool is a God Box. A God Box is a simple container in which you put little scraps of paper that have written on them certain troubles, problems, questions, or concerns. By putting them in a container, you are acknowledging that they exist, handing them over to the Divine, and taking a step back from the intensity of the situation.

A God Box can be as simple as a coffee can or as fancy as a decorated jewelry box. Mine is a small square box that was given to me as a present. I don't know what its original purpose was, but when I was looking for a God Box, there it was.

MAKING AND USING A GOD BOX

1. Find a container. Any kind will do: an Altoids mint can, a cereal box, a coffee can, a shoe box, an empty yogurt container, a glass jar, a small vase. My own preference is a box with a lid, to contain the energy.

2. Write your concerns, questions, or problems on individual slips of paper, fold them up, and put them in the box. That's all you have to do.

3. Leave the box for as long as you like. I find it interesting to empty out my God Box every few months and see what has changed in my life and what has been resolved. Then, depending on what has or hasn't changed, I throw some or all of the slips of paper away.

4. Have fun with it—be as creative as you'd like. Get some markers and glitter and do up a shoe box with drawings and images that comfort you.

Affirmation/God book dialogue. I have a great daily affirmation book called *In God's Care: Daily Meditations on Spirituality in Recovery:*

As We Understand God. As a way to connect to the Divine, I sometimes sit with the book and ask a question in my mind. I tune in to my spirit and wait for an answer in the form of a calendar date. For example, if I hear "May 9," I turn to the page for that date and read the message. More often than not, it answers my question directly. After reading the page, I ask another question in my mind, wait for the answer in the form of a calendar date, read the page, and so on, until the process resembles a conversation between me and my higher source. It's very comforting.

SPIRITUALITY TIPS

- One place to start a spiritual search is a health food store. Many of them have bulletin boards with listings of spiritual groups and workshops.

- Call your local church or synagogue and ask to meet with the minister or rabbi for a one-on-one discussion. Many houses of worship have youth ministers and spiritual direction groups. Most are free.

- Ask at your school guidance office or student services building for information. Most colleges have pastoral support for those in need.

- If you know someone with a strong, healthy belief system, ask that person to share his or her experience, and try going with this person to church or synagogue.

- Libraries are great resources for spiritual literature. Find the section on spirituality/self-help/religion and let your instincts tell you which books to pull off the shelves, based on their titles.

- If for some reason you feel connected to a particular spiritual figure, say Mother Teresa, Gandhi, Jesus, Mary, or Buddha, I suggest that you find an image of that person from a book or magazine and paste in on your wall.

- Set up a simple altar with a candle and a few things that have spiritual significance for you. It doesn't have to be elaborate. It can be on a windowsill or on the corner of the piano. I have a little Mary statue standing atop my computer monitor. She's about two and a half inches tall, with her eyes closed and her hands in prayer. I've got a special rock on the other corner. I have rocks and feathers throughout my house and in my car. These are all spiritual reminders for me.

- Carry special tokens in your pocket: rocks, beads, a religious card, a special crystal.

- Above all, trust your instincts. It's important that you feel safe and supported.

The more I get out of the way and let the sacred take charge, the better my life is. Not that I sit idly twiddling my thumbs. I do a lot of footwork and take many healthy risks, but while doing so I try to release my expectations and trust that whatever will be will be, just like the song says. Now, I'm no Doris Day, nor am I perfect at practicing this way of life, but whenever I let go and surrender my life and my will to the Divine—as I manage to do a lot of the time—I am happier, more productive, more connected with others, less burdened, and at greater peace.

One of the best parts about believing in a higher source is that it's always available, twenty-four hours a day, seven days a week. It's like having a therapist whose office never closes. I don't have to be kneeling by the bed praying to be in the presence of God. The sacred lives around and within me. It lives in and around you, too. All I have to do is think about my spiritual source and a direct line of communication is opened. I can be walking in the woods, sitting at my desk, eating dinner, taking a bath, playing with children, sitting still. I can always talk to the Divine, and when I do, I am always heard. Answers may take time to surface, but they usually do if I remain open to them. I may not get the answer I *want*, but I'll get the answer I need.

One of my favorite sayings is "God knows." This reminds me that God is well aware of the goings-on in my life and knows how hard I'm trying to live well. I am not alone in my struggles or triumphs. Help is always there for the asking.

Over the past fifteen years I've heard, read, or witnessed certain spiritual principles in action that keep me connected to the sacred. I offer them here for you in the hope that one or two will help you in your search.

- Every living thing is a sacred creation and deserving of love.

- Our breath is sacred.

- Spirituality works through people.

- The God of my understanding does for me what I cannot do for myself.

- This sacred being is here to help, not hurt, though I am given tests that challenge and deepen my spiritual understanding.

- My spiritual source is always with me. I am the one who walks away.

- Spirituality is anything I want it to be as long as it comes from love.

- My spiritual source can be anything as long as I know that I myself am not it.

In response to the question "Why do bad things happen to good people?" I offer two little poems from the book *Golden Nuggets of*

Thought, volume 1, compiled by Ezra L. Marler. (Please note that I believe "God" is neither "he" nor "she.")

> God never would send the darkness
> If He felt we could bear the light.
> But we would not cling to His guiding hand
> If the way were always bright;
> And we would not care to walk by faith
> Could we always walk by sight.
>
> —ANONYMOUS

Answer to Prayer

> We ask for strength and God gives us
> difficulties which make us strong.
> We pray for wisdom and God sends us problems,
> the solutions of which develop wisdom.
> We plead for prosperity and God gives
> us brains and brawn to work.
> We plead for courage and God gives
> us dangers to overcome.
> We ask for favors—God gives us opportunities.
> This is the answer.
>
> —HUGH B. BROWN

NATURE

All elements of nature have a reason for existence and live or die in harmony with the others (as long as humans stay out of the way). Nature can take care of itself, which is why being out in nature is so peaceful and appealing. Why do you think people are awestruck by rainbows, sunsets, shooting stars, and turning leaves? Why do we have such fondness for kittens, puppies, flowers, and babies? The innocence, comfort, and purity of these creations allow us to experience our connection to the sacred. Yes, chemistry and physics have a lot to do with it, too, but creations of nature remain miraculous, and their existence is out of our control.

Being in the presence of nature reminds me of how insignificant I am in the grander scheme of things. One afternoon while walking Nauset Beach, watching the Atlantic waves pound the shore—in, out, in, out—I suddenly realized that the waves continue their shore-bound journey even when I'm not there to see it happen. How's that for thinking I was the center of the universe?

One night I drove through Harwich Center and saw a clump of daffodils standing tall in the light of the street lamp, their yellow blossoms open to the sky. They were just standing there, doing what daffodils do, with or without any human appreciation. These moments humble me, and I am reminded that there is a greater force in charge, taking care of everything.

For a person with suicidal thoughts, nature can provide respite from the chaos and stress of everyday life. Nature puts very few demands on your psyche. Nature heightens our senses. We hear birdsongs, cricket chirps, frog groans. We feel textures and see colors that we often overlook. We smell grasses, flowers, wet leaves, damp earth. During our time in the wild we become part of nature's harmony and are spared for a while the stress of the fast-paced infomercial life of the twenty-first century.

All this flowery talk about nature might sound corny, but the natural world really does soothe the spirit and mind because there is very little conflict in the relationships between plants, animals, water, earth, sky. Soak it in.

EXERCISE: TREE CONNECTION

You will need to find a tree under which you can comfortably sit or stand. This could be in a park, your yard, a friend's yard, a playground, or a conservation area, or on the grounds of your library or a school campus. You will need a watch or timer and a journal. Writing about the experience isn't absolutely necessary but will help to keep it alive in your memory after you return home.

1. Sit beneath or lean on the tree you've chosen. Make a mental note of how you are feeling and the thoughts that are running through your mind in this moment, or make notes in your journal with a date and description of where you are. (Example: "Sitting under a tree outside the gym, May 8, 2001. Feeling sad and a little excited.")

2. If you like to draw, sketch a picture of yourself sitting beneath the tree. Keep it simple and quick.

3. Take several deep breaths and feel the connection between your body and the ground.

4. Listen to the wind blow through the leaves of the tree. If it's a calm day, look up through the leaves at the sun, seeing the intricate shadows and veins of life.

5. Feel the earth supporting you. How does your body feel? Tense, relaxed, tired, energetic? Lean back on the strength of the trunk. Touch the bark and notice its variations.

6. Sit quietly and breathe deeply for about ten minutes. If suicidal thoughts enter your consciousness, simply acknowledge them and say, "I hear you, now leave me alone. I'm sitting here under a tree."

7. See how many different sounds and smells you can detect. This will help refocus your thoughts. How does the air feel on your face?

8. When the ten minutes are up, make a mental scan of your body. How does it feel? Has anything shifted in your mood?

9. If you feel comfortable doing so, begin talking/praying to the sacred as if it were a friend by your side, or write to it in your journal. Say what's going on, what you feel, and what you need.

10. After a few minutes of writing, close the journal.

11. Take some deep breaths. Try to soak in the moment, knowing that your message has been heard.

12. Thank the tree and move on. You can always revisit the scene—in your mind, in the journal, or by returning to the tree.

This exercise can be done in any natural setting: on a boat, in a kayak, on the beach, on a bike, walking in the woods. The tree is helpful because it is a sturdy presence and can become your place for retreat. There is a beech tree I climb in Bells Neck Conservation Area that has seen me through some rough times. I love sitting in its branches and feeling that support. I've been up there in every season, during rain and snow, and at sunset. Seeing the buds burst into spring leaves is comforting. It reminds me that new life is happening all year long, even if I can't see it. Watching the leaves turn and fall in autumn reminds me that I am not in charge, and that everything has its place. I observe the cycle of life and am humbly reassured.

NATURE TIPS

• Having live plants to tend keeps us connected to nature and provides a sense of purpose. You don't need a botanical garden. One or two plants will do. Buy a plant that's easy to grow indoors (a spider or jade plant) and tend it. If money is an issue, ask a friend for a cutting. For a jade, break off a piece with stem attached and stick the stem in a glass of water. Change the water regularly. Within weeks it will sprout roots and then you can plant it in regular potting soil. To make a new spider plant, you can take one of the "babies" and stick it right into new soil. Pretty soon it will make babies of its own.

- Photographs of natural settings work, too.

- Instead of a labor-intensive garden, grow a tomato plant outside in a pot. Most nurseries sell them as seedlings for under three dollars a plant. It's exciting to watch them grow, and in the end you have free food!

- If you're into gardening, how about selling your goods at a farmers' market? It's a good way to meet like-minded people or, if you prefer, just be in the company of others without having too much interaction. Call your town hall or the local newspaper for a lead.

- Hang a colorful plant outside your kitchen window that will attract birds and butterflies. At the garden center ask for one that is easy to maintain.

- Many local newspapers list free nature walks. This is a good way to learn about new places to go, and you'll have companionship without having to make conversation.

- Most areas have birding or astronomy clubs. Call your local newspaper. Just show up and go for a bird walk or look through someone's telescope at the rings of Saturn.

- If there is a national park, nature reserve, or Audubon sanctuary nearby, volunteer to clear trails.

- Visit the animal shelter. Pet and talk to the dogs and cats, puppies and kittens.

- Outfitting stores like REI or Eastern Mountain Sports often arrange ski trips, kayak and biking groups, and walking and camping excursions.

Keeping it simple is always best when your brain is on overload, but it also helps to push a little and get yourself out there, even if you don't think you can do it. Remember, that's your brain talking, not your heart. Do in spite of how you feel. You never know whom you'll meet or what you'll see once you take the plunge. You might hear some words of wisdom that could change your life, or make a connection to someone who can help you in your career.

SOME THINGS TO THINK ABOUT

- One of the natural places I go to when I need support is Cape Cod Bay. One afternoon years ago I walked out on the sand flats at low tide. The water was up to my shins, and my head was swimming with messages of suicide. I was looking for some sign that I should try to stay alive. I looked out at the setting sun and said, "God, just give me a sign. Show me *something*. Show me that life is worth living and that I should stay." I dropped my gaze down to the water and there was a floating ten-dollar bill. Is that a message or what? To me, the message was "Your needs will always be met."

- One afternoon I was walking with a friend on Nauset Beach. I had just purchased new binoculars and was scanning the horizon while we sat and talked. Suddenly I saw a white vertical spray on the horizon line, miles away. At first I thought it was the spout of a humpback whale breathing, but I soon realized it was a humpback whale breaching—lifting itself out of the water, spinning and crashing down with a great splash. It literally took my breath away. It must have breached a dozen times. Had I not agreed to walk with my friend that afternoon, I never would have seen it.

- One evening at sunset I was sitting on a huge rock, meditating, down by Orleans Cove. I was contemplating life and asking the sacred whether I was on the right track. Moments later a huge great horned owl came swooping down in front of me, fifteen feet off the ground. It glided up to a tree and perched. To me, the answer was yes.

- This happens at least six times a year: I'm driving along, thinking about life, trying to work out a problem in my head about work, a friendship, anything. When I come upon an answer, a hawk swoops in front of my car and streams into the woods on the other side of the road. This tells me, "Go with that answer."

MEDITATION

It's important for suicidal thinkers to learn how to slow down the brain. Meditation has that effect.

As far as I'm concerned, the simpler the better when it comes to meditation. If I have to think about bells, pillows, incense, candles, crystals, and soft music, forget about it. I'll have the wrong color candle or a wick that won't burn. My crystals will need clearing. The incense will set off my allergies, the CD player will forget to repeat, and I'll wind up with show tunes in my ear instead of "Om Nama Shivaya."

One of my spiritual mentors said it best: "The only thing I need to meditate is my rear end." For me, meditation is about sitting quietly, with or without the above paraphernalia, closing my eyes or softening my gaze on an object, breathing deeply, and connecting to God. My goal in meditation is not to unlock universal mysteries or see Peter at heaven's gate, though I do reinforce my spiritual connection in this quiet time. My primary aim is to slow down my thoughts, release stress and troubles, breathe in love, and give my brain a break.

Before reading the meditation exercise, please review the chapter on deep breathing; breath concentration is a big part of meditation. Again, my instructions are simple and probably Zen-deficient, but they work for me, so I offer them to you.

EXERCISE: SIMPLE MEDITATION

You will need a quiet place, a clock or watch . . . and your rear end. Ask not to be disturbed for fifteen minutes or so. Try to make your surroundings as peaceful as possible. If you live with a big family, do this exercise when people are quiet—early in the morning or after they go to bed. You can also do this sitting on a bench, in your car, on the beach, or in the woods.

1. Sit comfortably on the floor or ground or in a chair, keeping your spine straight if possible. Do a mental scan to see what you're feeling.

2. Check the time and add ten minutes. Either set the alarm to ring in ten minutes or remember the time and check the clock periodically to know when to stop. Soft alarms are best because you don't have to think about the time while you are meditating and they don't blare you out of nirvana when it's time to stop.

3. Soften your gaze on an object in front of you, or close your eyes if that feels more comfortable.

4. Take several slow, deep breaths, counting to eight for the inhalation and eight for the exhalation, with a two-second pause in between. Practice purse-lip breathing on the exhale by pretending to whistle and slowly let the air out.

5. Now, as you breathe in and out, focus on the word "love." Breathe it in with your inhalation and exhale "love" with your exhalation.

6. Continue to breathe "love" until your alarm goes off or it's time to stop. Take several deep breaths, wiggle your toes, move your body, and slowly open your eyes. How do you feel? Do a mental scan. Has anything shifted?

For a variation, you can inhale love and exhale anger, fear, suicidal thoughts, or loneliness for the ten minutes, releasing them into the universe for positive transformation. The next exercise elaborates on that theme.

EXERCISE: SITTING MEDITATION WITH VISUALIZATION

Once again, you will need a quiet place, a clock or watch, and your rear end. If any of this feels too complicated, just stick to the deep breathing and forget about the other instructions.

1. Sit comfortably on the floor or ground or in a chair, keeping your spine straight if possible. Check the time and add ten minutes. Either set the alarm to ring in ten minutes or remember the time and check the clock periodically to know when to stop.

2. Soften your gaze on an object in front of you, or close your eyes if that feels more comfortable.

3. Take several slow, deep breaths, counting to eight for the inhalation and eight for the exhalation, with a two-second pause in

between. Practice purse-lip breathing on the exhale by pretending to whistle and slowly let the air out.

4. On the next exhalation, imagine a root growing from the base of your spine, down through the ground, and into the center of the earth.

5. With each exhalation, imagine the root going deeper into the center of the earth, grounding you.

6. On your next inhalation, imagine bringing the energy from the center of the earth up through the floor and your feet, through the chair, and into your spine, letting it flow right out of the top of your head.

7. See a connection growing between your head and the heavens. As you exhale, imagine the powers of the heavens coming down through your head, down your spine, through the floor, and into the center of the earth.

8. Continue this breathing for a few minutes, keeping the image of your connection to the earth and sky.

9. Now shift your focus to the word "love." As you breathe in, breathe in "love." See it rise from the center of the earth and float through you toward the sky. Breathe it in from the sky and let it float through you toward the earth.

10. Stay with the "love" breathing for a few minutes.

11. Now, as you exhale, exhale anything that is troubling you: fear, suicidal thoughts, anxiety, anger, a question, a situation. Let it drift to the center of the earth, where it is transformed into positive energy and returned to you as love in the inhale.

12. Continue this love exchange until your alarm goes off or it's time to stop. Take several deep breaths, wiggle your toes, move your body, and slowly open your eyes. How do you feel?

13. If you are a visual person like me, try drawing the images you saw, even if they are just colors and words. Write about the experience in your journal or simply tuck it into your mind.

EXERCISE: SIMPLE WALKING MEDITATION

When I do walking meditation, the goal is to quiet my mind and become focused on the breath while grounding myself and feeling my body push through space. I don't usually think of anything else, such as love or releasing feelings. You will need a small area in which to move that is quiet and where you will be undisturbed for ten minutes. This meditation can be done indoors or out.

1. Stand up straight and feel your feet planted on the ground beneath you. Take several deep breaths.

2. Make a gentle fist with one of your hands, keeping the thumb out, and place it on your stomach, above your belly button.

3. Lay the other hand softly over the back of the first hand, with your elbows resting at your sides. Your forearms should be parallel to the ground.

4. Soften your gaze and begin to lift your right foot slowly off the ground while taking in a deep breath. Hold your foot off the ground until the inhale is complete.

5. As you exhale, slowly place your right foot down in front of you, feeling it land very carefully.

6. As you begin your next inhalation, lift your left foot slowly off the ground; as you exhale, carefully place the foot in front of you.

7. Inhale up, exhale down. It's all very slow and methodical. You can walk in a large circle, back and forth across a room, along a nature trail, or in a field.

8. When ten minutes have passed, take a few deep breaths, wiggle your body, and jump up and down. How do you feel?

Trick #8:
Acting As If

Seize the opportunity by the beard, for it is bald behind.

—BULGARIAN PROVERB

Please remember that I know how hard it is to do *anything* when the brain is aching. The simplest thing feels remarkably difficult. A slight movement can feel like climbing a mountain. Making a cup of tea can feel like navigating a minefield. I lived with that mental grind for years; the mere thought of making a change could physically hurt. Still, I encourage you to take that first step. A tiny step. You can do it, even if you have to drag your brain along, kicking and screaming. I am offering these suggestions as ideas, proof that it is possible to outthink the brain.

Just as there's a fine line between feeling your feelings and being stuck in them, so a fine line exists between acknowledging your feelings and being ruled by them. Three important self-coaching axioms are: "Act as if," "Do in spite of how you feel," and "Fake it till you make it." They have more or less the same meaning: feel your feelings and move forward anyway. For example, I feel overwhelmed by a problem I can't seem to shake. I want to give up, but instead I "act as if" and keep moving forward, one little step at a time.

In the past, I spent thousands of hours in bed sleeping or planning my suicide instead of faking it till I made it, but when I did find the energy to act as if, quite often I felt markedly better just by giving it a try. The mere act of *trying* to act as if, or being *willing* to act as if, often lessened my angst because it showed my self that I could take steps to meet my needs.

When I say "fake it," I don't mean fake being happy if you're sad, or fake being certain if you're afraid. "Fake it till you make it" means to acknowledge, accept, and advance: note the feeling, accept it for what it is—a feeling—and move forward anyway. Do *in spite of* how you feel.

Trick #9
HALT
(Hungry, Angry, Lonely, Tired)

To halt means to stop. In this case HALT means to stop and take a look at yourself: Are you Hungry, Angry, Lonely, or Tired? These four states have a direct impact on the way we respond and relate to life. HALT is a reminder, a tap on the shoulder that says, "Wait a minute. What's going on in my brain and body? Are my thoughts running wild? Am I reacting strongly to an average situation? Is it hard to make decisions? Do I feel physically weak or shaky? If so, am I hungry, angry, lonely, or tired?" If the answer is yes, then I have to do something about it.

If you forget to put gas in your car, it stops running. If you don't get enough food or sleep or experience a buildup of anger or loneliness, your brain can stall like a car's engine. It backfires, chokes, stutters, and makes dealing with life that much harder.

If I am hungry, I need to eat. If I am angry, I need to process my anger. If I am tired, I need to rest. If I am lonely, I need to make a connection. If I ignore these fundamental needs, my brain gets the best of me. I become more vulnerable. I react rather than respond to external stimuli. I lose my center, and my general perception of reality is either spiked out of proportion or dulled to ambivalence.

Ironically, the brain voice has also become a healthy monitor. I'm sure most of you have heard of the "inner child" theory. Well, to me, another message this voice represents is my inner child, trying to get her needs met. If she feels neglected or scared because I'm ignoring basic self-care, I have to listen to that voice and meet those needs. Otherwise, she will resort to chaos to get my attention and the attention of others. If I am getting overwhelmed by all the things I think I *have* to do, so much so that I start slipping and sliding mentally, I have to *stop*, be humble, and say, "I can't do it. I need your help." Often one simple act of generosity (a yummy casserole or someone washing my piled-up dishes) will give me the energy to do three other tasks I'd been avoiding, because I no longer feel alone in my struggle.

HUNGRY

As recently as the day I'm writing this, April 27, 2001, I am challenged by food. I am coming out of a borderline personality episode

Note: The information in this section does not necessarily apply to those experiencing eating disorders such as bulimia, anorexia, or compulsive overeating. Some of my suggestions—for example, keeping peanut butter crackers, fruit, raisins, or trail mix on hand to ward off hunger and the effect it has on the brain—may not be appropriate. Please consult a medical professional if food is a significant challenge for you. Another resource is Overeaters Anonymous, 505-891-2664 (www.overeatersanonymous.org).

that began a week ago. Because I get disconnected from my self during a BPD flare-up, my relationship with food is temporarily compromised. I tend to postpone eating because it requires too much effort, or I crave sugar to soothe my fear and disconnection. And in the words of my Uncle Herbert, "Sugar is dynamite."

The thought of healthy food preparation is paralyzing at times like this: what to make, how to make it, doing the dishes, storing leftovers, emptying the compost. My brain jumps at the chance to take me down: "Oh, just go to sleep and wake up in the morning without having had dinner. It won't matter. You'll be *sleeping*, why do you need food?" "You don't need breakfast, just drink juice until lunch." When lunchtime rolls around, I hear, "You don't really need lunch. It's too hard to make a decision about where to go. Why don't you just wait until dinner?" Dinnertime arrives, and I'm so hungry I can't think straight. My blood sugar is so whacked that I'm light-headed, tired, irritable, easily confused, and unfocused; I just want to sleep, and I usually do.

When I get depressed, food is usually the first thing to go. I have trouble figuring out what to eat. I don't want to eat. I don't care. Plus, starving myself is one way to let my brain punish me. That is the extreme picture; it doesn't get that bad anymore. Usually.

Food is fuel, a basic need. Without enough of the right food, a simple task can seem enormous, especially to a brain that's already stressed and bent on self-destruction. On a deeper psychological level, hunger can say a few different things: "My needs aren't getting met. I'm all alone. No one will ever take care of me." Or "I have control over my body." Or "I'm not worthy of being taken care of properly." My response to hunger can fall into any or all of these three categories, depending on the situation.

On a physical level, hunger causes headaches, dizziness, weakness, stomach pain, and shakiness. Chronic starvation can cause serious long-term damage. Erratic food intake causes drastic highs and lows in blood sugar, which affects the thought process. If you're hungry, eat, but beware of eating too much sugar or ingesting too much caffeine. They have a whiplash effect and can cause a big emotional crash. The better you eat, the better you feel. See the "Food Tips" later in this section for ideas and information.

Today I try to eat well, though it still can be a challenge. I try to keep my insides as clean as I can. I have fish or chicken occasionally but try to stick with fruit, vegetables, grains, and soy products. I try to eat organically grown foods to keep pesticides and hormones out of my system. I drink soy milk rather than cow's. I rarely eat eggs or cheese, and I keep tabs on my sugar intake.

Back to sugar and dynamite: after a sugar binge, blood sugar levels skyrocket and later plummet, causing moods to spike, then crash. We may feel good while we're eating sugar, but the aftermath is predictably difficult. When I come down off sugar or caffeine, I usually feel tired, sad, or generally crappy. Instead of a candy bar, try a piece of fruit or some cereal. Instead of coffee, try juice or a fruit smoothie.

EXERCISE: FOOD CHECK-IN

1. Make yourself a sandwich, but don't eat it. Pour some juice and prepare a piece of fruit, but save them with the sandwich.

2. Wait until you're really hungry, and before you eat, do a mental check on how you feel. Do you feel irritable, tired, light-headed?

3. Eat the sandwich and fruit and drink the juice. Wait five minutes.

4. Now how does your mind and body feel? Does your stomach area feel warm? Do you feel more relaxed? Do you feel less irritable?

5. Keep a mental note about these changes and remember what it felt like to be really hungry and then what it felt like after you ate.

FOOD TIPS

Remember, these are just ideas. Pick and choose.

- When you start doing this kind of internal work, your body burns up more calories, so you might find that you get hungry more often. Listen to that and keep yourself feeling physically comfortable.

- If possible, keep fruit around or carry packages of peanut butter crackers, raisins, trail mix, dried fruit, popcorn, or energy bars.

- Keep bottled water with you. Drinking fluids is important. If you get dehydrated, you might get a headache. Try drinking some water and see if it passes.

- If you tend to skip breakfast like I do, leave cereal and fixings at work and eat on your morning break.

- Make a list of the meals you like to eat and keep it somewhere accessible. When you're really hungry and can't figure out what to prepare, read the list and be reminded of your options. Remember, it's okay to eat breakfast foods for lunch and dinner and vice versa. There is no rule book.

- Keep canned beans in the cupboard. You can throw them in soup or salad or mix them with rice for good protein. They are inexpensive.

- Go shopping before you run out of food. Shop with a friend for companionship.

- Eat before you go shopping; it helps you make better decisions.

- Shop with a list to avoid frustration. If you know you like a certain brand of something, stick with it for a while so that you don't have to keep making new decisions about what to buy. This saves time and mental energy.

- Keep lists of the foods stored in cupboards on the cupboard doors to avoid the "out of sight, out of mind" syndrome. I did this for a while to remind myself of what I had on hand to eat. When I used something up, I'd cross it off and add it to my shopping list.

- Volunteer to prepare a meal for a homeless shelter and make a double batch, keeping one for yourself.

- When you cook dinner, prepare enough for two or three meals; put leftovers directly into individual containers to take to work or school.

- Have a soup-making gathering. Each person brings a lot of one ingredient, and you all prepare the soup together, going home with containers full of delicious memories.

- Eat "comfort" foods when it's hard to eat: soup, smoothies, yogurt, soft foods, warm foods, scrambled eggs, PB&J sandwiches.

IF MONEY IS AN ISSUE

- Visit your local food pantries for veggies, bread, cereal, pasta, sauces, eggs. Call a local church or the department of social services for food pantry connections. All of the food is free. I went to food pantries for a couple of years before I got back on my feet again. Volunteer at the food pantry for companionship and a self-esteem boost.

- Many communities offer food exchange programs. You receive forty or fifty dollars' worth of groceries for a low fee in exchange for community service. Ask at churches or food pantries for more information.

- Look into food stamps. Often you can get emergency food stamps without being on welfare. Call your department of social services for information. If you don't qualify for food stamps, ask about alternatives. Social services people usually have good leads.

- Offer to barter with a friend. You could clean her house for two hours a week or do yard work in exchange for a homemade casserole.

- Volunteer at a church supper or a weekly church luncheon. See local newspapers for listings or call the church. Along with free food, you'll find sweet companionship, a chance to be greatly appreciated (boosting self-esteem), and an opportunity to help others through service.

- Volunteer to serve meals at a homeless shelter. Along with receiving a free meal, you may find that the hardships of others shed light on your own.

ANGRY

Anger is a wind that blows out the lamp of the mind.

—ANONYMOUS

If I can't turn off my anger, I can turn it over to God.

—*IN GOD'S CARE*, MAY 26

Anger is powerful. Some people say that depression is anger turned inward. It's the heat that can eventually leave you cold. Anger is an explosive feeling for me and can do extensive damage if I don't take care of it. To survive I had to find outlets for my anger.

If you feel angry, there are reasons for it. Anger, like all feelings, is an indicator, an internal response to an external situation or event. Because I wasn't taught or allowed to express my anger appropriately, mine eventually grew so out of proportion that it started to eat me alive. And I didn't even know I was angry! That's the astounding part. My anger got twisted into self-hate and self-destruction. To top it off, because I didn't know how to deal with uncomfortable feelings in general, most feelings turned into anger, which just magnified the whole situation.

It took a while to learn what anger feels like. In the body, anger causes teeth to grind, cheeks to flush, the heart to race. It causes heat, which is the dilation of blood vessels due to a hormone surge. Sometimes I can feel the heat start in my chest and rush up my body to the top of my head. Or my face feels hot and fuzzy. Anger causes the body to clench. It can cause stomachaches or diarrhea, general irritability, high blood pressure, headaches, fatigue, insomnia. I believe a lot of physical illness is due to suppressed anger.

Turn back to page 90 and take a look at my Feelings Time Lines. Notice how my feelings used to generalize into anger. Read through the steps. Does any of that sound or feel familiar to you? It's okay if it does. Actually, it's good that it does, because now we can start to pick the process apart and put on the brakes. The initial feelings of anger, fear, or sadness were healthy and normal, by the way. But my brain would reroute those feelings and turn them into suicidal thoughts. This happened so often, and for so long, that the entire sequence began to take as little as ten seconds.

When I learned what anger is and how to identify it, then I found ways to express it appropriately, without hurting myself or others.

Have you ever felt anger? If you're not sure, think of it this way: Do you ever have the urge to slam doors, break things, throw things, or scream? Do you ever feel a hot rush in your face followed by fatigue or disconnection and confusion? Does your heart race? Do you suddenly have uncontrollable energy?

At the beginning of my healing process, the most important thing was to get the anger out of my body rather than analyze it and find the source. It didn't matter if the anger was out of proportion. I just had to release it so that I wouldn't turn it on myself. As I got better, my therapist and I worked on identifying anger the moment it happened.

Even now, however, it sometimes takes me an hour or even a day to realize I feel angry about something. In the meantime, I usually feel disconnected, confused, and slightly overwhelmed. Then I try to recall the event and say, "Oh, that's right! I got really angry back there and didn't do anything about it." Sometimes just saying those words makes the disconnection go away. Other times I have to confront someone or try to remedy the situation. Today, for the most part, the anger stays relatively small and simply confuses me for a while.

If you're angry, let it out, but be sure to let it out in a way that hurts no one, including yourself. Here is a list of safe (and fun) ways to release anger. I'm sure your imagination can devise others. Some of these might sound strange, but they work.

TRICKS THAT RELEASE ANGER

- Throw rocks into the woods, water, or into the ground. If you feel comfortable doing so, scream out the reason for your anger when the rock leaves your hand. If you can't scream, just say it aloud in a regular voice. If you're mad at a particular person, speak to him or her as if he or she were standing right there. (You can verbalize your anger this way while doing any of these tricks.)

- Take several slow, deep breaths and on the exhalation make a long sound.

- Pray for help in removing anger from your body, replacing it with forgiveness, compassion, patience, or clarity.

- Scream into a pillow.

- Scream in your car or while you're walking in the woods or on the beach.

- Keep an anger journal, separate from your regular journal, and write about the anger—scrawl about the anger if need be. Write it down and rip it up.

- Write your angry feelings on raw eggs (or draw someone's face on them) and then throw the eggs at trees or large rocks.

- Hit raw eggs with a bat, as if they are baseballs. (You don't have to worry about littering because animals will eat the eggs.) Be careful not to hit into the wind or you'll wind up with egg on your face like I did!

- Throw pillows.

- Punch pillows, making sure they are thick.

- Write about your anger, then rip up the paper.

- Stomp around the house.

- Go for a fast walk or a run.

- Talk about the anger out loud alone, with someone else, or to a pet or tree.

- Draw the anger. You can draw simple shapes, scrawl certain colors that represent anger for you, splotch colors, whatever works.

- If you play an instrument, "play" the anger. I play the piano, and when I need to, I improvise an expression of my anger through musical notes.

You can add a few of these anger release tricks to your Crisis Plan if that would be helpful. A word of caution: be sure that none of these tricks hurt you or anyone else. If while doing any of these you begin to feel worse, stop what you're doing and try something else. Choose an enjoyable task from your Crisis Plan and do that instead.

I honor your anger. It is very real. Please remember, you don't have to hurt yourself to express it.

LONELY

When I was in the throes of suicidal ideation and depression, too much alone time was dangerous. I had to make connections with people or animals, even if I had trouble feeling the connection. I would sleep on a friend's couch, find a companion for a movie or a walk, or go to the animal shelter to pet the dogs and cats. At times I needed to be around other people just so I wouldn't hurt myself.

I encourage you to find people who are open to hearing about pain and confusion, who will let you talk without interruption and won't try to "fix" you. Be choosy. If you meet someone you like who seems to have what you want in terms of inner peace, ask that person how he or she found peace; then try doing the same thing.

In addition to friends and family who take the time to understand your situation, there is also tremendous support available from the wide community of people who attend Twelve Step meetings or other support groups. Clergy can be helpful too, but be sure they are open to hearing about suicide. Some religions see it as a sin. I disagree. Guidance counselors, coaches, and doctors are also available for help.

After I got out of the hospital in 1991, I began to build a support network of friends and family. It was essential that I have those early relationships to get me through the tough times, and it was essential that some of them fall away in order to permit growth.

I believe people are put into our lives for a reason; they don't all stay forever. Parting ways says nothing about the inherent worth of either person. Their presence has a purpose in our lives, as does ours in theirs: to teach us a lesson, to be a bridge, to give us an important nugget of wisdom, to challenge us, to set us on a new course.

When I began to get irritated if people called just to check on my mental health, it was a *good* sign. It meant that I wanted and needed more from the relationship than a one-way ticket. Unfortunately, the changing roles of friends would set off my borderline personality disorder, even if I was the one who initiated the change. I became angry at both ends of the equation: angry that they kept seeing me as weak (so I'd push them away internally), then angry because it felt like they were abandoning me. Ugh.

There will always be times when everyone in your support network is busy or hard to reach. My own experience has taught me some other ways to deal with loneliness at those times:

- Loneliness can be temporarily relieved in a crowd. If I can't find someone to hang with and I feel uneasy being alone, I go to a public place like a library, the beach, the supermarket, a concert, a restaurant, or the movie theater. Sometimes I just need to see that I'm not all alone on the planet. In the past this type of outing sometimes made me feel worse because I saw couples and families together and I started comparing my insides to other people's outsides. Most of the time, however, getting out in public distracts me long enough to let something shift internally.

- For a long time I visited the animal shelter almost every day. Some people find it terribly sad, but I saw my presence as a gift to the needy animals. I would talk to them, pet them, tell them they would soon have a new home. They always gave me unconditional love. Some shelters let you take the dogs for a walk. Remember pets in your own times of need. They are great friends and companions.

- Volunteering is another way to remedy loneliness. It gets you out of yourself and puts the focus on something external. One place I used to volunteer was at the local library, shelving books. No one had to know what was going on for me mentally. I just showed up, rolled my cart around, and did a good deed. My mind was diverted with the task of organization and I felt good about myself. Volunteers are usually welcome at animal shelters, schools, literacy programs, community gardens, camps, civic organizations, nature groups, choir groups, theater groups, or nursing homes. Remember, your input can be as small or as large as you want it to be.

- Another trick to deal with loneliness is keeping yourself busy. Once again, keeping the mind focused on things other than your loneliness can help it lessen or pass. See the Tasks and Activities List on page 143 for suggestions.

As I've already mentioned, one of my chief challenges has been learning how to hold on to the essence of people and events when they are no longer physically present. By listing their qualities and remembering special events, I reinforce their presence, rekindle the warmth I feel with them, and remind myself of the connection we share. Here's a fun exercise to try.

EXERCISE: CREATING CONNECTION

You will need a piece of paper and a pencil. If you want to make a collage, you will need scissors, white glue, and a large piece of heavy paper.

1. Make a list of people (or animals) you admire or those with whom you feel comfortable. They could be friends, relatives, schoolmates, coworkers, the bank teller, a professional athlete, a film star, or a historical figure. Include yourself on the list. Leave space under each name.

2. Starting at the top of the list, read each person's name and think about what it is that you admire about him or her, or why you feel comfortable in the presence of that person. How is each one of them special? List these qualities under each name. If you have a special memory of an event, add that, too. For example: "Julie Pina—I appreciate her friendship and love. I remember the time Julie showed up in her pajamas to my come-as-you-are birthday party. It made me laugh. I enjoy her humor and willingness to play." (FYI: the qualities we see in others we already have in ourselves.)

3. After you have listed the qualities and memories, read the list aloud and let it sink in. Post it on the wall or keep it handy so you can review it if you start to feel lonely again.

4. If you have pictures of these people or animals, take them out and look at them. Post the pictures somewhere easily seen.

5. Make a collage with the pictures, words, and/or images from maga-zines. Post the collage on your bedroom wall and look at it daily. This will further reinforce the presence of these individuals in your life.

I also do this exercise in person, speaking directly to the person with whom I want connection. For example, I will tell someone, "I really appreciate your sense of style." Or, "I appreciate how well you relate to people. You are a powerful example for me." Or, "You guys are the greatest. I really love working with you." Not only does this strengthen your connection to them, it also makes them feel good.

TIRED

Take rest; a field that has rested gives a beautiful crop.

—OVID

I love to sleep, but being tired does not always mean I *should* sleep. Fatigue can mean a lot of things: emotional overload, low blood sugar, lack of exercise, too much stress, too much busyness. I have to be care-ful to listen to all of my sleep messages. Then again, sometimes I just have to give in and sleep, like I did recently, until 2:30 P.M.

Some people require more sleep than others. I try to watch my inner clock and keep tabs on externals, too. Am I working too much? Am I pro-cessing new emotional information? Have I just gone through a major stressor? If the answer to any of these questions is yes, I need more sleep to stay caught up with myself. If I deny myself enough rest, I lose my center and become irritable and easily overwhelmed. Self-care starts to slip. More important, too much fatigue triggers the notion that my needs aren't get-ting met and never will, opening the door for my mischievous brain.

When I was depressed, I spent hours in bed, days in bed, but depression differs greatly from general fatigue. Depression sleep wasn't about recharging or regrouping. It was about isolation and giving up.

Today when I'm overtired, I show up for life to the best of my ability, but once I'm back home I rest. My therapist encourages me to exercise when I'm fatigued, but I can't say I heed her well; I prefer to get horizontal. Sometimes I reward myself with sleep *after* exercising. If I'm lucky, the exercise lifts my energy and I head down a different road, but most often if I'm tired I need to sleep.

I recently made an important sleep discovery: instead of seeing sleep as a waste of time and feeling guilty about it, I now see it as essential to life, like eating, working, and playing. I don't have to feel bad about sleeping half the day if it helps me function better. I happen to be a person who needs a lot of sleep, and that's alright.

Sometimes sleeping was the only way I thought I could survive suicidal thoughts. At least if I was asleep I wouldn't be hurting myself, right? The trouble was that staying in bed too long led to severe loneliness and hopelessness because my brain would have nothing to think about other than how bad I was feeling.

To meet sleep needs without feeding a self-destructive brain, it's important to create structure and routine. It's also important to practice moderation. If you are super-tired most of the time as a result of depression, here is a deal you can make with yourself.

EXERCISE: SLEEP DEAL

1. Take a look at the Tasks and Activities List on page 142. Find ten that you enjoy and make two of them a form of exercise.

2. Write the list on a piece of paper and beneath that list, write: "I agree to _____ for half an hour before I get into bed or lie down on the couch. Once that half hour has passed, sleep will be my reward. I will sleep for an hour, then I promise to get up and choose something else to do for another half hour."

By doing an activity, you can refocus your brain and some of your fatigue may lift. You may find after the first half hour of activity that you want to continue with another task. That's fine. If you're on the fence between wanting a sleep retreat and wanting some interaction, call and ask a friend to come over to watch a movie. That's a passive activity, requiring little effort, but you will have company while you do it.

One afternoon I was lying in bed, churning with thoughts of suicide. As I wondered how I could ever survive my life, I got this image of being on a ship caught in the middle of a hurricane with forty-foot seas. At the time I thought the sea represented my life, but in actuality it represented my *perception* of life. The boat's mast stood firm despite the violent water and represented my ability to withstand pain.

In the image I had both arms wrapped tightly around the large, wooden mast, and my body was flapping from it like a flag, slamming into the deck with every plunge of the bow. I could only keep my grip, close my eyes, and wait for the weather to clear. Somehow I knew the boat would not capsize. It was just a matter of time before the wind would relax and the water's surface would become more manageable. In that moment I realized that however bad things may appear and however crazy it feels to be inside my body and brain, the weather will always clear. All I have to do is hold on and wait long enough to see the sun again. Then I can let go of the mast and sail to dry land. After all, the sun is always shining—somewhere.

Here is another image I use when I need support and reassurance.

EXERCISE: CURLED UP IN THE HANDS OF THE SACRED

You will need a comfortable place to lie down—a bed, a couch, grass, or the rug on the floor. You can be lying on your back, your stomach, or your side.

1. Close your eyes and picture yourself sleeping peacefully in the hands of a loving sacred being. You are being cradled, held like a precious jewel. A treasure. You are totally safe and protected—there is nothing to be afraid of. This peaceful place is for you alone. This sacred being supports you, asking nothing in return.

2. Feel the weight of your face, arms, and legs on the surface beneath you; feel the weightlessness of your whole body being supported physically.

3. If you have trouble picturing hands, simply bathe the entire picture in pink. Surround the image with a warm, protective glow and enjoy the safety and comfort it brings.

4. Stay with this image for several minutes—let the comfort really sink in. Know that when you face life, this strength is beneath you and standing at your side.

5. Practice this imagery after you get into bed at night or before you get out of bed in the morning. To me, it feels wonderful. It's a great way to start the day.

SOMETHING TO THINK ABOUT

- If your brain is focused on suicide, being hungry, angry, lonely, or tired can give the Grim Reaper stronger legs to stand on, putting you and your safety at a disadvantage. If you are hungry, angry, lonely, or tired, take a small step to meet the need. If you cannot find the energy to take action, reach out to a friend for help; one day you will have the energy to do the same in return, just as I am doing for you.

Trick #10
Keeping a Journal

The Centers for Disease Control and Prevention (CDC) have suggested a good way to help prevent suicide: "Write down your thoughts. Each day, write about your hopes for the future and the people you value in your life. Read what you've written when you need to remind yourself why your own life is important."[1]

Journal-keeping saved my ass.

I go through stages of journaling a lot and then journaling very little. Journaling is a *great* way to vent feelings and thoughts. It's a way to ask for what I need, to clarify needs, to trace feelings back, to "talk" to people I'm afraid to talk to, to practice confronting those I need to confront. It is a great place to record progress, keep helpful sayings and ideas, make daily schedules. I often write letters to God in my journals, asking for guidance on a specific challenge or goal. If I can't find the words to express myself, I draw images to represent my thoughts and feelings.

I've held on to most of my journals, so I have stacks of them. Reading over past thoughts can be enlightening. I can see how far I've come, or whether I'm still struggling with a particular issue. Writing down feelings and thoughts is another way to dissect them. Seeing things on paper can take the sting out of a moment and give you a chance to step back, take a breath, and readdress a situation from a different point of view.

Throughout this book, I encourage you to jot notes into a journal. I think you will find that this helps reinforce the experience. When my head gets clouded with confusion, anger, loneliness, or fear, I can often forget all I've accomplished. It's so easy to lose sight of a breakthrough when life feels hard again. By keeping a journal, I have *written PROOF* that my life is cyclical. It is not a straight line. Feelings come and feelings go.

JOURNALING TIP

- I prefer to use the 9¾-by-11-inch composition books with thick cardboard covers that are marbled green or black and white. These notebooks lie flat when opened, and you can fold them over on themselves without breaking the binding. Two manufacturers are Mead and Pen-Tab; they can be found at most drugstores or supermarkets in the school supply section for two to three dollars.

TYPES OF JOURNALING

There are many kinds of journals, just as there are many ways to journal. Here are a few ideas. I encourage you to use your imagination and explore this form of expression as a way to release and examine uncomfortable feelings.

One word of caution: If you begin to feel worse while writing and start to focus on negative, self-defeating, or self-injurious thoughts, *stop*, close the journal, and find something else to do that you can enjoy.

Daily journaling. For years I found it extremely helpful to keep a daily account of my activities and feelings, the people I saw, what I did, when I did it, how I felt. This helped me internalize my life and hold on to life essence. These days I use my journal to process stress or difficult feelings. Seeing it on paper helps to get it out of my head and give me a more objective view. I usually converse with myself as I write, until I get to the root of the feeling or the stress. Then I figure out what I need to do to relieve it.

Nondominant writing. Some say that the nondominant hand represents the voice of the inner child. If you are a "rightie," try writing with your left hand. Again, when you're writing this way, try to be open and refrain from self-judgment. You're the only one who ever has to read it. You can even take nondominant writing one step further: try having a "conversation" between your dominant and nondominant hands. For example, with my dominant hand (my right hand) I may write: "How am I feeling right now?" Then with my left hand I write a reply, such as, "I feel afraid that no one is going to meet my needs." Then with my right hand I ask, "How can I meet my own needs? What do you (my inner child) need from me?" With my left hand, I may answer, "I need you to feed me better." Get the drift?

Talking to God. I strongly suggest that you try writing to the God of your understanding for guidance and direction, or to simply vent feelings.

Free-flow journaling. Write without stopping, without picking the pencil or pen up off the page; keep your hand moving until you run out of things to write. If you get stuck, write, "I am stuck, I don't know what to write," until something else comes along. It's amazing what comes out when I write this way. Often a deep-rooted fear will pop into the picture, something that I hadn't realized was on my mind. Then I'll say, "Oh, so *that's* why I've been feeling so insecure." Sometimes just seeing it on paper helps to lessen the intensity. Try not to judge it even if what you're writing makes no sense at all. The point is to get this stuff *out* of your head and *onto* the paper.

Art journal. Some people use their journals purely for artful expression: collage, painting, drawing, coloring. This is another excellent way to release pent-up feelings and manifest change.

Anger journal. When I was processing a lot of anger about sexual abuse, I had a separate anger journal. I didn't want the intensity of the "anger energy" to cloud my other thoughts. This was a practical way of "compartmentalizing" the anger (separating it out so that it didn't consume me). You could do the same for fear, anxiety, stress, or any other feeling that threatens to be overwhelming.

Affirmation journal. At the top of each page, write an affirmation from the Sayings and Affirmations List on page 167, or make up some of your own. Decorate the margins of the page to personalize the saying. Beneath the affirmation, describe what it means to you and why it is important. Write the affirmation several times at the bottom of the page to reinforce the image in your brain.

Wildflower or bird-watching journal. If you like to walk in nature, try keeping track of all the birds or flowers that you see. Most libraries have bird and wildflower books. It's a nice way to connect with nature, while having a focus for your mind.

Dream journal. People keep dream journals so that they can examine their dreams and try to interpret the symbolism. One suggestion is to keep your journal and pen right by your bed. When you wake up, begin writing immediately, before the dream slips away.

Therapy journal. For about a year my therapist and I rotated two of my journals between us. I would leave one with her at the end of a session and she would read and prepare written comments on it before our next session. Meanwhile, I would be writing in the other one, knowing she would eventually read my words and respond to my questions and concerns. This was a great comfort to me. It felt like I always had access to her safety—especially when I saw her handwriting alongside mine. Journal-swapping proved to be one of the most effective tools Sylvia and I used during my most fragile times.

Over time the journal-swapping stopped completely, but not by force or design. Gradually I forgot to bring my journal to session, or I would choose not to leave it with her, because I no longer needed that form of reinforcement to feel to her essence. Just like my Crisis Plan, journal-swapping eventually became obsolete, but it certainly served me well when I needed it.

Trick #11
Tasks and Activities—Healthy Diversions

A key part of your Crisis Plan is choosing eight to ten tasks and activities that will get you out of your head by redirecting your thoughts and distracting your brain. Completing a task provides a sense of accomplishment and boosts self-esteem and self-trust. I've gotten a lot done in my life because I've had to keep my brain occupied. Difficult situations often prove productive!

When feelings are super-intense, choose a simple task: folding the laundry, making the bed, going for a walk, petting the dog, drawing a picture, praying, lying still in a quiet room, brushing your hair. If you choose a difficult task and get frustrated trying to complete it, difficult feelings and thoughts might intensify, thus defeating the purpose. You can also choose to do *part* of an activity—cleaning just one corner of a room, starting a gift for someone, starting a jigsaw puzzle—if the whole thing is too much.

Take a look at the Tasks and Activities List on page 142. They range from simple to involved. Most of them can be done solo or with another person. Choose ten tasks and activities for your Crisis Plan, or make

TASKS AND ACTIVITIES LIST

Send yourself flowers.

Send someone else flowers.

Make a simple gift for someone.

Make a card for someone.

Make simple notecards.

Pray/meditate/practice deep breathing
and relaxation.

Do a jigsaw or crossword puzzles.

Draw, paint, or color.

Listen to music or make music.

Blow soap bubbles.

Clean the bathroom or part of the
bathroom.

Throw eggs at trees.

Go to a movie.

Go to a library and sit and listen.

Volunteer to shelve books at a library.

Visit the animal shelter.

Volunteer to walk dogs.

Fold laundry or iron clothes.

Play a board game.

Play a sport.

Pet or comb your dog or cat.

Clean your car or a part of the car.

Sing "Oh, What a Beautiful Morning"

Take a bath or shower.

Splash cold water on your face.

Wash and massage your feet.

Rearrange your closet.

Thin out your wardrobe.

Turn on all the lights; this "brightens"
your immediate surroundings.

Throw rocks into the woods.

Have a cup of tea.

Clean out part of the refrigerator.

Offer a compliment to someone.

Wrap yourself in a blanket and read.

Read inspirational books or magazines.

Listen to inspirational tapes.

Offer to help someone do something.

Jump up and down; really feel the weight
of your body when you land.

Leave yourself a nice message on your
answering machine.

Write yourself a nice note and carry it.

Drop coins on the sidewalk
for people to find.

Play cards/hacky sack/pool.

Juggle.

Cook something for yourself or others.

Do the dishes.

Make your bed.

Go for a brisk ten-minute walk.

Put on some music and dance.

Call a friend.

Invite someone over.

Organize your CDs.

Get outside and observe nature.

Make yourself smile every few minutes.

Rearrange your bedroom.

Water/weed/work in the garden.

Water/tend to the plants around the house.

Sew, knit, or crochet.

Work on a hobby (photography, stamps).

Do yoga or gentle stretching.

Watch an uplifting or funny video.

Rearrange the living room.

Send yourself a greeting card.

Make a collage with positive images.

Write affirmations and post them.

Work on your car.

Put photographs in an album.

Imagine something positive that you'd like
to have happen. Make a collage about it.

Write in your journal.

Write a positive poem.

Give yourself a facial.

Paint your nails.

Watch for birds outside the window.

Make a gratitude list.

Scream into a pillow.

Go to a support group meeting.

Plan menus for the week.

List the important people in your life.

Do a small home improvement task.

Go to a nursing home and visit people.

Volunteer in a children's art class.

Swim/run/jog/bike.

some up yourself. What works for me might not work for you. These are only suggestions. Please add your own interests and hobbies to the list.

REMEMBER

- Do in spite of how you feel if your brain tries to get in the way. Act *as if*.

- In addition to doing things for yourself, it helps to do things for others.

- Choose simpler tasks when feelings and thoughts are more severe.

- Praise and reward yourself when you've completed the task or activity, For example: "Well done. Good job! Good for you."

Trick #12
The Telephone Lifeline and Phone Lists

The telephone and phone lists are both crucial parts of your Crisis Plan. They are number-one ways to connect with life, for both emergencies and day-to-day living. A short or long conversation with someone can carry you through critical moments long enough for the feelings and thoughts to pass and for your moods to change. You can then take the steps necessary to improve the situation. If the feelings and thoughts don't pass, a phone conversation can link you to other help: medical attention, a support group, prayer, hospitalization, contact with a therapist or psychiatrist.

How often have you thought about calling someone but by the time you found the number you were either too afraid or too doubtful to pick up the phone? I've probably spent a year's worth of time sitting by the phone too afraid to dial. A phone list provides immediate, orderly access to the names and numbers of people and places in your support system. Instead of searching through dog-eared address books or scraps of paper jammed between couch cushions, when the need arises for a call you have the information right in front of you. Easy access.

Go back to page 72 for instructions on how to put together your Crisis Plan phone list. Write out a separate phone list, perhaps with more non-emergency contacts, and post it by the telephone, or tape it to the inside of your address book, journal, locker, or briefcase.

The days of midnight marathon calls are now over, but when I was fresh out of the psych unit, the telephone became a lifeline. I spent four to five hours on the phone daily, talking to new friends from the hospital, calling people from support groups, getting support from family, leaning on my therapist, reaching out to old friends. Whether I overdid it or not is not the issue—it worked and that's what counts.

As I slowly remodeled my brain, the need for constant external reassurance was replaced with internal strength. This evolution took place quietly and slowly until one day I noticed I was spending less time on the phone and more time with myself or in the presence of others sharing activities unrelated to my mental health.

SOME THINGS TO THINK ABOUT

- Every time I overdosed I eventually picked up the phone and called for help because my feelings changed. I started to feel afraid; the suicidal thought passed, and I no longer wanted to die. Had I passed out completely, I might have died or been left with permanent physical damage.

- Had I picked up the phone *before* I acted on suicidal thoughts, my life would have been far less complicated. Once I made the move toward suicide, I altered my life in a way that no phone call could easily rectify.

Trick #13
Contracts for Safety

I have sometimes been wildly, despairingly, acutely
miserable . . . but through it all I still know quite certainly
that just to *be alive* is a grand thing.

—AGATHA CHRISTIE

When I was in significant periods of crisis and instability, my therapist, Sylvia, insisted that I "contract for safety." By signing a simple one-line no-harm-to-self agreement at the end of each session, I made a commitment to maintain personal safety until the next time we met. If check-ins were needed between appointments, I verbally contracted over the phone. Sometimes the best I could do was contract for an afternoon or an evening, with check-ins two or three times a day.

Occasionally I toyed with the possibility of not signing, but the consequence was clearly understood: immediate hospitalization. This was a bittersweet consequence because I *loved* being hospitalized—the feeling of safety, the structure, having my immediate needs met— yet it caused such havoc within my support network. This stubborn streak was really just a war of wills—my self against my Self—a bit like teenage resistance to parental love.

A no-harm-to-self contract involves more than a promise not to *commit* suicide. It means no attempts, half-attempts, and quarter-attempts; no cutting, burning, bruising, and starvation. By signing on the dotted line, you commit to maintaining complete personal safety for a given amount of time: a day, two days, an hour, a week. It's not an open-ended commitment.

By remembering the agreement in times of turmoil and following through as promised, I demonstrated the ability to "internalize" Sylvia's presence in my life. Given my personality disorder, this was a significant step toward solidifying my bond with her. At times my heart wanted to keep her trust, but my brain had other plans; the harder I tried to do the right thing, the louder it screamed. Other times the contract was a source of comfort, a lifeline; pain and confusion seemed less frightening and more bearable.

Honoring the contract also put new information into my brain: not only *could* I take action against suicidal thoughts, but I *would*. Both of these ideas reinforced self-trust. When I found that I couldn't last until the agreed-upon time, I would call Sylvia and she would help me stabilize. Then we would set a new contract.

You can have a contract with anyone in your support system. I had a contract with Sylvia only, but I've heard of people using contracts with parents, siblings, and friends. I cannot make a direct recommendation; I can only state that it was vitally important that I had this form of agreement with a professional. She had the training to guide me through suicidal thoughts when I couldn't do it on my own. Had I kept contracts with nonprofessionals, there was no assurance that their responses would have been as trustworthy or effective. In fact, the manipulation games I played would most likely have escalated as I tested their limits. I've also heard of situations in which personal safety contracts didn't work at all. They worked for me. It's really up to the individual.

On page 148 is a sample contract. Feel free to copy it or use it as a guideline to create your own; I trust you have a great imagination. Here are some ideas to maximize its effectiveness.

CONTRACT FOR SAFETY IDEAS

Remember, these are suggestions.

- Make two copies of your contract, one for yourself and one for your caregiver. Sign both. Seeing your own signature reinforces the commitment.

- Ask your caregiver to sign it; seeing his or her signature may reinforce the bond.

- Post your contract in a visible spot as a reminder.

- Decorate the border to personalize it.

- If your therapist or caregiver wears a particular perfume or cologne, ask that person to spray some on the corner of the paper. Smell is a powerful sense. I used to carry around a sample of Calvin Klein's "Escape" because Sylvia wore it. When I needed reassurance, I'd take a little whiff and the safety of her presence would momentarily return.

The need for a contract eventually fades; we get better and we grow. We learn how to divert our thoughts and put our feelings on a shelf for the moment. We find strength through experience and start to believe that feelings do pass, with or without any help from us. We begin to trust others, and we finally trust ourselves. Until then, a contract for safety reminds our subconscious that we want to be alive even when our brain screams otherwise.

PERSONAL SAFETY CONTRACT

Date:

I, _____, promise to keep myself safe

from all harm or injury until the next time I see or speak to

_____.

SIGNATURES (YOURS AND YOUR CAREGIVER'S)   **DATE**

_____

_____

_____

_____

_____

_____

_____

_____

_____

_____

_____

Trick #14
Brain Food

I was going to buy a copy of *The Power of Positive Thinking*,
and then I thought: "What the hell good would that do?"

—RONNIE SHAKES

Some people say the self-defeating brain does push-ups when we're well so it has more strength to clobber us when we're down. Maybe. But if that's true, then the opposite is also true. When we are down and lost in the dregs of suicidal thoughts, the self-*affirming* brain is doing push-ups to strengthen and lift us out of the muck. As I mentioned earlier, I've experienced the "I want to die" moment thousands of times over the last eighteen years, which means suicidal thoughts have passed *just as many times*. That's a lot of push-ups. My brain has been busy.

It can get murky in a suicidal mind, can't it? Strange as this may sound, I think it can also be exciting to some degree, because in the chaos of the moment, we think we have control over whether to live or die. That's pretty heady stuff. But the reality is that in those moments we have no control.

Happily, the intense mental energy required to contemplate suicide is the same energy that now fuels my positive change—and it can for you, too. The depths of my sorrow now feed my joy. By refocusing the direction of the energy toward life rather than death, I catch the gusts in my sails and move forward, despite the many obstacles in my course. It's all about faith and the willingness to be open to the abundance of the universe, the willingness to say *yes*. Over the last several years I've made a conscious effort to become a yes person rather than a no person. Instead of responding to someone's dream with, "That could never happen," I say, "So, how could you make that happen?"

In her great book *Creative Visualization*, Shakti Gawain teaches us that creative visualization is "the technique of using your imagination to create what you want in your life." Her ideas expanded my vision of possibility and permanently changed the course of my life.

Gawain showed me that I have the ability to create my own reality based on what I feed my mind. By putting clear intentions out to the universe—this might get a bit New Agey, but hang in there with me—by putting clear intentions out to the universe through my imagination and faith, dreams really do come true. Not only *do* they come true, they *are* coming true. Let me clarify. I didn't create the sexual abuse or the death of my mother, but I do believe I created some of the lingering sorrow by continuing to make harmful choices based on self-destructive behavior.

Creative Visualization is the reason I'm living in my own home and it has nearly every quality I had hoped for; it's the reason I'm in an amazing love relationship; it's the reason I have a great job. Creative visualization is the reason this book is in your hands and not still in my head. With the help of the Divine, I am making dreams reality by choosing a life of possibility instead of one bound by hand-me-down constraints. Over the last ten years or so I've created most of what I thought would fulfill me by visualizing it, writing about it, praying on it, focusing positive energy on the desired outcome through meditation and collage, and speaking about it as if it's already happening.

Even during the worst times my nature was resilient but my reality was easily shattered, as was I, and the knockdown voice of my brain would often outdo me. Still, a glimmer of chance would pop into my head whenever I was on the brink of acting out. It was the old "what if?" syndrome. What if my life could get a lot better? What if I die right before something great happens? What if these suicidal thoughts go away and stay away? What if my dreams become reality?

———

Just as our body responds well or poorly to good or bad food, so our brain responds to the information we feed it. If we consume negativity, we get negative results. If we feed it positive energy, we create positive change. If we watch violent movies and listen to negative messages through music, we see the world with a more cynical eye. If we focus on serving others through word and deed, we generate love and feed our souls.

BRAIN FOOD TIPS

- When I go to the movies, I try to arrive ten minutes late so I miss the violent, explosive previews. Should I happen to arrive on time, I plug my ears and close my eyes so as not to infect my brain.

- I watch very little television, only videotapes on my thirteen-inch VCR/TV set. If I have access to TV, I watch public broadcasting, documentaries, or nature programs. Television advertising is a tremendous insult to the brain, particularly in the way it eats at our self-esteem so that we feel the need to buy some "magical" product.

- I try to shop locally and support small businesses.

- I avoid malls, department stores, and large supermarkets—way too much stimulation for this brain. The crowds, the dry heat or freezing air-conditioning, and the noise and congestion do me in. Once again, I dislike the way the advertising industry bombards us, to say nothing of using sex as a measurement of personal success.

- I try to surround myself with positive people who find joy in life and are working toward their dreams.

- I am choosy about the people with whom I share my deepest ideas and desires.

- I try to think positive thoughts about people.

- I barely read the newspaper or listen to radio news. When I do listen, it's National Public Radio. If I focus on what's wrong in the world—which is primarily what is reported—I feel markedly worse. If you do watch the news, I suggest you do so in the early evening rather than just before bed.

- I try to practice the philosophy of thinking globally but acting locally. I do what I can (like writing this book) to improve my immediate community.

- Reading something inspirational before going to sleep or first thing in the morning is a good way to clear the decks and create a good attitude.

- If I'm trying to manifest something positive in my life, I talk about it as if it's already happening. For example, instead of saying, "*If* this book gets published," I always said, "*When* this book gets published." These days it's "When I go on *Oprah*" rather than "If I go on *Oprah*." Can you feel the difference? Speaking about something like it's already happening puts that much more positive energy into the universe and shows my brain I really believe in my dreams.

It may seem like I shut myself off from the world. On the contrary, I do not ignore reality; I just ignore the reality fed to me by traditional media. I believe in creating my *own* reality, which is a world of positive, life-affirming alternatives, and I choose to focus my energy as such. I believe in *simple living*, supporting other people's dreams, social justice, animal rights, environmental protection, creating beauty through art and music. *That's* where I want to put my energy.

The abundance of the universe is limitless. It is I who put boundaries on my share of it. As I continue to focus on positivity, I create more and more of it in my life, and *I'm worth it.*

Trick #15
Therapy

More people go to therapy than openly admit. Perhaps it wouldn't take others so long to gather up the courage and make that first call if therapy were "normalized" (whatever "normal" is). Everyone needs help. None of us was born with a how-to book for living tucked into our bassinet. Nor was Life 101 a mandatory class in high school or college. Life is a challenge. For people dealing with depression and suicidal thoughts, life can sometimes feel unbearable. It's okay to ask for help. We wouldn't be human otherwise. If more people let down their guard and reached out for help, maybe there would be less suffering in the world. Maybe there would be more love.

Therapy is a great thing. Over the past eighteen years I've seen ten different therapists, at least five psychiatrists (for medication), and two group therapists, but not until Sylvia did I find the right match.

I walked into Sylvia's office on May 10, 1990. Over the past eleven years, she has supported and believed in me 100 percent as I leaped, stumbled, regressed, tested, catapulted, plateaued, crashed, and leaped again. She stood strong when people doubted her effectiveness. She fought for my independence when others wanted to lock me in a long-term facility.

Sylvia tolerated the tremendous chaos that ensued from my behavior. She faced the real fear of legal action had I ended my life, but throughout all of it her treatment of me remained constant: loving, direct, strong, gentle, appropriate, reliable, clear. Despite whatever chaos I created, she always kept our therapeutic relationship separate from the added stress. Certainly she set boundaries and held to them, but her way of relating to me hardly—if ever—wavered. She was the consistent parent I never had. She earned my trust, and I earned hers.

The bulk of my foundation work with her was rooted in the eight stages of personality development as defined by Erik Erikson (for a clinical explanation, try your local library or the Web) and can be translated into the following therapeutic areas:

- *Daily living skills:* Self-care (nutrition, bathing, rest, learning about my body, personal appearance, self-expression); learning how to meet my physical needs (food, shelter, clothing) consistently.

- *Stress management and behavior modification:* Setting limits; moderation; breath work, inner dialoguing, meditation, exercise, and prayer; maintaining focus; identifying and addressing feelings; anger release; developing inner barometer and coping skills; learning how to recognize, name, and change behavior patterns.

- *Sexual abuse work:* Memory recall through light hypnosis, imagery, drawing, and dream recall; processing memories and integrating the experience, releasing the anger, fear, and frustration; learning what is and what is not appropriate sexual behavior; developing self-affirming sexual beliefs; improving self-image and self-care.

- *Confrontation skills:* Facing fears; learning how to take safe risks; asking for what I need (whether or not I get it); finding the voice to state my truth with clarity; developing trust in self.

- *Intimacy skills:* Speaking my truth without shame or guilt; developing trust with others; learning how to let people get close to me while maintaining healthy boundaries; keeping some people at a healthy distance; opening my heart to healthy love; learning how to love appropriately without losing self.

- *Finding and maintaining identity and sense of self:* Looking within to find and nurture my strengths; revisiting my likes and dislikes; learning how to make choices by listening to myself; building self-trust and self-acceptance; setting and achieving goals; exploring ideas and having my beliefs supported as I test the waters of the world; expanding my spiritual connection; developing an attunement to my body and health; finding satisfying occupations and establishing financial security.

A TYPICAL THERAPY SESSION

For those of you who have never been to therapy, I thought it might be helpful to describe a typical session, based on my experience. Contrary to what we see in the movies, I've never been to a therapist who had me lie down on a couch. Also, not all therapists take notes during session.

Most of my therapy has been one on one, though I have been in two groups as well as couple's counseling. I prefer one on one, though I did enjoy the role-playing opportunities of a group.

One of the things to watch for when shopping for a therapist is how he or she handles confidentiality. Sylvia's waiting room is located just outside her office door. To mask any voices that might be heard through the walls, she has a white-noise machine in the waiting room and in her office. (A white-noise machine resembles a small round air filter that emits a "blanket" frequency or hum to drown out other sounds.) I've gone to a psychiatrist and another therapist who had *no* form of white noise. As I sat in the waiting room, I could hear every word of the session! Needless to say, those therapeutic relationships didn't last very long.

Typically, Sylvia sits in a chair facing me and I sit on her couch, facing her. There are about six or seven feet between us. In her office are books, plants, fresh flowers, big pillows, her desk and file cabinet, a big stuffed animal, two small clocks (one facing her, one facing the client), the white-noise machine, and some lamps. Sessions vary: sometimes I do the talking, sometimes she says quite a bit. At times we have done light hypnosis and dream recall, visualizations, role-playing. Members of my family joined me in therapy several times. She even met with my father alone once or twice.

Sessions are usually fifty minutes in length. At the end of the session I pay her (or I have her bill me), and we schedule my next appointment. Some therapists assign "homework" based on the treatment plan, or they may suggest that you read a certain book (like this one!).

Therapy tends to be expensive, but many insurance plans are starting to cover it. Also, some therapists take on pro bono work (free treatment). Always ask whether a therapist has a sliding scale. For example, a therapist may charge between forty and seventy-five dollars a visit, depending on your circumstances. I also know of therapists who barter for their fee: in exchange for a session, the client does cleaning or makes some other kind of arrangement.

There were times when I saw Sylvia up to three times a week. In addition to those sessions, we also had daily phone check-ins. As I got stronger, my treatments shifted to twice a week for a long time, then once a week for several years, then once every two weeks, and now it's once every three to four weeks. If you had asked me five years ago whether I thought I'd ever feel okay about stopping my sessions with Sylvia, I probably would have said no. In addition, just the *question* would have thrown me into a tizzy.

Today I can say, with a deep breath and a sigh, that one day soon I probably won't be seeing Sylvia anymore. If I need help with an issue—particularly pertaining to sexual abuse—I will certainly make an appointment to see her, but in general, much of what we do in therapy I can now do on my own. At this point I see Sylvia more for the fine-tuning work of reassurance and reinforcement. I am slowly but surely leaving the nest.

Here are some important things to consider when shopping for a therapist:

Boundaries. From the start I was informed that our relationship would stay within the bounds of therapist-client. In other words, we would never be friends. At first I felt rejected, but over time I saw the value in having such clear boundaries between therapist and client, particularly when dealing with transference and borderline personality disorder. Transference is defined as "the redirection of feelings and desires and especially of those unconsciously retained from childhood, toward a new object (as a psychoanalyst conducting therapy)." Some of the symptoms of BPD outlined on the website of the National Alliance for the Mentally Ill are "unstable, intense personal relationships with extreme, black and white views of people and experiences, sometimes alternating between 'all good' idealization and 'all bad' devaluation; marked, persistent uncertainty about . . . friendships and values."

My sessions with Sylvia are always about me, never about her, unless I ask. I've been to therapists who talk about their weekend plans, their grandchildren, and so on. And I'm paying to hear about it! If a therapist talks about himself or herself a lot, beware. *You* are the focus of your therapy. *You* are paying them to help *you*.

I know it sounds obvious that a therapist would keep what's said in therapy sessions confidential, but I've heard otherwise. I've heard therapists talk about their clients by name outside of session. I overheard one therapist ask someone else whether I was still seeing Sylvia. That was a breach of confidentiality. I've also been to a therapist who started crying when I said I was terminating our therapeutic relationship. I'm sure there are many good therapists out there. Just be sure to find someone you can trust who has good boundaries.

Availability. Sylvia and her associate have an excellent system for keeping themselves available to their clients outside of session. They use an answering service, so messages are taken by a human being instead of an answering machine. They check the answering service between sessions, in the evening, and several times throughout the weekend. She and her associate rotate being on call every weeknight and alternate weekends. If you call and leave a message on a weekend, either Sylvia or her associate will get back to you. Sometimes it takes hours, but they get back to you. If it is an emergency, you must say so, and the one on call will be beeped directly. And they *always* return their messages.

When I was really struggling, Sylvia and I had daily phone check-ins scheduled between sessions (sometimes twice a day). These were five- to ten-minute conversations to see how things were, get reassurance, and so on.

Consistency. As I've already mentioned, Sylvia has been remarkably consistent from day one. That may not sound unusual for a therapist, but it can be. Sylvia has seen me through a lot. I have tested and tested and tested her. She saw me in the hospital twice; I used to call her (via the answering service) at all hours of the night in crisis; I once showed up at her office drenched and barefoot after walking out of the emergency room. Through it all, she remained loving, accepting, and nonjudgmental. She is *clear.*

Sense of humor. Sylvia and I have shared a lot of laughter together because we both can see the lighter side of life. Had she not been so open with humor, I doubt I would have bonded as closely with her.

Reliability. I have seen Sylvia for eleven years. If you figure an average of at least once a week, that's 752 visits, maybe close to 1,000. In all that time, she has been late to only two appointments. One time she double-booked me with another client by mistake. She *always* returns my calls promptly, is flexible about rescheduling appointments, and gives plenty of notice for her vacations. In fact, she tapes a notice on the edge of her desk weeks in advance (facing the client) so that if any psychological prep work needs to be done around abandonment issues, the client has plenty of time to work on it. And even when she's on vacation, her associate is on call, so the client is never left in the lurch.

Intellect and intuition. I trust Sylvia's ability to treat me clinically. She is a smart woman who knows what she's doing. I also trust her ability to connect with the Divine and answer to an inner voice. I appreciate the balance she demonstrates between strength and softness. Over time these two qualities have played important roles in helping me fill my parental gaps.

Imagination. Ideas spark through me constantly. Sylvia has always supported my ideas, as long as they were self-affirming. When I was exploring my first developmental stage, I even ate baby food and drank from a baby bottle for a few months to relive the experience of being an infant. She never said a word (although she thought I went a bit too far with the bottle). She just let me do what I needed to do to fill in the blanks. Had she seen my little experiment becoming a problem, she would have stepped in and offered suggestions, but I went through it unharmed. In fact, I think the whole bottle-sucking thing *did* do me some good. I think it satisfied a mother-bonding need that I lost when my mother died. Who knows? I just know it worked for me.

Flexibility. One thing I really appreciate about Sylvia is that she didn't box me into a category in terms of treatment approach. If I wanted to explore certain things, she supported me in that work, keeping track of my stability and coping ability. She was open to my desire to get second and third opinions when I doubted her effectiveness. She stuck by me and ducked around my fastballs.

We both believe in the power of creative visualization and manifestation, so we've done a lot of work around visualizing goals, making collages, affirming goals, and so on. She has been open to spirituality and art therapy as well. Knowing that it helps me to understand my process or "see it," she has always taken the time to give me clinical explanations. She is also flexible about money if I'm in a bind. She once told me years ago, "Of course I will see you if you don't have the money. We'll work it out. You can pay me five dollars a week for the next twenty years if that's what you need to do."

I know several people who see Sylvia and think she's great. I also know a few who have gone to her and she didn't work for them. That is why I say it's important to find the right match. It's fine to try out or interview several therapists until you find one who seems to suit your style. How do you start looking? One place to start is by asking for a recommendation from someone you know who is in therapy and demonstrating positive changes. That's how I found Sylvia—word of mouth.

Therapy saved my life. Therapy taught me how to figure out what my needs are, how to meet them, and how to ask for them to be met. Therapy taught me how to live, how to be a person on this planet. I heartily encourage you to find good professional help.

SOMETHING TO THINK ABOUT

• When I first started working with Sylvia, I struggled a lot—refusing to talk, dwelling on despair, resisting change, creating crises just prior to or following positive breakthroughs. Then something shifted. I can't tell you exactly how or when, but suddenly I started to get the fact that it was up to *me* to determine how miserable I was—give or take some hormonal imbalance and the need for antidepressants. The biochemistry I could treat and monitor. The behavioral stuff—what I used to do to get in my own way—I could change by *choice* and practice. I just had to be willing to do it.

Trick #16
Vitamin "P"

Vitamin P, you've helped me see
that life was never meant to be
so hard and full of misery.
Great thanks to thee, O Vitamin P.
—A SUSAN ROSE BLAUNER ORIGINAL

I've never substituted antidepressants for therapy, nor do I want to take medication for the rest of my life, but for the time being it works and that's what matters. I resisted medication for years, then went on and off countless times. Finally I accepted the fact that for now I need it.

Prozac does not cure me, nor does it create miracles in my life. I take Prozac to keep my mental bridges intact, pay my tolls, and lube my brain so the neuron superhighway runs smoothly, without traffic jams or pileups. Prozac does none of my work for me; it just acts as a safety net for bridge construction, giving me the breathing room, clarity, and energy I need to manifest consistent change, take risks, and make self-affirming decisions. I still have to do the footwork and be diligent about my mental health to stay well.

As I mentioned earlier, had I been diabetic, I would have been taken to a doctor, tested, treated, and monitored, but because my affliction was psychological in nature, it was ignored. Diabetics take insulin to help their condition. I take Prozac to help mine. Prozac helps my brain function more efficiently, particularly in times of stress.

Remember the FedEx truck full of packages (thoughts and feelings) getting stuck at the river's edge? The neurotransmitter serotonin acts like a ferry that transports the the FedEx truck (the electrochemical messages) across the river (across a synapse from one neuron to the next). Prozac is a selective serotonin reuptake inhibitor (SSRI), meaning that it slows the reuptake of serotonin in my brain so that I will have more on hand when I need it. Prozac also helps my brain produce serotonin, which adds to the ferry transport fleet. I've been told that this drug also "caps" the emotional highs and lows, acting like a safety net.

I know little to nothing about brain chemistry or about antidepressants, other than what I've stated thus far. There are plenty of resources—libraries, your physician, the Web—through which you can learn more. The purpose of this chapter is to say that, in my opinion, if you need meds, it's okay to take them. Just be careful not to substitute meds for therapy, where all the long-term work gets done.

Also, some meds work better than others, depending on the individual. I've tried four different antidepressants but came back to Prozac. The only immediate side effect I ever experienced was dream intensification, but that passed after a few weeks. At present, my memory is slightly compromised, and that can be a drag. (I think this is a common side effect.) Quite honestly, I am a little afraid of the possible long-term ramifications, but I hope that by continuing to live a positive, self-affirming life, I will alter my brain chemistry and eliminate the need for medication altogether.

There are many alternatives to Western medicine, but I am not qualified to make recommendations. Again, I encourage you to ask questions and find out about all the options. On the website www.hopeline.com, you can find information on alternative treatments, including a fascinating letter by Gillian Ford, author of the book *Listening to Your Hormones*, which tells of her battle with suicidal depression and her use of estrogen to treat her symptoms. She says that "estrogen worked overnight and has worked uniformly for over 20 years. Be encouraged. I longed for years to die. And after age 29, I never felt that way again."[2]

I tried everything from homeopathy to gotu kola and polarity, and either I didn't wait long enough for these alternative therapies to work or I couldn't wait because I got too depressed. Certainly I'm aware that it's important to get enough "light" and eat foods that help support my mind, but in terms of altering brain chemistry, I'll stick to Western medicine for now. I don't want to mess around anymore.

MEDICATION TIPS

- *Important note:* If you *do* seek antidepressant medication and are actively suicidal, the prescribing physician or psychiatrist *must* know about it. I overdosed on my antidepressants.

- *Another important note:* If you're going to go to all the trouble of getting a prescription, take the medication as directed. It does you no good if you refuse to take it or overdose. Here's one time I'll use the word "don't": *Don't mess around.* You are far too important a person to deny yourself appropriate help. If you skip meds for a few days, you might not feel an effect right away because certain meds have what's called a half-life. I used to play around with this. Then my serotonin level dropped, and I would start to flounder. It would take a little time for the meds to build up in my system, so I'd be on an emotional high wire for a week or so. Not good. (This just happened, actually. With all the busyness of writing this book and working full-time, I forgot to take my medication. I didn't realize it until I suddenly dropped into a depressive slump and felt like I was walking through molasses all the time. Then I counted my meds and realized I was two weeks behind. I haven't felt this way in a while. It sucks!)

- *If money is an issue:* Most physicians and psychiatrists have samples they can give you. Also, many drug companies have what's called "indigent" programs for people experiencing financial hardship. I was on an indigent program for a while. See the National Depressive and Manic-Depressive Association website (www.ndmda.org/PAP or www.phrma.org) for a list of drug companies that offer assistance and ask your doctor for a form. It can be overwhelming to fill out the form, but remember, you *can* ask for help.

- Refill your prescription a couple of days *before* you run out so you're not stranded.

- Remember to get prescriptions filled before you travel.

- Let someone close to you know you're on medication so if you get in a slump and forget to take it, they can remind you.

- Take your medication at the same time every day (if it's prescribed as such). I can easily forget to take my medication if I don't do it first thing in the morning.

- If you are prescribed medication, ask about the side effects and how long it will take for the medicine to go into effect. Ask your doctor or psychiatrist whether she or he has had good experiences in prescribing the drug and what you can expect. Make sure to schedule follow-up appointments to monitor your status and report anything odd or unsettling.

- *Decreased libido:* I switched back to Prozac after my 1998 overdose and have been taking it daily ever since. I have experienced very few libido problems since then. In fact, my sexual life is stronger and healthier than it's ever been. In my case, decreased libido is not due to medication but related to the sexual abuse of my past and to relationship dynamics.

Trick #17
"Oh, What a Beautiful Morning"
—Sayings and Affirmations

One of the chief tools for lifting my spirits used to be singing "Oh, What a Beautiful Morning" from the musical *Oklahoma*. It really works—try it! If you don't know the lyrics, you can find them on the Web by typing "*Oklahoma* lyrics" in the search engine, or you can probably get a CD at the library. One place I love to sing is in the shower. It's a super release because the running water drowns out my fears of sounding funny to anyone listening. "Oh, What a Beautiful Morning" sounds great in the shower (I hope.).

I'm sure you have a favorite song or songs. Think of the ones that are uplifting and positive and sing them throughout the day or when you feel overwhelmed, lonely, or afraid. Not only do the words give your brain positive information, but the breathing involved with singing helps feed it oxygen, which can calm you. If you are into heavy metal or thrashy music, I encourage you to add music to your collection that is softer and life-affirming. Try to sprinkle such music into your ears now and then.

Sayings and affirmations (positive statements set in the present) help reassure the brain when it is running wild with feelings and thoughts. The following is a list of sayings I've accumulated from a number of sources over the past decade. Each one has helped me survive suicidal thoughts and daily challenges. I still use many of these sayings daily, and I have them posted around my house, in my car, on my computer. I speak them aloud when coaching myself and write them in my journal. I even make up sayings to help me through particular situations. For example, directly below my computer screen is a little piece of paper with "I am writing this book easily and effortlessly" typed on it.

When compiling this list, I did my best to identify the source. Some were scribbled in the margins of my journals or on scraps of paper stuck in books. Many of the quotes came from daily affirmation books such as *In God's Care: Daily Meditations on Spirituality in Recovery: As We Understand God* and the Al-Anon daily readers *Courage to Change: One Day at a Time in Al-Anon*. Several are taken from *Golden Nuggets of Thought;* others were found in fortune cookies.

EXERCISE: AFFIRMATION

You will need a pencil and a piece of paper or, if you would like, some colored paper, markers, and decorations such as stickers, glitter, and so on, depending on the flow of your creative juices.

1. Read through the following list of sayings and affirmations. When you get to one and find yourself nodding your head in agreement

or making a *hmmm* noise, put a mark next to the saying. Write that saying on the piece of paper. Make a list of your favorite sayings.

2. Decorate the list if you'd like, or make several copies of certain affirmations to post.

3. This can be fun. Make a bookmark with some sayings on it, or make a card for someone with one of the affirmations.

SAYINGS AND AFFIRMATIONS LIST

- As my attitude changes, I become even more able to give and receive love.

- God allows us to experience the low points of life in order to teach us lessons we could not learn in any other way. (C. S. Lewis)

- I attract only positive, loving people into my life.

- I am now creating safe ways to express my anger.

- As I trust myself, money comes to me easily.

- I can become a love-finder rather than a fault-finder.

- If we don't change our direction, we are likely to end up where we are headed. (Chinese proverb)

- I love myself completely as I am, and I'm getting better all the time.

- I have no idea what the universe has in store for me, but it's far greater than anything I could ever imagine. (Susan Rose Blauner)

- Giving and receiving are the same.

- I am choosing to direct myself to experience peace regardless of the events in my life.

- Forgiveness is the way to true health and happiness.

- I can let go of my past and my future.
  Now is the only time there is.

- I have a wise and loving friend within me.

- I have all that I need.

- I am enough.

- I can focus on the whole of life rather than the fragments.

- We are students and teachers to each other.

- Today I am keeping the focus on me. I cannot change other people, places, or things.

- Just for today I will try to live through this day only, and not tackle all my problems at once. I can do something for twelve hours that would appall me if I felt that I had to keep it up for a lifetime. (Twelve Steps)

- Let go and let God. (Twelve Steps)

- My life is unfolding freely and with positivity through each day.

- What people think of me is none of my business. (Twelve Steps)

- Life's a journey, not a destination. (Twelve Steps)

- I am loved.

- I am a capable person.

- It takes what it takes.

- Expect a miracle.

- Believing is seeing.

- There is nothing constant in the universe. All ebb and flow, and every shape that's born, bears in its womb the seeds of change. (Ovid, *Metamorphoses*)

- People who expect nothing never get disappointed. (Twelve Steps)

- As I feel my anger, I reclaim my power.

- It's already fine.

- I am worthy of acceptance, forgiveness, and love.

- I am a child of the universe, no less than the trees and the stars, and I have a right to be here. (Desiderata)

- I am changing.

AFFIRMATIONS AND GOAL-SETTING

I usually make a list like this once or twice a year. Notice that it is all phrased in the present tense. This is very important. Rather than writing "I will walk on the moon," write "I am walking on the moon." If something hasn't manifested before I make my new list, I simply tag it and keep believing that it's in the universal works. This list was made January 24, 2000, and posted by my night table, where I read it often. As of June 16, 2001, half of the entries on my list had already manifested in physical form (in bold), a few had partially manifested, and the rest are in the process of manifesting. (See what I mean about speaking in the present tense?)

WHAT I'M DOING

- I'm climbing mountains.

- **I'm speaking** fluent **Spanish**.

- I'm traveling around the world.

- I'm finding a healthy, long-term love relationship.

- I'm getting my book published.

- I'm creating unlimited financial abundance in my life.

- I'm exercising and meditating every day.

- I'm writing a screenplay and selling it to a studio.

- I'm making music.

- I'm feeling professionally fulfilled at work.

- I'm learning about wildflowers and their properties.

- I'm selling my piano.

- I'm emptying out my storage unit.

- I'm learning how to survive in the wilderness.

- I'm doing large-format photography.

- I'm setting up a darkroom and using it.

- I'm finding magical places to walk.

- I'm doing more.

EXERCISE: AFFIRMATIONS AND GOAL-SETTING

You will need a piece of paper, a pencil, and an open mind. If you want to make a collage, you will need supplies for that too. For a visual reference, see the What I'm Doing List.

1. Sit quietly and take several deep breaths.

2. Think about anything you would like to accomplish in your life, even if your brain tries to tell you it's impossible. Take "impossible" out of your vocabulary.

3. Begin writing a list of what you'd like to accomplish. Write *anything,* even if your brain says it's far-fetched, like "Walking on the moon." You never know what the universe has in store for you.

4. Okay, now take this list and rewrite each sentence in the present. Example: "I am walking on the moon." "I am meeting _____."

5. Make a decorative border around the list, or type it out on a computer and give it fancy dingbats.

6. If you want to, make a collage of you doing some of these things. Cut images out of magazines—say, a picture of the moon—and get a photo of yourself and cut yourself out of it and glue it so that it looks like you're walking on the moon. I'm tellin' ya, this stuff works! You'll be amazed with the results as long as you keep an open mind.

Affirmations are great. If nothing else, they shift our mental energy for a few seconds to focus on something positive, and they let a sliver of light into the darkness of our thoughts. I encourage you to use them.

Trick #18
Mirror Work and Inner Dialoguing

In the Woody Allen film *Broadway Danny Rose,* Allen plays Danny Rose, a devoted talent agent who manages an eclectic bunch of would-be performers ranging from balloon folders to a cheesy nightclub act, to a guy with a bird that pecks tunes out on a piano. Danny Rose teaches his clients to look in the mirror every morning and say "the three Ss: Star, Smile, Strong." I'm my own Danny Rose.

Affirmations tie directly into mirror work and inner dialoguing. You may be familiar with the technique of speaking affirmations in front of a mirror to reinforce certain beliefs or to manifest goals. For example, "I am now creating the perfect relationship," or, "I love myself completely." That is one form of mirror work. Another type of mirror work is to use mirrored reflection as a way of separating our feelings and thoughts from who we are as physical beings. We *have* feelings and thoughts, but they don't necessarily define us.

Do you ever catch a glimpse of yourself in the mirror and ask, "That's *me*?" as if you've never seen yourself prior to that moment? I do. It's a strange experience. The other thing that occurs to me is "That's what people *see* when they look at me?" I spend so much time in my head that I sometimes forget that other people don't see me from my point of view; they see me from theirs. They don't see the mental whirrings. They see my smile, brown hair, and blue eyes. To them, Susan is not her feelings or her thoughts. Susan is a woman, a whole-person experience, thirty-five years old, funny, sensitive, smart, creative, pretty, sometimes sad, often cheerful, sometimes overwhelmed, generally strong. She occupies a certain amount of space in the universe. She is not the center of it.

Visually they see my exterior—what is reflected in the mirror when I stand before it. They don't see what goes on behind my eyes and between my ears. Looking in a mirror helps me separate my self from my feelings and thoughts. It reminds me that I am a whole person, seen by others as an animate object rather than as a walking inner dialogue.

EXERCISE: MIRROR REFLECTION

I suppose it's not all that odd, since most people spend time in front of a mirror every day applying makeup, brushing teeth, shaving, but what I do is a little bit different. I look at myself and try to see what other people see, not what I see. I examine the nooks and crannies of my face in a little handheld mirror. You can do it with any mirror; I just like the handheld kind, because I can use it while sitting comfortably or lying on the couch.

1. Look at your face in a mirror. Say, "Hello. So this is me."

2. Examine your skin, your eyes, hair, eyelashes, and so on. Watch your eyes blink. Raise your eyebrows and see your forehead crinkle. Smile, frown. Notice how your face adjusts to these expressions.

3. Turn your face to either side, and see what people see when they look at your profile.

4. Look at your teeth. Tap on them and run your finger across them. Examine your ears. Wondrous creations.

5. Note to yourself how amazing it is that our bodies take care of us so well.

6. Get closer to the mirror and examine your facial hairs, wrinkles, age spots. See if you can notice something about your face that you hadn't already seen: a scar, a pockmark, a new freckle or wrinkle, a renegade eyebrow hair.

7. Touch your face as you examine it. Tell yourself aloud, "I love you. You are wonderful." What does your skin feel like? Is it warm, moist, dry?

8. Touch beneath your eyes. Notice that the skin there feels different from the skin on your cheek. Press down and trace your eye sockets. There's a skull in there! You're made of flesh and bone. Run your fingers down your nose. Isn't the shape of the nose amazing? Touch your mouth. Look at your tongue. Curl your tongue. Look at the bottom of your tongue. Look at your taste buds. It's all such a beautiful, perfect creation.

9. Now bring your hands to your side and look straight into the mirror.

10. Smile at yourself, even if you don't want to. Say, "I love you completely in this moment." Practice some of the sayings from the previous chapter on affirmations.

This exercise—or a modified version of it—can be done anytime and anywhere; that's one reason why I carry a little mirror in my bag. If I start to feel lost in my head, I take a look in the mirror to ground myself. My feelings can easily get the best of me if I forget that they are just a small part of who I am.

Adapt this exercise to suit your needs. Skip over the facial exploration and simply stand before the mirror and repeat certain affirmations that ring true for you. "I am a worthwhile person. I am loved. I am a capable human being." It may feel embarrassing at first, but remember, no one is watching. Just you and the Divine.

When we look straight into our own eyes and affirm our being, I believe a new voice is born in the brain. Each time we practice this form of affirmation, the new voice is strengthened and reinforced. Over time it replaces the old broken record from the past.

A dialogue is "a conversation between two or more persons." An inner dialogue is a conversation with yourself. Example: "You can do it, sweetie. I know you can. What do you need?" I say that to myself a lot. "Everything's fine, Susan," is another. "Just keep moving, you can do it."

If you've ever been on an athletic team, inner dialoguing is a lot like being your own coach, like being your own best friend. When people are stressed or depressed, they often tend to speak to themselves harshly: "What's wrong with you? You're such an idiot!" Those are voices from the past—and look where they got us! What we need to hear when we're feeling so vulnerable is "It's all right. I'm here for you. What do you need? How can I help you feel better?"

The Brady Bunch Syndrome, HALT, Feelings Versus Facts, identifying your feelings, and other Tricks of the Trade all involve inner conversation: "What am I feeling? What is the fact? Am I hungry? Am I tired? What do I need? It's okay, I can do this." Inner dialoguing, carried on in a gentle, supportive tone, can help you through the hard times. If your volume starts to rise or your voice starts to mimic one from the past, *stop* and take a different tack. What's the use in treating yourself like you were treated in the past if it only makes you feel bad? No one enjoys misery *that* much.

Mirror work takes inner dialoguing and reflects back a solid, visual experience. If your brain tries to discourage you by saying, "You don't need that. What a waste of time!" just say, "Leave me alone," and do it anyway.

Trick #19
Service—Helping Others

As the ripples caused by a flung stone stir the surface of a
whole pond, so your joy-making shall spread
in ever-widening circles.
—*GOD CALLING*, MARCH 10

The magic of helping others is potentially infinite. By adding positive energy to the universe through kind words and deeds, I believe we alter the world's disposition. For suicidal thinkers, there's an added bonus: while you're busy doing a good deed, your brain is temporarily diverted and suicidal thoughts are put on hold. Acts of service build self-confidence, reinforce connection with living things, and remind us that we have the ability to be kind—to others *and* to ourselves.

It's easy to feel hopeless when faced with the problems of the world, but we *can* and *do* make a difference. Most good starts with one individual making one small step. I try to keep my mind off the bigger picture and keep it simple, keep it small, keep it close to home, and keep the faith. Sure, terrible things happen every day, and we are blasted with it by the media, but there is plenty of *good* happening too. I want to be a part of that, and there are several different ways to do it.

Doing a specific act of kindness for someone you know. Offering to help a friend or acquaintance with something you know that person needs is one form of service: moving furniture, lending money, cooking a meal, cleaning or washing a car, coming over for a visit, giving words of encouragement.

It doesn't have to be a huge effort. It can be as simple as dropping off a casserole, offering to clean for an hour, walking the dog, picking up the mail, returning library books. Extending myself puts the focus on the other person, gets me out of my own head, and often results in a closer bond with that person. I generally feel good about what I've done, the other person is appreciative, and I've passed an afternoon's time, temporarily relieving my brain from active suicide duty.

Doing a random act of kindness for someone you know. This form of service is more spontaneous. I generally do this when I'm feeling good, but it also helps lift my spirits when I'm feeling low. Again, it gets me out of my head by temporarily focusing my thoughts and energy on another person or situation.

Because such acts are spontaneous, the other person has no prior expectations, and that means no pressure, more flexibility, and no guilt. If I change my mind and decide not to go through with it, no one's the wiser. Random acts of kindness could include: sending flowers for no reason; leaving a nice note on someone's windshield; calling to say you appreciate that person's friendship; making someone a card; praying for someone's happiness and total health; making small surprise gifts; complimenting someone's appearance.

Doing a specific kindness for a stranger. It always warms my heart when I witness or participate in this form of service: holding the door open for the person behind me; giving someone change in the supermarket line; giving up a parking spot; helping a stranger find something in a store; letting someone cut in line; donating to charity; laughing with and appreciating children; helping someone into a car; listening intently to an elderly stranger tell a long story; buying lemonade from a kid's lemonade stand; helping someone take off a coat at the movies.

Perhaps I'm naive, but these simple forms of exchange reassure me that people are really good at heart, that they do care, and that deep down we are all one.

Doing a random act of kindness for a stranger. This form of service is the most playful for me. I might feel a little mischievous in the planning and a bit eccentric in the follow-through, but it truly connects me to the universal energy of love. Some of these acts I learned from other people, and some I've made up on my own: dropping coins on the sidewalk for someone to find; giving out flowers to people on the street; leaving a nice note on a slip of paper in a library book; leaving a dollar bill in a library book; telling a supervisor that his or her employee has done a great job assisting me; offering a wide smile to people on the sidewalk; putting coins in an expired parking meter.

Some of these activities are quick. If you need to occupy your mind for a longer stretch, choose something simple that takes more time, like visiting dogs and cats at the animal shelter, volunteering to shelve books at the library, collecting litter on the beach or in the park, or helping distribute food at a food pantry.

Doing for someone else exactly what you need done for you. If I need a particular thing and feel sad or frustrated because it's not happening, I offer it to someone else. Such an act affirms my belief in the abundance of the universe by putting my intentions in a positive light and allowing me to avoid self-pity. Another twist to this form of service is offering my*self* what I want someone else to offer me: a loving card; a nice message on the answering machine; a nice dinner; a compliment; a smile in the mirror or a pat on the back; a date at the movies.

On Valentine's Day 1994 I was feeling sad and lonely. *I wanted a valentine, dammit!* And no one was going to give me one. I wasn't severely depressed but could have easily slipped into isolation, which often lead to suicidal thoughts. After a half-hour of self-pity, I straightened up and said aloud, "Okay, what can I do about this? How can I shift my energy?"

I answered myself. "Why not give people what *I* want to receive?"

I sat down and made twenty-five little red paper hearts, with "You are special, HVD (Happy Valentine's Day)" written on one side. I went to my weekly meeting early, set up the chairs, and put a valentine on each one. When people arrived, they were surprised and delighted to find a valentine greeting. I loved seeing their reactions. After the meeting someone I had never met before approached me and said, "This made my day. It's the only valentine I got." I had given her what I wanted to receive and in doing so made a profound difference for both of us.

I know it's hard to get out of your head when the brain is focused on suicide, and that it seems *impossible* to do anything when you are depressed, but if you can break away for even half an hour, acts of service can be simple and the benefits great. Not only do we help others, we help ourselves. The more we give of ourselves in a healthy way, the more we receive.

If I'm having a hard day, I try to remember that I'm not the only one on the planet dealing with difficulty. If I see someone needing assistance, I offer it with a smile, despite how I feel inside. If I don't have the energy to help, I simply say a prayer for that person and keep walking; it's the best I can do at that moment.

Trick #20
Movement and Exercise

Sleep is my favorite sport. Unfortunately, sleep does very little to stimulate endorphins or release toxins from the body, two chief benefits of physical exercise.

I've never been a big sports fan, nor do I enjoy team athletics. I'm too afraid of losing the game-winning point—probably a legacy of eighth-grade gym and being graded A to F on athletic ability.

Since my physical form requires very little to keep it in shape, I have no real motivator other than the fact that exercise is good for me on all levels. It's funny: I practice the Tricks of the Trade, choose a healthy lifestyle, and take Prozac every day because I know it helps my brain remain clear, yet I resist exercise even though I know it improves mental functioning and self-confidence and creates a stronger, healthier body.

I've been told that physical exertion is preventive medicine for people with depression. I will refrain from spouting the biochemical benefits of exercise other than to say that while exercising, the body releases endorphins, defined as "any group of proteins with potent analgesic properties that occur naturally in the brain."

According to my pharmacist, an analgesic is a pain reliever. It reduces pain and elevates mood. In her book *Human Anatomy and Physiology*, Elaine N. Marieb states that endorphins "act as natural opiates or euphorics, reducing our perception of pain under certain stressful conditions. . . . Endorphin release is enhanced when an athlete gets his or her so-called 'second wind,' and is probably responsible for the 'runner's high.' [Endorphins are considered] pain-killing neurotransmitters."[3] Unfortunately for me, I've never run long enough to experience a runner's high.

Physical exertion also increases heart and breath rate, thus elevating body temperature and making us sweat to compensate for the excess heat. A natural response to sweating is to drink water, which in turn makes us urinate. Each of these physical responses—increased circulation, deep and rapid breathing, sweating, and urination—cleanses our bodies by releasing toxins.

On a feelings level, I believe that exercise moves blocked energy, freeing it up. If I feel stuck or emotionally disconnected, it helps to move my body and feel it push through space. When I *do* exercise, I prefer to stimulate endorphins out-of-doors. I like to walk in the woods or on the beach, jog, hike, kayak, climb trees, swim, garden. Feeling my feet hit the ground when I jog, or the resistance of the water against my kayak paddle, grounds me to the earth. This strengthens my spiritual connection and reassures me.

Because physical exertion is low on my priority list, I prefer to "multi-task" while exercising. I might offer to help someone with a physical task, like putting together a computer work station. I do nagging chores like cleaning the bathroom and kitchen, vacuuming, trimming the hedge. I connect with friends as we walk on the beach. I do my grocery shopping after I walk to market. I pray for an hour while I work in the garden. I clean up the beach as I stroll along the shore.

By the way, if your brain tries to sneak in and screw up your exercise plans, practice inner dialoguing and soothe yourself with words like "I hear you, brain, but I'm going to do this anyway. I am capable of following through with this, and it will make me feel better. What is my resistance? Fear. Okay, I recognize the fear, and I'm going to do this anyway. Okay, let's go!" If your brain keeps nagging you, tell it to piss off or just say, "I know, I hear you, but I have to do this for me. I want to do this. I'm not going to let you stop me."

Fortunately, my great skill at exercise avoidance has given rise to some creative solutions to the dilemma, and none of them requires a $300-a-year gym membership.

Make it fun. If I know I'm going to have a good time exercising, I'm more apt to do it, and do it again. Find something you like to do and try to do it three times a week, or pick two or three things you like and do them each once a week. It could be volleyball, jogging with a friend, lifting weights, walking, aerobics, ballroom dance, Rollerblading, yoga, boxing, karate, dancing in your living room or out at a club, bike riding, or swimming in a pond or at a fitness club. (Some hotels will let you use the pool for a minimal fee.)

Find companionship. It's much easier to be motivated if I have companionship. Having a set time to exercise with someone gets me out and moving. If I lose steam, my companion helps keep me going, and vice versa.

How do you go about finding exercise companions? Join a softball or volleyball league, play tennis, or join a hiking or walking club. Find a weight-lifting buddy or running buddy. Make a weekly date for a walk with a friend. Play community basketball. Go square dancing!

Most newspapers have listings of these types of activities, as do community centers, YMCAs, and YWCAs. Many towns have adult education programs that offer aerobics, tai chi, yoga, basketball, tennis, weights, dance, swimming, and more at very reasonable costs. Community centers are usually free to residents. Call your town hall for information. Also, local theater groups often offer dance programs.

Keep it simple. Some people like "toys." I'm not one of them; I like simplicity. The more planning and preparation an exercise requires, the quicker I lose interest. All that prep work puts me to sleep. I want to be able to show up, do it, and get it over with. That's why walking out-doors with a friend is one of my favorite things to do. In fact, I rarely think of it as exercise. Walking is simple and easy and requires little or no equipment or effort.

Jogging is simple, too, though not recommended for some folks with back or knee problems. I tend to jog in warmer weather because it seems less complicated than jogging during the winter. Figuring out appropriate jogging gear for cold weather and navigation techniques for slippery, snowy roads is too much for my brain to handle. I don't want to have to *think* about what I do for exercise.

Besides walking and jogging, other simple exercises include: danc-ing, gardening, cleaning, doing home improvement projects, Roller-blading, biking, hiking, and swimming. Here's an interesting idea that I got from my physician. It does require "toys," but I think it's quite inventive. Set up an exercise bike in front of the TV and VCR. Get a video and watch it only while you're riding the bike, for twenty min-utes a sitting. You'll want to come back and see what happens next, but you have to ride the bike to do it. Clever!

Set easy goals and create rewards. Dealing with this exercise prob-lem is yet another form of outthinking the brain. I do find that if I make a written commitment to myself or a verbal commitment to a friend, I am more likely to follow through. If I set easy goals at the start—for example, to walk two times a week—and reward myself when I meet that simple goal, I am more apt to exercise the next week and to set the goal higher. For a reward I might buy myself flowers or take a nap, send myself a greeting card, make a little sign to post, or simply say to myself, "Good job! I knew you could do it," and literally pat myself on the back.

Practice moderation. Like anything in life, it's best to be moderate in exercise. Perhaps in my case I've taken moderation a bit too far, but even I can get overzealous and overdo it when I'm on a roll. I need to allow for downtime so I can regroup. Being on the go-go-go has its benefits but in the end will wipe me out.

If while running I get tired and need to walk, I walk. I keep up the pace so my breathing remains fast, but I take it easy. After two weeks of run-walking, I walk less and run more. Pretty soon I don't have to walk at all and can run the whole distance. Had I tortured myself the first time out, I never would have gone back for more. Plus, I don't run-walk for hours on end. I run for twenty minutes tops; that's enough for me. I've filled my cardiopulmonary quota for the day.

Exercise does not have to be painful. I disagree with the theory "No pain, no gain." If there's pain involved with an activity, I want nothing to do with it, thank you very much. I've had enough pain in my life. I admit there's such a thing as good pain—like a long stretch in yoga or a sore muscle the day after tending the garden—but incapacitation is not my goal.

Volunteer. When people think of volunteering they envision candy stripers at the hospital or reading to the visually impaired. But there are countless other volunteer opportunities that involve exercise. For instance, you could walk the dogs at an animal shelter or clean the kennels; clean a part of your church with a friend; join a landscaping committee; sign up for a walkathon or bikeathon; mow your neighbor's yard, rake their leaves, or tend their garden; tend part of a nature trail; or help a friend move.

Part of my exercise dilemma stems from my early belief that I would not live past twenty-one. I was very active as a child, but after I became depressed, my motivation to move dropped significantly; just getting by was my main objective. Maybe you know how that feels. But just as I did, you can learn to lead a healthy, fulfilling life and take care of yourself. Even as I continue to work to get the hang of this exercise thing, I know that I want to be alive today. Why not feel the best I can while living?

Trick #21
Sound and Color

Dance with the muse; breathe life into the moment.
—SUSAN ROSE BLAUNER

Music and art have been my salvation. Each has provided a healthy outlet for self-expression, giving me the power to be free and touch the deepest part of my being.

SOUND

Both making and listening to sound can fill me up like nothing else. When I sing in a chorus, I feel the connection of my body and spirit to the Divine and know that I am one with everything in the universe. I know that I am safe and everything is going according to plan.

I play the piano. One form of expression I developed years ago was "playing" my feelings and thoughts to get them out of my body. I sit quietly with myself and let an image enter my mind; then I play the image, staying within a certain scale and progression of notes. It doesn't matter if what comes out is harmonious; even the disharmonies are beautiful—in many ways they are metaphors for life. Even in its ugliness, life can still be beautiful.

EXERCISE: "PLAYING" FEELINGS

1. Sit (or stand) with your instrument.

2. Take several deep breaths and think about how you are feeling.

3. Close your eyes and let an image come to your mind.

4. Stay with that image as you slowly open your eyes and soften your gaze.

5. Begin to play your instrument as if it were telling a story, as if it were describing the image in your mind. Feel the music speak through your body.

6. Continue with the image and sound as it swells or diminishes, stutters or flows. Try not to judge it; let anything happen. If you feel comfortable, make vocal sounds as you create the music—even humming is a good release.

7. After five or ten minutes, wind down and let the music drift off into resolution.

8. Stay in the stillness for a few moments.

9. Breathe and move on.

Even if you don't play an instrument, you can use music as an avenue of expression. It can be as simple as taking a wooden spoon and drumming on the bottom of an overturned plastic bucket. Give it a try.

EXERCISE: BUCKET MUSIC

1. Sit in a chair, with the bucket held upside down between your knees.

2. Take several deep breaths and think about how you are feeling.

3. Close your eyes and let an image come to your mind.

4. Stay with that image as you slowly open your eyes and soften your gaze.

5. Begin to make slow circles on the upturned bottom of the bucket with the wooden spoon. Listen to the sound as the spoon scrapes along the plastic.

6. When you feel so moved, tap the spoon on the bucket as you continue to focus on the image in your mind. What is that image trying to say?

7. Tap the bucket again. Create your own rhythm for the image. Gradually speed up your taps and try to generate some energy as you "play" the image. If you feel comfortable, hum or make other vocal sounds as you create the music.

8. Continue with this sound creation for about five minutes until gradually it starts to fade and find its way to resolution.

9. Sit in the silence for a moment.

10. Breathe and move on.

EXERCISE: BASIC SOUNDING

Sounding is a great release. Like playing an instrument, using your voice allows you to create sound for expression. This exercise can be done anywhere. It's great to do in the shower or when you get into bed. Basically it's a long sigh with sound.

1. Take a deep breath.

2. Open your mouth wide.

3. As you exhale, pretend you are saying "ahhhh" for the doctor.

4. Keep making the sound as you release the air from your lungs.

5. Take another deep breath and repeat steps 1 through 4.

6. Try this with other sounds, such as "eeee," "ohhhh," "oooo."

EXERCISE: BASIC OHM

Using the basic sounding technique go through three different sounds when you exhale: "ahhhh," "ohhhh," "mmmm."

1. Breathe in.

2. Open your mouth.

3. Exhale a deep "ahhhh" for about seven seconds.

4. As you continue exhaling, change the sound to "ohhhh" for about seven seconds.

5. As you continue exhaling, close your lips and change the sound to "mmmm" until you run out of air.

6. Pause.

7. Repeat steps 1 through 6 several times.

8. After the last repetition, sit in the silence and soak it up. Doesn't it feel good? This is a nice way to start a meditation.

COLOR

Colors are energy, and energy is vibrational. Aside from the color I apply when I put paint on a canvas or make a collage, I know very little about color theory in terms of the mind-body connection, other than to say that bright colors lift my mood and darker colors are more soothing. For example (and this may sound really strange), if I'm feeling sad, I intentionally wear bright underwear, I wear a brightly colored scarf or pin, and I change my bedsheets from dark colors to light. I have this great set of bright yellow sheets. How can I help but feel invigorated when I'm lying between them? The same goes for lavender: I've got a lavender flannel set that soothes and calms me. I choose to surround myself with pleasing, invigorating colors these days. I believe my body and brain are affected by the energetic color vibrations. Hey, I'll take all the positive energy I can get.

If you want to explore the positive effects of color, read a great little book by Louise Hay entitled *Colors and Numbers: Your Personal Guide to Positive Vibrations in Daily Life*. It explores how certain colors and numbers work together—for example, wearing orange on a day whose date adds up to a certain number, that kind of thing. This small book is fun, creative, and easy to read. I enjoyed the exercises, and when I applied Hay's suggestions to my life, I noticed improvements.

COLOR IDEAS

- For one week make a conscious effort to wear bright-colored clothes. If your clothes are mostly black, try getting some brightly colored underwear. It's cheaper than buying a new wardrobe.

- Try buying a bright pillowcase—solid yellow, pink, or orange. See whether you feel a difference, either sleeping on it or looking at it.

- If it's the holiday gift-giving season, tell people you want bright-colored towels for the bathroom or festive sheets.

- If you're repainting your house or apartment, choose a color that's a little bit different—perhaps something light and fun like light avocado green, strawberry, marigold, or lavender.

- Instead of writing with black ink, use blue, purple, or red pens.

- Get a bottle of bright red nail polish and paint your toenails.

Trick #22
Support Groups

When people are serving, life is no longer meaningless.

—JOHN GARDNER

Support groups are an A-1 way to meet people who can help and are willing and able to listen. Support groups add structure and routine to the week, provide emotional outlets and safe personal contact, and are a great place to get numbers for your telephone list. Had I not found support groups where I could air my feelings and share my thoughts in safety—sometimes *daily*—I would not be where I am today. In addition to therapy, support groups showed me that it's okay to be who I am, that change is possible, and that I am not alone.

There are support groups for just about every situation: divorce, cancer, alcoholism, weight loss, codependence, anxiety, gay and lesbian issues, drug addiction, you name it. Here are some ideas for finding and attending support groups.

SUPPORT GROUP TIPS

- Most newspapers have a Help Calendar in their Sunday edition, with a comprehensive list of local meetings.

- If you know someone who has made positive changes, find out how that person did it and then try doing the same. Most likely that person will have attended some form of support group and can point you in that direction. He or she might even accompany you to your first meeting.

- Places of worship often have support groups for men, women, youth, couples, or spiritual direction. If you attend one, check the bulletin or newsletter or ask the leader for guidance.

- In part 7 I list contact information for Twelve Step organizations. Whether or not you feel that you fit any particular category, you may well find the change you've been looking for in a Twelve Step meeting. By attending Twelve Step groups, I found a new lease on life. If the meeting has a phone list, pick one up and mark the names of the people you meet, or put a check mark next to the names of people who said things that rang true for you.

- One good way to connect with people at support groups is to show up early and help set up or stay late and help put things away. This is a form of service and boosts self-esteem while giving your mind a focus or purpose.

SOMETHING TO THINK ABOUT

- None of this has to be done alone. If it feels frightening or overwhelming to attend a support group by yourself, it's okay to ask someone for company, depending on the type of group. Usually a contact number is listed and you can call ahead to check this possibility out. Maybe your friend will learn something too.

Trick #23
Structure

Some people view structure and routine as boring or unimaginative. I disagree. When I was struggling emotionally, structure and routine were absolute necessities. If I faced a blank canvas of a day, I waffled, feeling confused and disconnected. I became easily overwhelmed and felt lonely without a plan of action. The Crisis Plan is one form of structure. For day-to-day existence, I learned to make schedules for myself—daily and weekly—and used goal-setting as a guide for my progress.

If I intentionally structured the day or week, my brain had less room to mess around. I had a purpose, a mission. If my brain started to nag at me with words like "Don't do that, Susan. What's the point?" or "Come on, it's not worth it, just go to bed," I would pray for those thoughts to vanish from my head, tell my brain to fuck off, and do it anyway. I had to be strong.

There was a time when I scheduled something to do for every night of the week because it was too hard to be alone. Monday night was a meeting, Tuesday night was a movie or a visit with a friend, Wednesday night was chorus, Thursday night was a meeting, and so on. Weekends were especially rough; I had to try even harder to keep focused. If I retreated to my room (or tomb) I usually stayed there— barring trips to the fridge—sometimes for days at a time. This habit usually spelled disaster. It was almost as if I thought I had to reach a certain threshold of emotional pain before I could release it and try to feel better. To prevent this phenomenon from occurring, it was vital that I *plan* to have places to go and things to do.

I also learned how to participate in activities without exerting much effort. I didn't have to bow out because I felt overwhelmed. I could just show up. I didn't have to carry the conversation. For example, if someone invited me to go to a picnic or to the beach I could join them on the beach, but do my own thing, like read a book, write in my journal, take a walk, or just listen to the conversation. The point was to find companionship. I had to learn to "do in spite of how I feel."

Today my brain is pretty cooperative unless I'm overtired, hungry, or suffering from chapped lips. (No kidding, it drives me nuts.) When I'm faced with a big stressor, however, I turn straight back to structure and keep myself on track—writing things down, setting realistic goals, keeping track of what's left to do and what can wait, prioritizing. I don't need a fancy date book. I do all this stuff in my journal, on scraps of paper, or on the back of paper place mats at restaurants. I also plan a reward for myself to balance out the stress.

I know how hard it feels to set goals or make plans when your brain is trying to squash you, but I believe in you 100 percent. You can do it.

STRUCTURE TIPS

- *Plan ahead.* Make weekend plans *before* Friday night rolls around. Try to get things set up as early as Wednesday so that you have something to look forward to, even if it's just a movie with a friend Saturday night or a walk in the woods Sunday morning. If your brain tries to convince you to stay in bed, tell it to leave you alone. Then drag yourself out the door.

- *Keep it simple.* Break things down into small, manageable parts; it's easier on the brain. When you think of completing a whole big *anything*, it can seem impossible to get started. If you pick one part of it and do that, the larger picture is more attainable. For example, if you have to read six chapters of a book for school, break it down into two chapters at a time, with a break in between. Instead of planning an elaborate dinner, arrange nice settings, order take-out, and have friends pick it up on their way to your house.

- *Schedule rewards.* All this structuring is tough stuff. Be sure to schedule healthy rewards for yourself when you make an effort to change and follow through with it. I absolutely love movies, so that is often my reward. Or I'll take myself out to dinner as a reward for working hard on the book. A bath is a great way to slow down and unwind. Taking a walk in the woods can be a reward for working inside all day.

Trick #24
Hospitalization

As I said earlier, I loved being hospitalized in the psych ward. Why not? Stripped of all personal responsibility and the stress of everyday life, I readily accepted my role as live-in patient. Like a kid, I soaked up the round-the-clock attention on the ward. I needed that structure and feeling of protection, however impermanent and artificial. It was like being on vacation, except that I was locked up like a convict. Believe it or not, being locked up actually felt better than being a civilian. (I recently learned that some psych hospitals are horror shows. I guess I was very fortunate in that regard.)

Each patient was assigned to a team consisting of a psychiatrist, a psychologist, a psych nurse, and a social worker who met in the morning, discussed our cases, and came up with questions and assignments for the patient. The psych nurse recorded this information in a "focus journal" for each patient before distributing them to us. By the end of the day we had to have answered the questions and completed the assignments. The journals were collected the following morning for review and the process started all over again.

All told, I spent about forty days locked up. The longest stretch was twenty-one days, following my first gesture in 1991. On the psych ward I met everyday folks, people like you and me doing their best to make sense of this crazy world. Rich folks, poor folks, men, women, young, old, criminals, executives. Mental illness does not discriminate.

There were two wards, one upstairs, one down. Patients under sixteen were rehabilitated downstairs. One day while heading out for an activity, our adult group crossed paths with the kids. I'll never forget the sight of a young girl laughing. She was about fourteen years old, wearing a white T-shirt and blue jeans. Both of her wrists were wrapped in gauze. I can still see her smiling face, blond hair, skinny arms, and those bright white bandages. "How sad," I thought, "that such a beautiful girl would want to kill herself. She's so young! What could be so *bad* in her young life that she would want to die?" How quickly I forgot.

We had to get up at 7:00 A.M. to begin our day, which included group and individual therapy along with morning psychiatrist visits and the medication lineup at the nurses' station. Yes, the doctors asked me questions like "What is meant by 'A rolling stone gathers no moss' or 'Don't count your chickens before they hatch'?" We had to fill out lengthy personal evaluations, design Crisis Plans, report the status of our bodily functions, and get permission to use knives in cooking class.

I recently watched the film *Girl, Interrupted,* based on the book of the same name, about a young woman with borderline personality disorder who makes a suicide gesture, is abruptly hospitalized, and spends the next sixteen months facing her illness while incarcerated with the unpredictable yet comforting behaviors of fellow patients. It brought it all back to me: bed checks every fifteen minutes, medication lineups, institutional furniture, scary strangers, instant friends, subculture groupings, and the torment of wanting to get better but feeling at ease in an artificial, structured environment.

I latched onto this world so readily that room decoration began the minute my personal belongings arrived: photos, books, knickknacks, clothing, greeting cards. It was against the rules, however, to keep the houseplant: someone could have eaten it.

It was a comfort to know there was a safe place where I could cast anchor, but hospitalization *did* disrupt my life. Every time I wound up in a johnny gown I reshattered the trust that had grown between me and the people in my life. It was like starting all over from square one every time. I totally resented this loss of trust, but it was all my own creation. If I had been in their shoes, I probably would have responded the same way.

The trouble was that once I had a taste of hospitalization, going back was an option I craved. I can't tell you how many times I asked Sylvia to hospitalize me, but she would encourage me to hold on and continue to support me 100 percent as I fumbled through life trying to find my way. While in the psych ward after my 1992 overdose, I even asked to be sent to a long-term psych facility and was all but shipped off until Sylvia stepped in on my behalf. She adamantly maintained that our client-therapist relationship needed to remain intact, that returning me to mainstream life after stabilization was in my best interest, and that long-term hospitalization would prolong the process. The goal of hospitalization for me was stabilization and discharge. I hated her for making this assessment at the time, but she was right.

Life on the psych ward was far from perfect. In fact, sometimes it was frightening. There were sudden outbursts; people often screamed in solitary, their wails echoing through the corridors. One patient escaped. One afternoon I was sitting in the lounge when I heard loud shrieking and loud, crashing noises. Someone was throwing furniture across her room. When I found out it was my roommate, I was terrified.

They may have taken her out that night, I don't remember. Nevertheless, they eventually brought her back, and when I crawled into my bed her first night back I asked, "You wouldn't hurt me, would you?" "No," she said, "I would never hurt you." I believed her completely. We shared our stories, and I soon fell asleep without any lingering fear. There was an understanding between patients in the hospital, at least in my experience.

Another roommate hardly spoke and had a tendency to steal. The afternoon I arrived, she started screaming and stood, twirling around in our closet, with her arm outstretched over her head. That night I found her seated on the floor beside her bed with an overturned chair propped in front of her like a table (and for protection, I suspect). She was dangling a crystal pendulum over a piece of paper.

I noticed that she had taken my snow boot and set it on the floor beside her. I took it from her, returned it to my side of the room, and left for the lounge, only to return and find that she had taken it again. This happened several times, once while a nurse was present. Finally, in frustration, I said to her, "I don't care *what* you do with my boot, as long as you don't eat it!"

Toward the end of my stay I found out that she had a fondness for animals, so I made her a collage of animal pictures I ripped out of magazines. (We didn't have access to scissors in our rooms.) One night, before going to sleep, I handed her the collage. She looked up at me, smiled, and said something about the innocence of animal life. I agreed with her, and we wound up talking well into the night, about God, nutrition, the universe, art, creative visualization, life, anything.

The next morning she crawled back into her shell but left an opening for me. The day I was discharged we hugged each other good-bye and wished each other well. I see her once every few years in the local supermarket. Sometimes I say hello.

That experience taught me an important lesson: I never really know what's inside another person, even if his or her behavior is wild and strange. Most people are good, with histories and reasons for acting the way they do.

I don't broadcast my history via the Goodyear blimp, but if anyone asks whether I've been hospitalized in a psych ward, sure, I tell them. That's one way I can demystify mental illness and help people see it for what it is—a part of everyday life.

Trick #25
What About an Afterlife?

One can survive anything these days except death.

—OSCAR WILDE

I was given another important gift at the hospital. Joan, one of my favorite psych nurses, found me crying in my room one afternoon. "It's so hard, it's so *hard!*" I sobbed. She sat on the edge of the bed, softened her gaze on my spongy face, and asked, "*What's* so hard?"

"Everything! *Everything!* It's just so *hard!*"

"*What's* so hard?"

I couldn't give her an exact answer.

She held my hand, and we sat in silence for a while. Then she spoke these words: "I probably shouldn't be telling you this, but do you want to know what *I* think happens when a person commits suicide?" I nodded yes. She said, "I think they turn *into* the feeling they're trying to escape."

Picture that! Turning into anger for the rest of eternity. No thanks. Even the *possibility* of a never-ending anger existence has stopped me from acting on suicidal thoughts hundreds of times since that moment. Thank you, Joan.

Life after death can be a sore topic for suicidal thinkers. I suppose some people believe that after we kill ourselves we move on to a peaceful better place, or we start another life without the problems that currently cause such pain. That's not my understanding.

Some of the following theories and ideas may sound strange. And depending on your age, I might even sound like a throwback to the sixties. Please bear with me; these beliefs kept me safe and alive during times of great crisis. I offer them as food for thought, not mandatory communion. Take what you like and leave the rest.

I believe our physical bodies exist to give souls earthly transportation. In physical form our soul can interact and experience life, learning the lessons necessary to achieve deep understanding before moving on to a higher plane of existence. Whatever haunts us now will be carried on to the next life and the following life as long as it is left unfinished. So what's the point in dying today if I'm just going to return immediately with the same challenges?

I also believe that the ultimate plane of existence is pure love energy. The fame, money, power, and material possessions we acquire on earth provide temporary comfort, yes, but in the bigger scheme of things they are quite unimportant. My goal in life is a direct connection to a spiritual source. I want to learn how to love as fully as possible so that I can give back the gifts bestowed upon me. By doing my small part, perhaps the world will be a better place.

To reach a universal destination I have to face my fears and discover inner truth. I have to learn to love and not hate, to accept and not judge, to support and not oppress. It is also critical that I accept every part of my being, improve whatever I can, and see all creatures as sacred without compromising the dignity or safety of a single one. Until I accomplish these goals, I will carry any fears, challenges, issues, or stumbling blocks that remain untended with me when I start all over again. I believe the longer we take to face our fears and learn how to love, the more often we return to this earthly existence to work it out. For a glimpse into this theory as well as a good hearty laugh, rent the video *Defending Your Life* by Albert Brooks. It's great.

Let's take this idea one step further and apply it to suicide. If we kill ourselves, aren't we just adding time to our lives, quickening our arrival to the next lifetime, where any unfinished business remains? Further, if we come back as human babies, we have to go through every developmental stage all over again—imagine another adolescence! If we come back as an ant, we could get squished under someone's shoe. Why not stay here, work out what we can, and have less to deal with when we return?

Maybe suicide victims don't get another lifetime. Maybe what my psych nurse Joan said is true: people who kill themselves turn into the feelings they are trying to escape.

Some people give little or no thought to afterlife. When you die, you're dead, they say, and that's it. Seems like an awful waste of time and energy to me: live a whole life, die, turn back into earth, and that's that? Maybe it's the overachiever in me, but life *has* to be more than a linear existence, traveling from point A to point B. I see it as circular, or spiral, in nature. Each one of us is here to learn certain lessons, and until we do we keep circling back to have another go at it. In the process we touch people with love and spirit, and that's what lingers on, not the car we drove, the money we made, or the big job we held. Love remains, that's all.

———

Thank you for sticking with me and reading the material in parts 1 through 3; I know it's a lot to digest. Just remember that none of it has to be done perfectly, and none of it can be done all at once. You are a strong and capable person. I'm so glad you let your heart outshine your mind. Please read on and continue your journey toward freedom. Part 4 illustrates how suicidal behavior affects those around us and part 7 is a comprehensive resource list of books, organizations, websites, and hotlines.

PART FOUR

There Is Hope! Letters from My Therapist, Family, and Friends

Journal drawing, 1994

The soul walks not upon a line,
neither does it grow like a reed.
The soul unfolds itself, like a lotus of countless petals.

—KAHLIL GIBRAN, *The Prophet*

Honesty

Hold on to your bootstraps. I've asked friends and family for honest feedback about how they experienced my suicidal behavior. Some of it is hard to read because it brings up anger and embarrassment, but it's crucial that you and those who love you see information like this: it illustrates that you are not alone. You *do* make a difference in people's lives; your actions do have an impact.

The first segment, "Sylvia's Perspective," was written by my therapist. It is followed by words from my brother Bob, his wife Julie, three friends—Ellen, Jeff, a birthday song from my friend Jennifer Stratton—and finally, an unusual perspective from my friend and once-landlord/housemate Dorothy, who happens to work in the mental health field.

Here is an excerpt from the letter I sent to friends and family:

I want to include short notes and/or letters from family and friends to illustrate the effect suicidal behavior has on loved ones. When someone is contemplating suicide they feel completely disconnected from others and themselves. And most likely their loved ones aren't being entirely truthful about their own feelings because they're afraid it will push the suicidal thinker over the edge. I'd like you to tell your side of the story—openly and honestly. Don't worry about hurting my feelings; I can handle it. The more open you are the better . . .

. . . I know I made it hard for everyone. It's okay to say you were pissed, scared, and/or frustrated; I also know you loved me (I didn't know it then). By sharing the fact that you felt anger and love toward me simultaneously, you would show the readers that it's never all or nothing. It is possible to be loved even if people are scared and angry.

Sylvia's Perspective

Susan has asked me to write of my clinical and personal experience while working with her over the past eleven years. Embedded in the process are a collage of successes and inherent difficulties, all of which contributed to the hoped-for and deliberately intentioned outcome: integration.

Integration is the process of unifying the aspects of a personality which have been fractured due to trauma or stunted because of the inability to complete appropriate stages of development. For the person struggling with borderline personality disorder, it's rather like living life through a thick, multicolored stained-glass window, all the while trying to understand, experience, and interpret it. The goals of treatment are a unified self experience and world view.

While this sounds simplistic, the concept is fraught with emotional landmines originating within the patient, the correspondingly larger system, and the treatment process itself. Just as no two snowflakes are alike, people follow the same principle. Treatment, while adhering to certain proven theoretical constructs, is tailored to the strengths, differences, and needs of each person.

One of the puzzlements I experienced with Susan was her ability to maintain, from the beginning, appropriate boundaries with me during the treatment hour. Her testing was done indirectly and generally through another source. This indicated that she had the ability to connect *in person* and that the connection was important to her, thus giving an example of how one of Susan's strengths could be used as an asset, but also could prove difficult to manage in anticipating the sources of her testing.

There were times midtreatment when I experienced what I imagined to be the voluntary world of a circus ringmaster, particularly during one period of time that tested my own boundaries, stamina, and creativity. Over a period of four days, in addition to two direct sessions with Susan, I fielded seventeen "crisis" calls from the other people in her system: family, physicians, and other health-care professionals she had elicited to meet her needs as she began to escalate the testing process. One of Susan's strengths has been her ability to organize people and systems to meet her needs. Not realizing the extent of her problems, however, many of the people who responded to the engaging Susan bailed out when she escalated her emotional demands.

Throughout treatment, an attitude that worked with Susan was to compensate for and mirror-balance her extreme emotional states. Structure and boundaries were always understood to be part of any work we did. For long periods of time I used weekly no-harm-to-self contracts with Susan to maintain connection and support the therapeutic relationship. At times we had to contract day to day. When phone check-ins were established during particularly critical times, Susan understood that if she failed to call at the agreed-upon time, I would phone the police. This had to be done twice.

Another construct that entered into the foundation of our work was understanding and recognizing developmental levels as they applied to Susan's dynamics and regressive episodes. Susan would fill her self-experience of "feeling empty" with suicidal thinking and behavior. To override this, we would mutually devise a list of activities which could be changed or added to as developmentally appropriate.

Some of these activities were based on the particular daily living skills she needed to learn or to have reinforced, for example, nutrition and taking care of her physical needs. When Susan was ready to learn more independent-oriented skills, a cotherapist was used as a transition object to minimize testing the primary therapist relationship and to allow Susan easier advancement through stages of self-confidence.

Trying to accommodate Susan's ever-changing needs and presentations produced three particularly useful tools which were threaded throughout the course of treatment.

Relaxation techniques and imagery proved useful to control panic as well as to help her regain and experience memories of her mother, who died when she was fourteen.

Being a talented multimedia artist, she readily accepted art therapy as a medium to express, organize, and balance highly charged emotional states.

Watching Susan struggle to maintain a connection with me during one particularly suicide-obsessed period elicited the idea of recycling her journals. She kept two overlapping journals—one would be left with me to read before our next session, the other she kept to free-float with her writing during the interim, as well as to write to me directly. We would exchange journals at each session. I'd receive her latest thoughts, and she'd receive my written comments. This proved to be one of the most helpful techniques.

The most difficult challenge was the ongoing struggle for Susan to give up the option of dying, both cognitively and spiritually. There was a turning point many years into treatment when she was able to state during a session that dying was no longer an option: "Not that the thought still doesn't occur," but "it is no longer okay to act on it."

I remember experiencing gratitude to my spiritual source, pride in Susan's growth and strength, and a profound sense of peace. This is the moment in therapy that reinforces meaning and gives purpose to the work we do.

—SUBMITTED BY SYLVIA, R.N., M.E.D., L.M.F.T., JANUARY 2001

A Brother's Walk on Eggshells

To begin with, I would say that during the worst of your situation I had a mixture of emotions toward you ranging from extreme empathy and sadness to, at times, a sense of disillusionment with your plight, which was due to what I felt had become your somewhat narcissistic attitude.

Consequently, at times, my compassion toward your situation was tested whenever I perceived that you were exhibiting a "woe is me, life has dealt me a bad hand and all of you are responsible" attitude. While I realized that this self-absorption with your own problems is a common and understandable trait among people dealing with deep depression and suicidal feelings, I was still put off by an apparent mind-set that you were the only one dealing with life's various daily problems. In this regard, I think that no matter how much one loves and cares for another that is in your situation, it is common for their sympathies to be strained when they are, as in my case, struggling to raise a family, deal with a job, pay the bills, and so on.

Unfortunately, it got to a point where I did not enjoy your company, which was tough for me, because in the past I had always felt that we had a lot in common and I missed sharing thoughts and laughter with you. But when I was around you, I always had that "walking on eggshells" feeling, fearing that whatever I said would be the wrong thing. So I just felt it was easier to avoid contact with you altogether. But of course then I would feel guilty that I was *not* staying in contact with you, the old "damned if you do, damned if you don't" syndrome.

Thankfully, over the past couple of years, I have happily watched you start to enjoy your life, culminating in your highly responsible job, the purchase of your first home, and the publication of this book. I think I can speak for the entire family in saying that we're all proud of your accomplishments. As for myself, I am thrilled that our relationship as brother and sister has strengthened, and I'm looking forward to sharing thoughts, laughter, and our lives together in the years to come. Congratulations, Sue.

Love, Roberto XO

P.S.: Teedent!

—SUBMITTED BY MY BROTHER BOB, NOVEMBER 2000

Watching Her Husband, My Brother

Okay, Sue, here it is. I've read it over, and it is a little painful. Isn't it hard for you to read these? To the best of my recollection, this is how I felt.

I'm writing this as an extended family member who was affected by your suicide attempts and depression. I am married to your brother and am aware of the close bond you two share, and how important that is to him.

I'll begin at the time when he received the phone call telling that you had tried to kill yourself. After hearing this, he called me in a frantic and distressed state. I listened dumbfounded, unable to offer any comfort. I was worried about you, worried about him, worried about the effects on your father and siblings.

Your family responded immediately—the enormity of the situation and the volatile emotional state that you were in created a sense of urgency. I remember at that time experiencing an unusual mix of emotions—fear, guilt, aggravation, and sadness—and the resulting fatigue that followed.

I had conflicting feelings toward you. I was unable to comprehend the depths of your despair. I was afraid at any moment you would kill yourself, and I was afraid of the aftermath. It was unclear to me how much control you had, and I began to question your motives.

I began to sense a barrier between us. I felt awkward and ineffective, not knowing what to say or how to respond. Also at this time I experienced some hostility toward you. I could see the effects your condition had on my husband, whom I love deeply. I was angry at you for causing him so much anxiety and stress. Being a parent, I could identify with the anguish your father felt. It was a tumultuous time for our family.

The tragedy is, at a time when you needed support and understanding from me, I was pulling away from you. Looking back, it is clear to me why I responded to you in that way, but it remains sad and unsettling. Now I think of where you are, and I am so pleased and proud. Our relationship is strong, and I consider you a friend and a sister.

In hindsight, I now have a better understanding of your struggle and, in turn, have been reminded of my own shortcomings during this crisis.

—SUBMITTED BY MY SISTER-IN-LAW AND FRIEND JULIE, NOVEMBER 2000

Like a Holiday from Adulthood

I'm so happy you're writing this book. I hope what I'm sending you will be of use. The pictures that come to mind are:

1. I met you through *The Lark*, a play we were rehearsing together. It was such a leap of faith for both of us—for me to direct and for you to play the lead. What I saw in you at the audition was your inner world. You were able to let us see that, your depth,

your vulnerability, your faith. So it was a shock to suddenly hear you couldn't play the part and you were in the psych ward.

When I visited you, I was surprised that you were just yourself, only a bit dulled maybe from the drugs. I was apprehensive that you would be spooky in some way. The only odd thing was that you were in pajamas in the afternoon, which actually seemed fun, like a holiday from adulthood.

This experience was very early in my knowing you, so right away I had some reservation in my heart. Like, "Be careful, you don't know who/what you're dealing with. You can't cure her, save her, or control her destiny with your love. So be careful of your own heart, don't invest too much."

2. I remember that I wasn't in touch with you when I wrote an article about *The Lark*. Only after it was in print did I ask if you'd mind that I mention "the first Joan ended up in the psych ward." You *did* mind, and I regret my insensitivity.

3. In the years afterward I felt that making contact was too emotionally complicated for me. I felt like I had to be so clear and sure and able to justify everything I said and did, like walking on eggshells. I didn't feel strong enough in myself to love you unconditionally just as you were, without expectations. This remains a challenge in life!

4. I remember visiting once and you were playing the piano, which I'd never heard you do—it was beautiful. That same purity and inner reverence came through your music. At the time I wondered, "How can it be? How can someone who has *that* inside her want to die?"

Today I wouldn't ask that question. I'd ask, "What beauty in myself wants desperately to live? Do I allow it to?" "When I stifle what's beautiful in me, what am I saying to myself? That something else is more important? What's more important? That my beauty isn't wanted? Doesn't fit? Is inconvenient?" "Who believes in my beauty? Do I insist on finding them, spending time with them? If not, why not?" "How can I daily respond to what's beautiful inside myself and others?" "How can I really feeeeel the connection? That every time I believe in me I believe in you. Every time I let me down, I let you down."

This is how I can prevent suicide moment to moment.

Thank you so much, Sue, for inviting me so boldly back into your life. Back into your commitment to allowing your own beauty to flourish!

Love, El

—SUBMITTED BY MY FRIEND ELLEN, AUTUMN 2000

God Doesn't Make Junk!

It amazed me when we discussed your most recent suicide gesture because I had completely spaced it out. I guess that puts me in the category of having been shocked and disbelieving.

What comes back to me now is how powerless I felt. I did know I could tell you I loved you and cared for you. I think the thing that was most amazing to me about talking with you then was how different you sounded and seemed. Your description of yourself as disconnected seems perfect. You seemed completely out of the moment.

I never felt anger toward you, just compassion. I was, however, scared for you. I have known you for about nine years, and I consider you one of my closest and most trusted friends.

I don't think my treatment of you changed as a result of your gesture. It did help me to realize how much we all need each other and how important it is to be present for friends who are struggling. We have always been this for each other, and I value that greatly.

As for how I have seen you change, here is what I've noticed: You built yourself a network of friends to support you. You still hit lows, but you don't stay in them. You empower yourself rather than view yourself as a victim. You ask for help. You give yourself permission not to be perfect, to have downtime, to have uptime, to be authentic. You have great willingness to learn about yourself, and you are one of the most honest people I know.

I guess the most important of these from my perspective is your recognizing that you are a powerful woman with choices; you can advocate for yourself.

What would I like to say to a suicidal reader? You are a miracle—God doesn't make junk! You're not alone, even though you may feel that way now. There is love all around you. Life is one day at a time, one moment at a time.

As for their loved ones . . . it's okay to be afraid. It's okay to feel powerless. It's okay to not have the answers. The greatest gift we have is our love, and that is enough.

—SUBMITTED BY MY LONGTIME FRIEND, NOW COMPANION, JEFF,

JANUARY 2001

Sue's Song

A child was born to wonder,
and a child was born to cry.
A child was born for laughter,
and a child was born
to learn how to fly away
from all the darkness that surrounds.

And as we grow a little older
we have to look a little deeper in ourselves
to chase away some of the monsters
that hold us down and keep us
from breathing in the light of love.

Thank God, you decided to stick around
a little longer than you ever thought you would.
Thank God, you decided to stick around
a little longer than you ever thought you could.

A child was born to play.
And a child was born to grow in her own way.
A child was born to grow older.
And a child was born to bring back the light of day.

And as we grow a little older
we have to reach a little farther than ourselves
to chase away some of the monsters
that hold us down and keep us
from breathing in the light of love.

Thank God, you decided to stick around
a little longer than you ever thought you would.
Thank God, you decided to stick around
a little longer than you ever thought you could.

A child was born to play.

—WRITTEN AS A BIRTHDAY GIFT FROM MY FRIEND JENNIFER STRATTON,

OCTOBER 1999

Rich with Humanity, Hope, and Change

When I first learned about your overdose, I was at work and found your name in the computer as an evaluation. I work for a mental health crisis intervention program and the fact that someone I lived with had been evaluated by our team was a shock to me. I was shocked and scared and worried that you had harmed yourself badly. But then again, it wasn't a shock, because you had been so upset for some time. It hadn't occurred to me that you might harm yourself in your depression and anguish, and this made me feel stupid—that I hadn't seen the signs, should have done something more, especially since I'm "in the business," so to speak. I felt inadequate.

Once I knew you were all right, I allowed myself to feel the anger as well. I felt betrayed somehow, intruded upon, trapped at home by the same intensity that I had to deal with at work. I was also angry on behalf of our other housemate—thinking about how Bob would have felt if you had died; thinking that one of us would have found you and the devastation of that experience. I felt responsible for everyone— you, and my inability to help or even recognize the signs of danger;

Bob, in all his innocence and the pain he might feel; and Lizzie, my friend and previous housemate who once shared this living space.

Of course, this was partly my codependency raising its ugly head. I actually spent some focused time at work processing out the codependence and letting go of my needs and wants enough to go back to my compassion for you, rather than stay pissed off and distracted in my adrenaline-addicted way, so that when we talked later I was able to tell you clearly and calmly how I felt, without being resentful or trying to fix it. I very much appreciated your willingness and courage to take the initiative to find out how I felt, to hear me out with grace and dignity. I really respect you for that—it was real and good. And I have great respect for the recovery you have embraced since that attempt. It was a frightening experience, but also rich with humanity, hope, and change. Peace . . .

—SUBMITTED BY MY FRIEND AND FORMER HOUSEMATE DOROTHY,

MARCH 2001

PART FIVE

Helping the
Suicidal Thinker

Journal drawing, 1994

Love is the only sane and satisfactory answer
to the problem of human existence.

—ERICH FROMM

Introduction

Thank you for wanting to help a suicidal thinker. You play an important role, requiring patience, stamina, and perseverance. Bearing witness to his or her pain is no easy task, but however strange this may sound, it's important to realize that suicidal thinkers most likely want to live. They just *think* they want to die because their brains are bent on killing them.

When my mind focused on suicide, it was craving relief—from psychological pain, or "psychache," a term coined by Dr. Edwin S. Shneidman.[1]

Whenever I had suicidal thoughts, I was in one or more of these feeling states: I felt painfully alone; I felt volcanic anger and wanted to punish someone; I felt free-floating anger and had no healthy outlet for it; I felt afraid of being abandoned (so I thought I'd abandon *first*); I felt afraid that my needs would never be met (so I'd create a crisis to get them met); I felt overwhelmed by responsibility or financial stress; or I felt completely hopeless that my life would ever improve. At times it hurt to live.

My heart craved love, yet when offered appropriate love, I often refused it for a number of reasons: habit, depression, my personality disorder, the need for control, a fear of rejection, a fiendish brain. My rejection of love intensified the psychache and raised the stakes on suicide, which made me crave love even more. Living in a suicidal mind is incredibly complicated. And tiring.

On its website (www.suicidology.org), the American Association of Suicidology states: "People having a crisis sometimes perceive their dilemma as inescapable and feel an utter loss of control. These are some of the feelings and things they experience:

- Can't stop the pain

- Can't think clearly

- Can't make decisions

- Can't see a way out

- Can't sleep, eat, or work

- Can't get out of depression

- Can't make the sadness go away

- Can't see a future without pain

- Can't see themselves as worthwhile

- Can't get someone's attention"

In *Definition of Suicide*, Dr. Shneidman describes ten common suicide characteristics:

1. The common *stimulus* for suicide is *unendurable psychological pain*. Pain is what the suicidal person is seeking to escape. It is psychological pain of which we are speaking; metapain; the pain of feeling pain. The main clinical rule is: Reduce the suffering, often just a little bit, and the individual will choose to live.

2. The common *stressor* in suicide is frustrated psychological *needs*. Suicides are born, negatively, out of needs. Psychological needs are the very color and texture of our inner life. Most suicides probably represent *combinations* of various needs. The clinical rule is: Address the frustrated needs and the suicide will not occur.

3. The common *purpose* of suicide is to seek a *solution*. First of all, suicide is not a random act. It is never done pointlessly or without purpose. It is a way out of a problem, dilemma, bind, challenge, difficulty, crisis, or unbearable situation. It is the answer—seemingly the only available answer—to a real puzzler: How to get out of this? Its purpose is to solve a problem, to seek a solution to a problem that is generating intense suffering. It is important to view each suicidal act as an urgently felt effort to answer a question, to resolve an issue, to solve a problem.

4. The common *goal* of suicide is *cessation of consciousness.* In a curious and paradoxical way, suicide is both a moving toward and a moving away from something; the something that it is moving toward, the common practical goal of suicide, is the stopping of the painful flow of consciousness. The moment that the idea of the possibility of stopping consciousness occurs to the anguished mind as the answer or the way out in the presence of the three essential ingredients of suicide (unusual constriction, elevated perturbation, and high lethality), then the igniting spark has been struck and the active suicide scenario has begun.

5. The common *emotion* in suicide is *hopelessness-helplessness.* In the suicidal state [the common emotion] is a pervasive feeling of hopelessness-helplessness. I believe that this formulation permits us somewhat gracefully to withdraw from the (sibling) rivalry among the various emotions, each with the proponents to assess that *it* is the central one of them all. To the extent that suicide is an act to solve a problem, the common fear that drives it is the fear that the situation will deteriorate, become much worse, get out of hand, exacerbate beyond the point of any control. Oftentimes, persons literally on the ledge of com-

mitting suicide would be willing to live if things—life—were only a little bit better, a just noticeable difference, slightly more tolerable. The common fear is that the inferno is endless and that one has to draw the line on one's suffering *somewhere.*

6. The common *internal attitude* toward suicide is *ambivalence.* We can now assert that the prototypical suicidal state is one in which the individual cuts his throat and cries for help at the same time, and is genuine in both of these acts. This accommodation to the psychological realities of mental life is called ambivalence. It is the common internal attitude toward suicide: To feel that one has to do it and, simultaneously, to yearn (and even to plan) for rescue and intervention.

7. The common *cognitive state* in suicide is *constriction* (tunnel vision). . . . Suicide is much more accurately seen as a more or less transient psychological constriction of affect and intellect. Synonyms for constriction are a tunneling or focusing or narrowing of the range of options usually available to that individual's conscious when the mind is not panicked into all-or-nothing thinking. The range of choices has narrowed to two— not very much of a range. The usual life-sustaining images of loved ones are not disregarded; worse, they are not even within the range of what is in the mind.

8. The common *interpersonal act* in suicide is *communication of intention.* Clues to suicide are present in approximately 80 percent of suicidal deaths. It is a sad and paradoxical thing to note that the common interpersonal act of suicide is not hostility, not rage or destruction, not even the kind of withdrawal that does not have its own intended message, but communication of intention. The communication of suicidal intention is not always a cry for help. First, it is not always a cry; it can be a

shout or a murmur or the loud communication of unspoken silences. And it is not always for help; it can be for autonomy or inviolacy (to not be violated) or any number of needs. Nonetheless, in most cases of suicide there is some interpersonal communication exchange related to that intended final act.

9. The common *action* in suicide is *egression*. Egression is a person's departure or escape, often from distress. Egression means to leave, exit, or escape. Suicide is the ultimate egression. Suicide is a death in which the decedent removes himself or herself from intolerable pain and simultaneously from others in the world in a precipitous fashion.

10. The common *consistency* in suicide is with *life-long coping patterns*. In almost every case what one does see are certain displays of emotions and use of defenses that are consistent with *that* individual's reactions to pain, threat, failure, powerlessness, impotence, and duress in previous episodes of that life. In general, . . . suicide, although enormously complicated, is not totally random and it is amenable to a considerable amount of prediction.[2]

If suicidal thinkers are trying to end psychache, and psychache stems from frustrated psychological needs, your job is to help them *meet* those needs.

When I confided in someone about suicidal thoughts, I did so out of trust, even if my general treatment of that person was erratic. If the other person had the ability to give and receive help openly, both of us benefited from the exchange. If, on the other hand, that person's ability was limited (for any number of reasons), his or her feelings of inadequacy or frustration often collided head-on with my feelings of rejection and abandonment, fueling the suicidal situation.

When a suicidal thinker or depressed person comes to you asking for assistance, be aware of your limitations; it's okay for *you* to ask for help. I suggest that you do what you can for the person in the moment, then seek additional support and guidance. It is both dangerous and impossible for a layperson to try to remedy the situation alone. See part 7 for a comprehensive listing of prevention organizations and resources.

You'll quickly see that this part of the book has little to do with changing the suicidal thinker. Rather, I discuss how the rest of us can change *ourselves* so we can better support the suicidal thinker. The only person who can "fix" the suicidal thinker is the suicidal thinker, with your loving support and the guidance of a professional.

After a review of the risk factors, warning signs, and statistics of suicide, the rest of part 5 is divided into three sections: words, beliefs, and actions—what works, what doesn't, and why.

By holding to certain beliefs about the suicidal situation, I believe that our actions and words contribute to a more (or less) productive atmosphere for growth. By engaging in certain actions—good listening skills, for example—we convey the belief that it's okay to talk about it. By choosing appropriate words rather than words that don't work, we take the suicidal person seriously, practice patience, and affirm the belief that change is possible.

My personal examples are supplemented with guidelines from professional suicide prevention organizations. If anything I say sounds simplistic, know that I am well aware of the difficulty involved. My road to freedom was wracked with obstacles and setbacks.

I'm sorry that someone you love is considering suicide. If it's any consolation, I put people through the wringer before I finally "got it" and stopped the suicide cycle. I've come to realize that I had to go through what I did in order to get to where I am today, which is a place of profound gratitude and lasting peace.

May your love and compassion reach the heart of the suicidal thinker, and may your willingness to grow aid in that person's transformation. I can say from experience you're in for a bumpy ride, but it is definitely worth the effort. So are you.

Change is possible and love heals. You *can* make a difference. So hang in there, breathe, find support, get educated, and remember: there is no need to go through this alone. This book is dedicated to all of you; I wish you well.

Risk Factors and Warning Signs

To give and receive are one in truth.

—*A COURSE IN MIRACLES*

In 1999 the World Health Organization estimated that approximately 1 million people would die from suicide in the year 2000, a global mortality rate of 16 per 100,000. That's one suicide every forty seconds.[3]

More people take their own lives than die from homicide in the United States.[4] In 1999 suicide was the eleventh leading cause of death for all Americans, and the third leading cause of death for young people age fifteen to twenty-four. Homicide ranked fourteenth.[5] Each year in the United States approximately 500,000 people require emergency room treatment as a result of attempted suicide.[6] There are now twice as many deaths due to suicide than due to HIV/AIDS.

Although mental disorders (particularly depression and substance abuse) are associated with more than 90 percent of all cases of suicide, there is no typical suicide victim.[7] It can happen to anyone in any family. If someone you know is suicidal, the American Association of Suicidology reminds us, your ability to recognize the signs and your willingness to do something about it could make the difference between life and death.

The following list of risk factors and warning signs—many of which are symptoms of depression—were gathered from the websites of the American Association of Suicidology, Befrienders International, the Centers for Disease Control and Prevention, and Focus Adolescent Services; a report by Dr. John McIntosh, a professor of psychology at Indiana University, South Bend; and "The U.S. Surgeon General's Call to Action to Prevent Suicide."[8] The categories under which I present this information are taken from Befrienders International: "Situations," "Behaviors," "Physical Changes," and "Thoughts and Emotions."

No one of these signs alone indicates a suicidal person. The people most at risk for committing suicide are those who exhibit or have experienced several of these signs. Generally, the more signs a person displays, the higher the risk of suicide, according to Befrienders International.

SITUATIONS

- Previous suicide attempts. Four out of five people who commit suicide have made at least one previous attempt. Half of all children who have made one suicide attempt will make another, sometimes as many as two a year until they "succeed."

- A family history of suicide, violence, depression, or substance abuse.

- Access to a firearm. If you have a gun in your home, you are *five times* more likely to have a suicide than if you did not have a gun in your home, according to the website Suicidal.com. Surprisingly, even when a child has made one attempt with a firearm, parents often fail to remove guns from the home.

- Experienced violence in the form of physical, sexual, domestic, or child abuse.

- Experienced poor parent-child communication.

- Experiencing unusual stress due to traumatic life events and/or major life changes such as death of a friend, spouse, or family member, separation, divorce, the end of a relationship, job loss, problems at work, impending legal action, impending loss, loss of honor, failing academic performance, impending exams.

- Recent imprisonment or upcoming release.

- Medical condition, chronic pain, long-term illness.

- Barriers to accessing mental health treatment.

- Co-occurring substance abuse and mental disorders.

- Unwillingness to seek help because of the stigma attached to mental and substance abuse disorders and/or suicidal thoughts.

- The influence of significant people—family members, celebrities, peers who have died by suicide, both through direct personal contact or inappropriate media representation.

- Life events commonly associated with elderly suicide are: the death of a loved one; physical illness; uncontrollable pain; fear of dying a prolonged death that damages family members emotionally and economically; social isolation and loneliness; and major changes in social roles, such as retirement. The widowed, divorced, and recently bereaved are at high risk, as are depressed individuals and those who abuse alcohol or drugs. (Depression is *not* a normal part of aging.)

• Many children who commit suicide are anxious and insecure and have a desperate desire to be liked and to do well. Their expectations are so high that they demand too much from themselves and are constantly disappointed. A traumatic event that may seem minor viewed from an adult perspective—being jilted, failing a test, getting into an accident—can be enough to push a child over the edge into a severe depression.

BEHAVIORS

• Making remarks about committing suicide. For example, "I can't go on," "Nothing matters anymore," "What's the use in living?," "I'm seriously thinking about packing it in," "No one will miss me if I'm gone," or "It's never going to get any better."

• Crying for no apparent reason.

• Experiencing an inability to feel good about themselves or express joy.

• Withdrawing from family, friends, or social activities.

• Losing interest in hobbies, work, or school.

• Increasing drug or alcohol use or use of other medications. Sometimes teens try alcohol or other drugs to relieve depression. Unfortunately, the drugs themselves have a depressant effect by lowering inhibitions against self-injurious behavior. In any age group, drug and alcohol use can cause people to commit rash, impulsive acts that they most likely would not have committed when sober.

- Seeming preoccupied with death; writing or talking about death and suicide.

- Showing marked changes in behavior and attitude that have no apparent reason or last for a significant period of time: for example, a shy person becomes a thrill-seeker, or an outgoing person becomes withdrawn, unfriendly, and disinterested.

- Behaving recklessly; taking unusual risks and acting impulsively.

- Breaking the law; fighting (with parents); getting in trouble at school.

- Self-mutilating: Cutting, burning, scratching, pulling out hair, and so on.

- Failing to take prescribed medicines or follow required diets.

- Acquiring a weapon.

- Preparing for death by getting affairs in order. For example, making out a will and final arrangements, giving away valued possessions. Young people making such arrangements often give away treasured items such as a favorite book or a CD collection.

PHYSICAL CHANGES

- Change in eating or sleeping habits; sleeping too much or too little; loss of appetite; sudden weight gain or loss.

- Lack of energy and loss of interest in life.

- Change of sexual interest; loss of sex drive.

- Sudden change in appearance.

- Loss of interest in personal appearance.

- Increased frequency of minor illnesses.

THOUGHTS AND EMOTIONS

- Depressed mood—most of the day, every day.

- Mood swings—one minute high, next minute low.

- Mental disorders, particularly mood disorders such as depression and bipolar disorder.

- Irritability and restlessness.

- Unexplained fatigue or apathy.

- Thoughts of death, punishment, or the option of suicide.

- Deep sadness or guilt, feelings of worthlessness.

- Having trouble working, concentrating, making decisions.

- Feelings of helplessness, hopelessness.

- Inability to see beyond a narrow focus.

- Loneliness—lack of support from family and friends.

- Rejection—feeling marginalized, socially isolated.

- Experiencing anxiety and stress.

Suicide Facts and Statistics

The most recent statistical data compiled by psychologist Dr. John L. McIntosh notes that in 1999, every 18 minutes a person died by suicide in the United States. He also notes that an average of 730,000 attempts are made in this country every year.[9] Data compiled by the Centers for Disease Control and Prevention show that males are four times more likely to die from suicide than females, but females are three times more likely to make suicide attempts than males. Males are also more likely than females to die from their first attempt.[10]

Age is a significant factor in suicide rate. From 1952 to 1995 the incidence of suicide among adolescents and young adults nearly tripled. More teenagers and young adults die from suicide than from cancer, heart disease, AIDS, birth defects, stroke, pneumonia, and influenza and chronic lung disease *combined*. In 1999, approximately 1 out of every 13 United States high school students reported making a suicide attempt in the preceding 12 months.[11] For every completed youth suicide there are between 100 and 200 attempts.[12]

Suicide rates increase with age and in the U.S. are highest among seniors age sixty-five and older—more than 50 percent higher than for young people or for the nation as a whole, according to Dr. McIntosh, whose research focuses on suicide among older adults and on survivors of suicide.[13] The CDC notes that the 1980s was the first decade since the 1940s when the suicide rate for older Americans rose rather than declined. Dr. McIntosh's figures back this up: each year more than 6,300 older adults take their own lives. In other words, nearly 18 older Americans kill themselves every day. As noted in the previous chapter, Dr. McIntosh finds that some older Americans are at higher risk of suicide: the widowed, divorced, or recently bereaved, and those who abuse alcohol or drugs. Also at somewhat higher risk, the CDC finds, are Asian American women, who have the highest suicide rate among women sixty-five and older.

Race has played a significant role as well in the increase in suicide rates in the last twenty years. Although in 1999 white males accounted for 72 percent of all suicides (adding in white females, whites accounted for 90 percent of the total),[14] the suicide rate has increased most rapidly among African-American males age fifteen to nineteen: 105 percent from 1980 to 1996. Among Native Americans, one CDC stat is chilling: 4,718 American Indians and Alaskan Natives residing on or near a reservation died violently between 1979 and 1992, and more than half of those deaths were suicides.

What are the absolute numbers? Dr. McIntosh's figures from 1999 show that a total of 29,199 Americans died by suicide that year. Of that number, 21,107 were white men, 5,193 were white women, 2,351 were nonwhite men, and 548 were nonwhite women.[15]

Dr. McIntosh also compares statistics on suicide methods. This table shows who committed suicide and how in 1999:[16]

SUICIDE METHOD	TOTAL	YOUTH	ELDERLY	MEN	WOMEN
Firearms and explosives	56.8%	59.3%	71.4%	61.7%	36.9%
Hanging, strangling, and suffocation	18.6	24.8	10.8	19.1	16.3
Solid and liquid poisons	11.5	5.0	6.5	7.0	30.0
Gas poisons	5.3	3.4	3.9	5.1	6.0
Jump from a high place	2.4	2.9	2.3	2.1	3.3

Look at the figures for suicides committed with guns—nearly three in every five suicides in the United States. The CDC says that from 1980 to 1997, suicides committed with a gun accounted for 62 percent of the increase in the suicide rate among people age fifteen to nineteen. Firearms were also the most popular method among older Americans (71.4 percent in 1999).

All of the figures cited in this chapter are for the United States only. We are not the only nation, however, experiencing steep increases in the number of people who kill themselves. The World Health Organization reports that around the world suicide rates have risen 60 percent in the last forty-five years.[17]

Words

WHAT I HEARD VERSUS WHAT I NEEDED TO HEAR

> I don't let my mouth say nothin' my head can't stand.
> —LOUIS ARMSTRONG

The following excerpt is from a sermon I gave on suicide in 1996. It is a responsive reading between myself and the congregation. I spoke the words I often heard from certain family members and friends when I was struggling emotionally. The congregation spoke the words I needed to hear. I suggest that you read all of it aloud, and let yourself feel the difference between each set of sentences.

SUE: What is *wrong* with you?

CONGREGATION: I hear you. Do you want to talk about it?

SUE: Why do you keep *doing* this to yourself?
CONGREGATION: I hear you and I feel concerned. How can I help?

SUE: But you have so much *going* for you!
CONGREGATION: I believe in you. How can I help?

SUE: I just don't *understand* you!
CONGREGATION: I'm here for you. What do you need from me?

SUE: Why can't you *forget* about it?
CONGREGATION: I know it's hard, and I hear you. Would it help to talk about it?

SUE: Come on, it's not *that* bad.
CONGREGATION: I hear your pain. Is there anything I can do?

SUE: Don't you *know* I *love* you?
CONGREGATION: I love you.

Well, that just about sums it up right there. I feel sad just to read it. So sad for the girl who just needed to be heard and feel loved. So sad indeed.

I've divided this section into "whys," "whats," "shoulds and shouldn'ts," "don'ts," and "can'ts," with a few miscellaneous comments thrown in at the end. First I list the question or comment that didn't work, then I give an alternative. Read each sentence aloud. Do they sound familiar? Please try to use the alternatives *especially* when dealing with someone who is depressed or in crisis. That person needs to feel heard and accepted rather than judged or ignored.

Notice in the alternative wording that "you" is quite often changed to "I." *Feel* the difference.

THE WHYS	ALTERNATIVES
WHY do you keep doing this to yourself?	How can I help?
WHY do you make things so *hard*?	I hear you. What can I do?
WHY can't you snap out of it?	I understand you're in pain. How can I help?
WHY can't you let it go?	You are important to me. What can I do to help?
WHY do you have to make such a big deal out of everything?	I love you.

THE WHATS	ALTERNATIVES
WHAT is *wrong* with you?	I love you. Do you need anything from me?
WHAT do you *want* from me?	How can I best help you?
WHAT'S gotten *into* you lately?	I've noticed a change. Is everything all right? Is there anything I can do?

THE SHOULDS AND SHOULDN'TS	ALTERNATIVES

Basically, "should-ing" on someone is bad news all around. Try to avoid it.

You **SHOULD** think better of yourself.	You are important to me.
You **SHOULDN'T** feel that way.	I honor your feelings.
You **SHOULDN'T** think like that.	I'd like to know what you're thinking.
You **SHOULD** try harder.	How can I best support you?

THE DON'TS	ALTERNATIVES
DON'T feel that way!	I honor your feelings.
DON'T think that way.	Would you like to tell me about it?
DON'T you see how much you've got going for you?	I love you and I feel concerned. Would it help if I sat and listened for a while?
DON'T do this to yourself.	You are important to me. It's hard to see you go through this. Can I help in any way?

THE CAN'TS	ALTERNATIVES
CAN'T you get over it?	Would it help to talk about it?
CAN'T you see what this does to me?	I care for you and feel concerned.
CAN'T you see what this is doing to our family?	We are all concerned about you. Let us know what we can do.
CAN'T you forget about it?	I know it's hard. How can I help you get through it?

MISCELLANY	ALTERNATIVES
You're too emotional.	I appreciate your sensitivity. How can I help?
You know what your problem is?	I believe in you. You are important to me.
I just don't understand you!	I care, and I feel confused. Do you know what might help?
Cheer up.	I hear you.

Notice that most of the alternative comments give the power of choice to the suicidal thinker: "How can I help?" "What can I do?" "What do you need from me?" Notice also that, instead of denying the person her feelings with statements like "Don't feel like that" or "Come on, it's not that bad," the listener is honoring the suicidal thinker and remaining open to her experience. When you are more open to her, she is likely to be more open with you. Your openness creates a safe environment in which she can air feelings and thoughts. Once I found people who could *really* hear me, I was able to start the unraveling process and examine the tangled knot of feelings under my suicidal thoughts.

Here are some conversation guidelines from professional suicide prevention organizations:

- Don't be afraid to talk about suicide.

- Be direct. Talk openly and matter-of-factly about suicide.

- Don't dare the person talking about suicide to do it. This "common remedy" could have fatal results.

- Offer hope that alternatives are available, but do not offer glib reassurance. It may make him feel as if you don't understand.

- Your willingness to discuss it will show the person that you don't condemn him for having such thoughts. Ask questions about how he feels and about the reasons for those feelings.

- Don't worry that your discussion will encourage him to go through with a suicide plan. On the contrary, it will help him to know that someone is willing to be a friend. It may save his life.

- Remind the person, in a nonjudgmental way, that suicide is a permanent solution to a temporary problem. ("I know life feels really hard right now, and I understand that you're in pain. I know you'll get through this; we'll get through it together. How can I help?")

- Don't try to end the discussion or offer advice such as "Think about how much better off you are than most people. You should [there's that word!] appreciate how lucky you are." *Such comments only make the suicidal person feel more guilty, worthless, and hopeless than before.*

- Be quiet and listen! People who have suicidal thoughts don't want answers or solutions. They want a safe place to express their fears and anxieties and to be themselves. (See the chapter "Listening Well" for suggestions.)

DELIVERY AND TIMING

Whoever said, "Timing is everything," was absolutely right. Even the kindest thought can get skewed on delivery if the person speaking it is stressed, angry, tired, or overloaded.

In my experience as a suicidal thinker, I felt safer with a person who spoke clearly and calmly, with an even tone and a soft expression. The minute voices got sharp or eye contact started to fade, I felt nervous and on the edge of rejection. I'd tighten inside, my heart would start to race, and I'd clam up, shutting the person who was trying to talk to me out (and shutting myself out in the process).

When you begin to talk about the suicidal situation, try to be on the same physical level with the suicidal thinker. For example, if she begins to talk while seated at the kitchen table and you are standing up, looking down at her, take a seat and look her evenly in the eye. If you walk into his bedroom and he is lying on the bed, pull a chair over and sit down by his side instead of standing over him.

It helps to talk about intense feelings in a neutral place—not during a meal or in front of a lot of people. Set time aside. Go for a walk together.

It's best to eliminate distractions such as television or radio. The person confiding in you will feel rejected and invalidated if your attention swerves to catch a guy stealing third. Most likely he'll walk away, saying, "Oh, it was nothing. Forget about it," and he will leave, feeling sadder and even more frustrated. What is more important? The score of a ball game or his life? One of my chief competitors for my father's attention was TV sporting events. One day I got up the nerve to ask him to turn the TV off when I needed to talk, and he did. It brings tears to my eyes to remember the first time he turned it off without my prompting. I walked into the den, stood in the doorway, and said, "Dad, can I talk to you for a minute?" "Sure," he said, "just let me turn off the television."

Another suggestion: when talking with a suicidal thinker, do just that—talk *with* her, not *at* her. Keep your statements focused on yourself. "I feel concerned. How can I help?" "I love you. What do you need from me?" By using "I" instead of "you," you are less apt to say something that can be misconstrued as blame or shame. Remember, tunnel vision has severely narrowed her mental focus. Anything you say needs to be clear and direct.

Try to talk about other subjects, steering clear of the "whys," "don'ts," "shoulds," and so on. Try to point out positive things you notice about him, without being overzealous. For example: "I really appreciate how you were with the kids yesterday. You relate to them so well," or, "I like how you arranged the table setting. It looks beautiful." Anything to boost his self-esteem is great—remember to keep it positive. Instead of saying, "Don't you know how talented you are!" say, "I think you're so talented. I love the way you play the piano." Keep it soft, direct.

Sometimes you'll need to be not only clear and direct but firm. When I really tested the waters, Sylvia offered me very few options. If I didn't sign the personal safety contract, I had to go to the hospital. If I didn't call her for my scheduled check-in, she called the police. She didn't mess around.

Here are some more guidelines from the experts:

- Lectures don't help. Nor does a suggestion to "cheer up," or an easy assurance that "everything will be okay."

- Don't analyze, compare, categorize, or criticize.

- Rejection can make a problem seem ten times worse. Having someone to turn to makes all the difference.

- Ask questions gently; don't interrogate.

- Ask the person whether he has considered a method of suicide, made any specific plans, or taken any steps toward carrying out those plans, such as getting hold of some means of suicide. But don't act shocked, since this will put distance between the two of you. Stay calm.

- Don't change the subject, and don't pity or patronize. Talking about feelings is difficult. People who have suicidal thoughts don't want to be rushed or put on the defensive.

- Be nonjudgmental. Don't debate whether suicide is right or wrong, or feelings are good or bad. Don't lecture on the value of life.

EXPRESSING YOUR FEELINGS

I will remember that my words can help or hinder.
I will benefit from using soft words today.
—*IN GOD'S CARE*, SEPTEMBER 14

Being a suicidal thinker is a catch-22. Instead of masking their feelings, I wanted people to be up-front with me, so I could feel a part of their experience—so I wouldn't feel alone in mine. But when they told me how they felt, depending on how *I* felt, my response was usually anger, shame, or embarrassment, none of which would have been a problem had it not been for my suicidal thoughts. They were understandably concerned about "setting me off." See my brother's letter in part 4. (I've been on the other side of a suicide conversation many times, so I know what it's like to be afraid of pushing someone over the edge.)

Being honest about our feelings is important, not only to connect with the suicidal thinker but to let them know the impact of their behavior on our lives. The trick is to do it without casting blame or shame. For example, avoid "You make . . ." statements: "You make me feel so afraid!" "You make me feel crazy!" "You make me feel nervous." No one can "make" us feel anything. If we feel it, it's because of something within us, not the other person. Remember to use "I" statements: "I feel scared," "I feel afraid that you might hurt yourself," "I feel concerned."

Preface your expression of feeling with something like "I love you." Begin the discussion by stating something positive about the other person, perhaps a quality you admire. This helps take her off the defensive. End the discussion with another positive statement.

———

It's vitally important that you find avenues of self-expression *elsewhere*. Get it out. Let it out. Find a place to vent the anger, fear, and frustration. Find people who are going through similar situations and listen to how they're dealing with it. If you can do this, there will be less built-up tension in your interactions with the suicidal thinker.

TIPS FOR EXPRESSING YOUR FEELINGS ELSEWHERE

- Talk to a therapist on your own.

- Meet with a member of the clergy for spiritual guidance and comfort.

- Find a support group to attend.

- Read part 3 and find some exercises to practice.

- Pray about your feelings.

- Write them down in a journal.

- Be open about the situation with trusted friends.

- Talk openly about it with your spouse or companion.

- Get anger and frustration out of your body (see the "HALT" chapter in part 3).

Here is some additional advice from the experts:

- Many people find it awkward to put into words how another person's life is important for their own well-being, but it is important to try to do just that.

- Describe specific behaviors and events that trouble you. Noting particular ways in which a person's behavior has changed may help to get a dialogue started. (Remember, however, to avoid the "whys," "shoulds," and so on. Instead of saying, "Why are you acting so strange? Why don't you take a shower?" say, "I feel concerned about you. I've noticed that you haven't been showering. Is there something wrong? Can I help?")

ACKNOWLEDGING THEIR PAIN

Someone who knew what he was talking about once remarked that pain is the touchstone of spiritual progress.

—BILL W.

Pain is a hard thing. It can be hard to hear about; it's even harder to experience. It's even more difficult to be in pain when people tell you not to feel it. The suicidal thinker is in extreme mental pain. *You must acknowledge it;* it needs to be heard. Acknowledging the pain of a suicidal thinker is like giving her permission to breathe.

According to Dr. Shneidman, "psychache" is directly linked to frustrated psychological needs. One of my frustrated psychological needs was the need for people to acknowledge my pain. I had very few places to go with it save inward because I was taught it was wrong to feel and express.

First of all, every individual has a unique version of reality, based on her past and personality development. How can anyone know what another person *should* feel about a given situation? Telling a depressed person not to feel sad is like asking a color-blind person to find you a red shirt. It just won't happen. Moreover, if the suicidal thinker is anything like I was, she will raise the stakes and stir up more chaos the more her pain is denied, ignored, dismissed, or belittled.

I am convinced that people find it difficult to acknowledge someone else's pain because they don't or won't acknowledge their own. There is absolutely nothing wrong with feeling pain. It's a part of life, like joy and excitement. It's neither good nor bad, right nor wrong. It just is.

How to acknowledge someone's pain. What I'm talking about is simply acknowledging—not fixing, changing, or helping. This is all you have to do:

1. Look her straight in the eye.

2. Hold her hand if it's okay with her. If it's not, don't force it. Just smile.

3. Say in a loving, soft, nonjudgmental voice, "I hear your pain and I care."

That's it.

Experts point out that suicidal ideation is frequently accompanied by a self-absorbed, uncommunicative, and withdrawn state of mind, and the individual may be reluctant to discuss what he is thinking. Nevertheless, it's important to express empathy and *concern*, and to acknowledge the reality of his pain and hopelessness.

SPEAKING FROM LOVE

> Love doesn't grow on trees like apples in Eden—
> it's something you have to make.
> —JOYCE CAREY

It's interesting and sad to note that in all of the literature I've read thus far about suicide prevention, the word "love" is hardly ever used. What I mean is that the actual word "love" is rarely suggested as something the suicidal thinker might need to hear. I find that interesting; our reason for wanting our loved ones to stay alive is because we love them. If you love someone, I suggest that you tell that person before you lose the chance. Hearing your expression of love could mean the difference between life and death.

It's so sad that expressing love and affection is such an awkward thing in our culture. I wish there were an incentive plan or something: "Get a tax refund if you attend this self-expression course!" People need to know they are loved, especially suicidal thinkers. Here's how to do it:

EXERCISE: EXPRESSING LOVE

1. Look him straight in the eye.

2. Hold his hand, if it's okay with him. If it's not, don't force it. Just smile.

3. Say in a loving, soft, nonjudgmental voice, "I love you."

Beliefs

> "Came to believe": The three most beautiful words
> in our language.
>
> —ANONYMOUS

Beliefs alter our perception of reality. They also affect our language and direct our actions. Beliefs about suicide directly affect our treatment and understanding of the suicidal thinker.

If we believe in the suicidal thinker's capacity for self-improvement, he has a better chance of improving. If we believe his situation is hopeless, his chance for change is greatly diminished, and the situation is far more likely to end in disaster.

If we believe the suicidal thinker's problem will simply resolve itself, we are denying reality and refusing her what she deserves: our love and compassion. If we believe in our ability to grow and change as she does, we feel less threatened by her progress and are therefore less likely to compromise her achievements, however unconscious our actions may be.

We are more likely to use new communication skills, take a more effective course of involvement, and learn how to let the suicidal thinker fumble through life if we feel comfortable with ourselves. Such efforts contribute to a more productive healing environment, allowing him to do the work necessary to break the cycle of destruction.

The following beliefs are, I feel, crucial to establishing a healthy, loving environment in which the suicidal thinker can find relief, comfort, reassurance, and support:

- Secrets are deadly.

- It's okay to talk about it.

- It's a family challenge.

- Change is possible.

SECRETS ARE DEADLY

It's a given that secrets underlie most suicidal thoughts, secrets like sexual abuse, battering, or severe loss. Often the suicidal thinker can't even easily recall these secrets. Clearly those secrets need to be flushed out, but here I speak only of the crisis at hand. Beware: if the suicidal crisis is continually buried in secrecy, the suicidal thinker might end up buried as well.

We've all been trained to discount trauma, keep our chin up, look on the bright side. This attitude, however, can lead to fear, shame, and confusion, feelings that make it difficult to give and receive productive emotional support. By acting on the belief that secrets are deadly and establishing an open line of communication, you give the suicidal thinker an outlet for the turmoil that's eating at her soul. If you remain closed to the reality of her life, you contribute to her destruction. It's as simple as that.

Your loved one's suicidal thoughts are not going to disappear by shutting them out. This is not a game; she could wind up dead or with permanent physical damage.

If someone in your life has made a suicide gesture or has come to you talking of suicide, there's a good chance that person will continue in the same vein until he or she breaks the cycle, either by outthinking the brain or completing the suicide. It's hard to hear someone talk about suicide, I know. If you tend to squash or interrupt the suicidal thinker with words like, "Oh, come on, that's nothing," or "Why can't you forget about it?" please try the following exercise.

EXERCISE: COMMUNICATION

1. When a suicidal thinker or depressed person comes to you needing to talk, stop whatever you're doing (turn off the TV, put down the newspaper, close the book, turn off the radio, take the skillet off the stove).

2. Tell her you're there for her 100 percent.

3. As she talks, look her straight in the eye. Nod your head. Say, "Um-hmmm."

4. If she starts to cry, let her cry and sit in silence. You may feel compelled to fill the silence with words. Sometimes it's best to sit quietly and let her release the tears. Please do not say, "Don't cry," or, "Don't be so sad."

5. Breathe deeply while she shares. Most likely your level of discomfort will start to rise. Perhaps sip a glass of water while she talks to give yourself something to do without diminishing your attention.

6. As she speaks, cries, or vents her anger and confusion, look at her neutrally with love and compassion. Try not to display shock, anger, or fear.

7. If you begin to feel angry and defensive as she shares, remember to breathe deeply to keep your equilibrium. Wait until you are away from her before you let the anger out. Go for a drive and scream; call a trusted friend and tell him about it. Be sure to release any anger, but not in her presence.

8. If you need a breather while she's sharing because it's getting too intense, say, "I love you, _____, and I'm really concerned. Let me just take a minute and collect my thoughts." Ask if you can hold her hand during the silence. If she declines, say, "Okay, that's fine. I just thought I'd ask," and let it go. After a minute, ask to continue the discussion.

Often this type of discussion is spontaneous, and the listener has very little time to prepare. If you have the opportunity, however, I suggest that you practice this exercise with someone else to get a feel for it (called role-playing). A "dress rehearsal" can help lessen potential discomfort.

IT'S OKAY TO TALK ABOUT IT

Despite what I heard growing up—"No one wants to hear it"—talking about my feelings was the *only* way I got better.

In the beginning of my self-exploration (mid-1980s to early 1990s), I often felt shut out and rejected when I spoke openly to family members about the ways in which I was seeking help, particularly when I spoke about therapy. How sad it is that the effort to reach out for help—a powerful, courageous act—is often repelled because of another person's inability to witness pain.

Had I not found Sylvia, the people from Twelve Steps, a community at First Parish Unitarian Universalist Church, and other travelers on the road to self-discovery, I couldn't and wouldn't have made it this far. Because of their honesty and willingness to be vulnerable, I finally saw that I was not alone and there was nothing wrong with me for feeling the way I did. These people made it safe to vent all the crap I'd been carrying around for a good twenty-five years. They let me do and say what I needed to break the suicide cycle.

Because of the safety found in these arenas, I became strong enough to approach family members and begin to heal those relationships. After I was hospitalized and the truth could no longer be denied, things started to shift even further. But it was still a long, arduous haul. Over time my struggle was openly acknowledged and it felt safer to express my truth, though all of us were still fumbling our way through each step.

I began to voice questions and set boundaries. I said and asked many things. To nearly everyone: "I need you just to listen and not tell me how to feel." To my father: "How did you feel when Mom died?" or "I need you to turn off the TV when I'm talking to you." To my three oldest siblings: "What was it like when my mother came into your lives?" To my sisters: "I don't need another mother; my mother is dead. I need a sister, a friend." To people who liked to poke fun at me: "If that's how you express love, then I don't want it."

I began to feel like a person with feelings and thoughts instead of an outcast or damaged goods. I began to feel accepted for who I was and not judged for what I felt. I started to translate my distortion of reality into a language I could comprehend and clarify. The feelings and thoughts were no longer trapped in my cerebral pressure cooker.

It's okay to talk about it. While I advocate positive thinking and "acting as if," I say phooey to the theory of putting on a happy face despite internal strife. We all have problems, and we all need help. Anyone who claims otherwise is from another planet. The suicidal thinker needs to know he can share his experience with others: his friends, family members, and professionals. After all, what is more important, the "family image" or the life of your child, spouse, sibling, or friend?

In 1996 I was asked to give a presentation on depression and suicide to parents of teenagers. I used the illustration on the following page to show what happened to me as a teen when I tried to share difficult feelings with my father. I call the drawing "The Wall" because that's exactly how it felt.

The Wall was so high that my feelings and thoughts had nowhere to go. They just swirled backward, surrounded me and pulled me deeper into their web. Because I had no healthy outlet for my feelings, they inevitably turned to frustration and anger, which quickly boomeranged back at me—and were translated into suicidal thoughts.

When I was in my late twenties and my father and I began to heal our relationship, The Wall started to drop. I finally felt like my feelings were heard and respected. Instead of swirling back at me, they floated over the wall. Sometimes. Like any relationship, ours was far from perfect, but we both worked hard to improve it.

THE WALL

We are all members of the same human family, wanting and deserving love, respect, and acceptance. Believe that it's okay to talk about it, and show the suicidal thinker: "My door is open. Anytime you're ready to talk, I'm ready to listen." If she doesn't respond right away, try not to badger her for information. Just remind her that she is loved and when she's ready, you are there. (Of course, if the suicidal thinker is making gestures, it is imperative to seek professional support and guidance, even if she doesn't want to talk about it.)

Please remember: if you're opening the door to listen, *you must be prepared to do so*. See the "Actions" chapter for tips on listening well, practicing compassion, and setting boundaries. I suggest that you practice these skills with a friend.

IT'S A FAMILY CHALLENGE

Suicidal thoughts are products of experience, history, and genetics. Suicidal gestures manifest not from thin air but from a breakdown in the generational chain—a breakdown of biology, communication, behavior, understanding, trust, or circumstance.

To peg the suicidal thinker as the "troubled one" in the family is a severe disservice. Most often that person is highly sensitive, intelligent, and creative, with deep feelings and a finely tuned emotional radar that tends to intensify family undercurrents.

It's important to believe that suicide is a *family* challenge. Suicidal thinkers are not in it alone. They are card-carrying members of a family system, a direct product of their immediate environment and upbringing. The family is how and where our personality develops.

Instead of looking for causes outside the family structure or pointing the finger of blame at the struggling relative, I encourage you to look within the circle and within yourself. Be honest: Does someone in the family have an addiction problem? Is there a history of suicidal behavior in the family? Eating disorders? Depression or other mental illness? Was there severe trauma with the loss of a parent or sibling? Is there a possibility of sexual abuse? Was there divorce?

Is there something you can do to help the situation? There are many possibilities: renewing your commitment to meet your *own* needs; talking more openly with your spouse; addressing an addiction problem; finding more time for the suicidal thinker; learning how to be a better parent; finding grief support. I'm well aware that taking such steps is easier said than done, but the sooner the truth is approached and addressed, the sooner you *and* the suicidal thinker will find relief. If that person has already entered the cycle of suicide gestures and hospitalizations, it may be harder to break the pattern, but any positive change on your part is better than none.

This is a long journey—for everyone. Some say crisis brings people together. That is certainly true for the Blauners. We have weathered enough for several families, and I can honestly say that despite any unfinished business between us, I feel closer to my immediate family than I ever thought possible. That doesn't mean I have a perfect relationship with each and every person, but I do have friends within my family. I try to accept them for who they are, quirks and all, just as they try to accept me, quirks and all. We are all imperfect, and we all make mistakes, but after ten years of mending, stumbling, and embracing, when I'm in their company I look around and see loving people doing the very best they can.

CHANGE IS POSSIBLE

The only sense that is common in the long run is the sense
of change—and we all instinctively avoid it.

—E. B. WHITE

Change is definitely possible. I am living proof. Change is not only possible, it is inherent to our existence. Folks who refuse to change or think they're too old, too young, too whatever, are mistaken. If my father could begin changing at the age of seventy-nine, anyone can.

If we want to support the suicidal thinker, we have to believe in her ability to change and *our* ability to change with her. Had I listened to people's doubts in me I would have never accomplished some of the greatest achievements in my life: driving alone across the country; finding a place to live and work once I reached my destination; writing this book and getting it published; buying a house; leaving jobs for better ones. I wouldn't have had the guts to follow my intuition, to leave a long-term relationship that was over long before I finally left it, to believe in God, to trust in therapy.

Change begets changes. If we maintain the belief that change is a good and natural thing, then our resistance to the boat-rocker might lessen. We will let the boat-rocker outgrow his old role as a suicidal thinker and embrace him in the new.

Actions

LISTENING WELL

I needed someone to listen to me,
even if I made no sense to them.
—SUSAN BLAUNER, SERMON ON SUICIDE, 1994

To listen is "to hear something with thoughtful attention." One of the greatest gifts you can give a suicidal thinker is to listen well. The sooner her feelings and thoughts are accepted, the sooner her suicidal thoughts will have a chance to quiet down. The longer her thoughts and feelings are denied or rejected, the louder she'll think she has to scream.

In an everyday situation, mediocre listening skills are frustrating but tolerable. For suicidal thinkers, mediocrity can be deadly. It's not that being rejected will kill the suicidal thinker, but the anger generated might escalate into an "I'll-show-you" attitude, resulting in a rash, impulsive act.

Even after I made suicide gestures, people still met my feelings with remarks like "Don't feel that way," or "You shouldn't feel that way, you have so much going for you." I still wasn't being heard by some people. Whenever that happened, I felt rejected, unheard, unloved, and angry. These reactions fueled my feelings of isolation and the sense that no one really cared.

I've already talked about the importance of choosing words carefully. In this chapter, I share my own listening tips followed by suggestions from suicide prevention professionals.

EXERCISE: LISTENING WELL

This is an expansion of the listening exercise in the "Secrets Are Deadly" Section.

1. Begin by giving your full attention to the person speaking.

2. Look him straight in the eye.

3. Let him talk without interruption. Nod your head, occasionally making a "Um-hmm" sound.

4. Use other verbal cues like "Okay," "I hear you," "Uh-huh."

5. If you start to feel uncomfortable, remember to breathe deeply and try to refrain from interrupting as he shares.

6. While he is talking, pay attention to what he is saying instead of trying to figure out a solution. If you start to get lost in your head, *stop*, take a breath, and return to the moment.

7. Even if what he's saying makes no sense at all, keep nodding your head and offering comfort.

8. When there is a pause, say, "I hear what you're saying. I just want to be sure I understand you correctly," and repeat back to him what he has just said, without interpreting what he said into your own words. Use his words as closely as you can. In this way, he will *really* feel heard and safe. If you start offering advice, he will most likely clam up and walk away.

9. After you have "reflected back" to him (this will take only a minute or two), stop talking and let him start again, or ask a clarifying question like, "So, when do you think this first started?" or "What do you think brought this on?" Remember to steer clear of blame, guilt, shame, and judgment.

10. When he answers, let him do so without interruption, until there is a gap and you can "reflect back" to him again.

11. Be sure to tell him "I love you" or "I care."

When I am the listener, I try to stay focused on the speaker's words rather than drift off mentally searching for solutions. Whenever I start to drift, it means I'm not really listening. If I get an idea or have a suggestion, I ask, "Would you like some feedback?" instead of blurting it out and interrupting the other person.

If she asks for advice or to hear my thoughts and feelings, I try to make "I" statements. For example, "I feel concerned (scared, surprised)," or "I think this is a serious matter." I try to avoid statements like "I feel like you are _____," or "I think you should _____."

Generally, I try to ask the speaker what *she* thinks or wants. For example, "What do you think would help?" "How can I help you with that?" "Would it help to talk to a counselor?" "Have you called your therapist?" If she is totally overwhelmed and answers primarily with "I don't know," then I offer solutions. "How about if I call someone for you?" "Can I come over and sit with you for a while? I could cook you dinner." "I'm really concerned. I would like to call a professional. Is that okay with you?" "Would it help if I called your mom?" See the next section, "Respecting Boundaries While Taking Action."

Here is some listening advice from the experts:

- Listening—really listening—is not easy. We must control the urge to say something—to make a comment, add to a story, offer advice. We need to listen not just to the facts that the person is telling us but to the *feelings* that lie behind them. We need to understand things from the other person's perspective, not our own.

- Allow expression of feelings. Accept the feelings. Show interest and support.

- Suicidal thinkers want someone who will take time to really listen to them—someone who won't judge or give advice or opinions, but will give undivided attention. They want someone who makes himself available, puts the person at ease, and speaks calmly, someone who reassures, accepts, and believes. Someone who says, "I care."

- If someone you know expresses suicidal thoughts or feels depressed, hopeless, or worthless, be supportive. You may encounter negative reactions from the individual, who may believe that her condition is hopeless and will never get better. Let her know you are there for her and willing to help her seek professional help.

RESPECTING BOUNDARIES WHILE TAKING ACTION

On its website, the American Association of Suicidology writes:

"No doubt you have heard that people who talk about suicide won't really do it. It isn't true. Before committing suicide, people often make direct statements about their intentions to end their lives, or less direct comments about how they might as well be dead or that their friends and family would be better off without them. Suicide threats and similar statements should always be taken seriously.

In some cases you may find yourself in the position of having to get direct help for someone who is suicidal and refuses to go for counseling. If so, do it. Don't be afraid of appearing disloyal. What at the time may appear to be an act of disloyalty or the breaking of a confidence could turn out to be the favor of a lifetime."

Befrienders International states on its website: "Suicidal thinkers want someone to trust. Someone who will respect them and won't try to take charge. Someone who will treat everything in complete confidence."

Issues of loyalty and confidence blur when it comes to a suicidal situation. On the surface these two messages appear to conflict. However, there's a big difference between breaking a confidence through gossip and breaking a confidence to save a life. All the suicide prevention material I've read thus far states plainly, "Don't be sworn to secrecy."

The Teen Education and Crisis Hotline (TEACH) offers another approach on its website (www.teachhotline.org): "Be honest with the person if you plan to call a family member or friend. Make the call in front of him or her so that he or she won't wonder what you're saying. Ask the person to agree to postpone the decision for a while; in return you might offer to accompany them to find support or help."

I like that idea. Here's a similar take on this perplexing dilemma from the American Foundation for Suicide Prevention (www.afsp.org):

QUESTION: Apart from talking to a suicidal person and encouraging him/her to go for counseling, what else can we do to prevent this?
ANSWER: Going with someone to the counselor often helps. If the person won't listen to you, you may need to talk to someone who might influence him or her. Saving a life is more important than violating a confidence.

When I'm in contact with someone who is having suicidal thoughts, particularly if the situation appears to be escalating, I continually ask the person certain key questions whenever we meet:

1. Have you told your therapist about this?

2. When do you see your therapist again?

3. Have the feelings gotten worse?

4. What can I do to help?

5. What do you need?

6. Are you able to meet that need?

7. How can I help you meet that need?

I always ask the person if he has a plan of action for the suicide. A yes answer is a major four-alarm warning signal. People who have gone so far as to have a plan are far more likely to carry it out. I follow this question with, "Who else knows about this? Can I talk to them?" (This gives me an outlet for *my* stress around the situation.) Then I ask, "Do you have a crisis hotline number to call?" If the person doesn't, I give him one.

I make sure to hold his hand if he will let me, look him straight in the eye, and tell him how important he is. I let him know I will do whatever I can to help, that I will drive him to the emergency room or psych ward, any time of the day or night, and that I will sit with him in a doctor's waiting room.

Sometimes just hearing that someone cares enough to offer that kind of help will buoy a suicidal person through another crisis. When you're thinking about killing yourself, it's really hard to know what you need or how to get help, even if you want it! Knowing there's someone you can turn to no matter what makes a big difference.

The experts say:

- Parents are bound to have trouble understanding a depressed teen's confusing signals. After all, what parent wants to think of his child as anything but happy and confident? Parents must pay close attention to serious depression; the risks are too great if they don't.

- Any suicidal gesture, no matter how "harmless" it seems, demands immediate professional attention.

- Get professional help. Get involved. Be available.

- Don't be sworn to secrecy. Seek support.

- Take action. Remove means, such as guns or stockpiled pills.

- Suggest that the suicidal thinker call 1-800-SUICIDE or a similar organization that serves your area.

PRACTICING PATIENCE AND COMPASSION

Whenever you feel exasperated by the situation (and you will), try to remember that the suicidal thinker is living on an internal battlefield in addition to navigating everyday stress. I wanted to be alive, accepted, loved, and understood, but for one or many reasons my brain tried to convince me I was useless, worthless, unloved, pathetic, and that I *really* wanted to die.

The goal is to accept the suicidal thinker—suicidal thoughts and all—rather than judge or try to fix him. What you can offer is non-judgmental compassion as he stumbles down the road to freedom. You can be there when he trips and falls, and when he finds relief. You can embrace him with outstretched arms, saying, "I love you. I am here for you."

As long as he isn't hurting himself or anyone else, let him fumble his way into the light without trying to convert him to your way of thinking; each person's reality is different.

I suggest that you take a look at the Tricks of the Trade in part 3, particularly the chapters entitled "HALT," "Spirituality, Nature, and

Meditation," "Service—Helping Others," "Keeping a Journal," "Therapy," and "Support Groups."

GETTING EDUCATED AND FINDING
YOUR OWN SUPPORT

Give what you have. To someone, it may be better
than you dare to think.
—HENRY WADSWORTH LONGFELLOW

Getting educated. How I Stayed Alive When My Brain Was Trying to Kill Me is meant to be a guide for suicidal thinkers and their loved ones, not an alternative to professional counseling. In addition to practicing the suggestions offered here, I encourage you to become educated about your particular situation. See part 7 for resources. There are many specialized organizations, books, mental health professionals, and social services available to assist you.

Your own inner awareness helps. The people best able to handle my situation were the ones who understood not only my illness but their own inner dimensions. The following is an excerpt from a letter written by Dorothy, my friend and former housemate/landlord, describing her reaction to my overdose that took place in her home in November 1998.

> I actually spent some focused time at work processing out the codependence and letting go of my needs and wants enough to go back to my compassion for you, rather than stay pissed off and distracted . . . so that when we talked later I was able to tell you clearly and calmly how I felt, without being resentful or trying to fix it.

When I returned home after being discharged from the hospital, I went straight to Dorothy to apologize and talk about what happened. Because of her own self-awareness and our honest relationship, I knew we would talk openly, and although I was afraid of her reaction, I knew I was safe. Her entire letter is printed in part 4.

Quality outshines quantity. More important than the *quantity* of time you are available for the suicidal thinker is the *quality* of the support you offer. Much of this book deals with stress management. One of the best ways to help the suicidal thinker is to work on your own stress management skills. By finding healthy outlets for your feelings and devising ways to ease stress, you are more apt to create an atmosphere of safety, trust, and acceptance during times of crisis.

Support yourself and you can better support the suicidal thinker. As human beings we can't help but have reactions to and judgments of suicidal thinkers, and that's why I suggest you find healthy outlets for your own fear, anger, and confusion. In this way, you can meet the situation with a cleaner slate and a clearer heart. See parts 3 and 7 for suggestions.

———

Thank you for opening your mind and heart to my ideas and suggestions. I hope they will be useful as you embrace the suicidal thinker and help that person find a way back to life. Please read through part 7 and find the resources to help you on this challenging but amazing journey.

PART SIX

Until We Meet Again

Journal drawing, 1994

The noontide is upon us and our half waking has turned to

fuller day, and we must part.

If in the twilight of memory we should meet once more,

we shall speak again together

and you shall sing to me a deeper song.

And if our hands should meet in another dream

we shall build another tower in the sky.

—KAHLIL GIBRAN, *The Prophet*

geese

we stood there watching
the geese were unafraid

life is so wonderful sometimes

they took off honking all the way
over the rivulets then the harbor
my heart melting, I watching them
fly wing to wing
my heart streaming
as the water flowing from the pond
into the body of the sound
of the birds flying above, no—
skimming over the water
wing to glorious wing
flapping up and down, no—
making an arc through air
quickly but not so quickly
that you couldn't see them
not like a hummingbird
not like an eagle
somewhere in between

"My grace is sufficient for you."

—CHRISTOPHER BREHL, MARCH 21, 1993

(*WRITTEN THREE MONTHS BEFORE HIS SUICIDE*

ON JUNE 29, 1993)

I Recognize . . .

Love, for only in its presence can gifts like this be realized. Inez (Harrig) Blauner was the vessel that brought me into this lifetime. Because of the love she shared with my father Stuart, I was born.

Honesty, for it walks hand in hand with insight and connection. I am grateful to the seven people who wrote letters for this book, particularly my brother Bob for his bravery and willingness to speak his truth.

Humility, for it is coupled with quiet greatness. The Reverend Jim Robinson teaches me to love beyond fear by reminding me that everything in life is sacred. Thank you, Jim, for looking into my eyes, holding my hand, and seeing the sacred in me when I lay crying in the emergency room after my last overdose.

Wonder, for it fuels the mind, body, and spirit. Herbert and Ruth Douglas, two of my life mentors, always encouraged my mind, nurtured my spirit, and supported my curiosity. I can only hope to feel a fraction of their zest for life when I reach eighty-five.

Compassion and fairness, for both allow people to be who they are—people. Hank Hyora leads a remarkable staff with his generosity and unyielding humor. To all of my coworkers—so talented, loving, and dedicated—I say, thank you for everything.

Commitment, for it is the backbone of any great achievement. I honor and thank the hardworking people dedicated to suicide prevention, particularly Reese Butler, executive director of the National Hopeline Network, Kristin Brooks Hope Center, for helping to refine my resource list and connecting me with all the right players; and Dr. Paul Quinnett, president and founder of the QPR Institute, for his genuine enthusiasm. With great respect, I thank Dr. Edwin S. Shneidman for his incredible fifty-year devotion to suicidology.

Professionalism and faith, for together they create great things. Several key people opened the literary door for me and led me through it with marked enthusiasm. To author Anne D. LeClaire, agents Meg Ruley and Stephanie Tade of the Jane Rotrosen Agency, and all the great folks at William Morrow, thank you for catching my dream and helping to make it reality.

To my fast friend and editor-goddess, Jennifer Brehl, what can I say? It is no coincidence that, unknowingly, I sent the first draft of this manuscript to you on the eighth-year anniversary of your brother Chris's suicide. It's been an honor to work with you on this project, so deeply personal for both of us. Because of our willingness to embrace the truth, we are giving to the present what we both needed (but couldn't find) in the past. Thank you for your laughter, humanity, dedication, and excellence.

I am grateful to Dr. Bernie S. Siegel for offering to write the foreword, and for letting me pester him in Star Market six years ago. I thank Christopher Seufert of Mooncusser Productions for capturing my essence on video and creating a vehicle for the book's promotion. I also thank Amy Tagliaferri, Maryanne Raye, and Marie Marley for proofing early portions of the manuscript; and Jeff, for his complete support and help in editing the first draft.

Friends, family, and community, for they are the flavors of life. To those with whom I share my journey, it is a privilege to know and love you. I would especially like to honor Julie Pina, for her long-standing, trusted friendship, and Jeff Schwartz, my friend and companion, for showing me the true meaning of unconditional love.

Above all, I thank the universe, the Divine, the unexplainable, for carrying and supporting me through this wild and fascinating ride. To you I attribute everything.

Do you have a call to sing?

Do you have a call to dance?

Whatever your great calling is,

it demands another chance.

It has a place. It has a face. It is your own.

Embrace and own it.

Give it a home. You're not alone.

You've found yourself

You've found your destiny.

—JEFF SCHWARTZ, "DESTINY"

PART SEVEN

Hotlines, Websites, and Other Resources

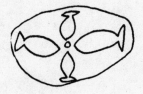

Journal drawing, 1994

You are a child of the Universe,
no less than the trees and the stars:
you have a right to be here.
And whether or not it is clear to you,
no doubt the Universe is unfolding as it should.

—FROM *DESIDERATA*, 1692

Hotlines and Suicide Prevention Organizations

I personally contacted these hotlines and organizations and asked them to describe their target audience, goals and directives as well as provide their telephone and fax numbers, postal, e-mail, and website addresses. Those marked with ✳ are geared specifically toward youth. All are confidential and the hotlines are available twenty-four hours a day, seven days a week. I thank the many people who embraced this project with enthusiasm and support.

For Internet access, most libraries offer free Internet use at public terminals. (Some require a simple sign-up.) There are also Internet cafés that give patrons access to the web for a minimal fee. Colleges and universities have computer labs as well.

CRISIS HOTLINES

Note: If you ever get a busy signal when dialing a crisis hotline, hang up, keep your hand on the phone, and try again, or try another crisis number.

- **National Hopeline Network: 1-800-SUICIDE, 1-800-784-2433** "The National Hopeline Network links the caller to the certified crisis hotline nearest to them. You can expect to reach a trained crisis line worker who will do a lethality assessment, make appropriate referrals, and provide intervention if needed. You can also expect to reach a non-judgmental empathetic listener." In the year 2000, 1-800-SUICIDE routed over 250,000 calls. After a twenty- to twenty-five-second recorded message followed by five seconds of recorded music, you are quickly connected to a human being.

✳ **Covenant House Nineline: 1-800-999-9999**

"The Covenant House Nineline provides crisis intervention, referral, and information services to troubled youth and their families throughout the United States. In the year 2000, the Nineline received over 58,000 crisis calls from youth throughout the country." The Nineline has a short, five- to ten-second recorded message, offering the option of English or Spanish; then you are immediately connected with a friendly human being.

✳ **Girls and Boys Town National Hotline (hotline@boystown.org): 1-800-448-3000**

"Highly trained counselors provide free confidential services twenty-four hours a day, seven days a week. Calls range from relationship and parental discipline to depression and suicide. In crisis situations, counselor assists callers and provides community resources and emergency intervention." A fifteen-second message offering the option of English or Spanish is followed by five seconds of recorded music before you are connected with a friendly human being.

✳ **Trevor Project: 1-800-850-8078**

"Helpline for gay, lesbian, bisexual, or questioning youth." If all the counselors are currently helping other people, the phone rings a while, then you get a friendly fifteen-second message asking you to call back in ten to fifteen minutes or to leave a message with your name and phone number so that a counselor can call you back as soon as one of them is free.

• **Befrienders International: www.befrienders.org**

"Befrienders International has a network of 361 centers in 41 countries, providing a free, confidential, and nonjudgmental listening service to people who are lonely, despairing, and suicidal. Its centers are run by 31,000 volunteers." Available in ten languages. People are befriended by telephone, in face-to-face meetings, by letter, and by e-mail. Start by going to the website, then scroll down and click on "Enter." After you enter, you can choose from several options. Click the top option, "Feeling Suicidal or Depressed?" and you will be given another list of choices, including support by e-mail, finding a crisis hotline near you, and more.

* Cop 2 Cop (COP2COP@cmhc.umdnj.edu;
www.cop2coponline.org): 1-866-Cop-2Cop, 1-866-267-2267
"Cop 2 Cop is a 24 hour/7 days a week stress hotline/helpline for law enforcement officers. The line is answered by retired officers who provide peer support, as well as clinicians that specialize in dealing with law enforcement officers."

911

If you have already *acted* on suicidal thoughts and need immediate medical assistance or ambulance transport to a hospital, call 911. If you are *considering* acting on suicidal thoughts, please note that 911 is not staffed by trained counselors. To reach a trained listener sensitive to the needs of suicidal thinkers, call 1-800-SUICIDE or another hotline number.

HOTLINES IN CANADA

* Kids Help Phone (www.Kidshelp.sympatico.ca):
1-800-668-6868
Kids Help Phone Parents' Hotline: 1-888-603-9100
"Kids Help Phone is a national bilingual and anonymous phone counseling and referral service for children and youth [of Canada]. Their professional counselors answer an average of 1,000 calls every

day. Kids call about a range of concerns, including relationships, substance abuse, violence, and suicide. Any problem, big or small, they are here to help you through." This number works only in Canada. If you are in the United States, please dial 1-800-SUICIDE.

ORGANIZATIONS

Included in this section are self-descriptions of various suicide prevention organizations and my comments on their websites. All of these organizations are available to people of any age, sex, race, sexual orientation, socioeconomic status, or spiritual belief. Please note that the telephone numbers listed below are *not* crisis hotlines. If you are experiencing a crisis, please call 1-800-SUICIDE or one of other hotline numbers listed here. Most of the following organizations are linked with other resources on the Web. The youth-oriented organizations help people of *any age* find the resource they need.

American Association of Suicidology (AAS)(www.suicidology.org)
"National membership organization with mission to understand and prevent suicide as a means of promoting human welfare. Five divisions: research, clinical, crisis centers, prevention programs, and survivors. Publishes quarterly peer-reviewed research journal and two quarterly newsletters (one for and by survivors), sponsors annual Suicide Prevention Week, holds annual national conference, distributes public and media education materials, participates in collaborative research and prevention projects, etc."

This is a thorough, user-friendly site for those considering suicide or people wanting to understand and help suicidal thinkers. Provides links to crisis centers, hotlines, resources, and specialized organizations.

American Association of Suicidology

4201 Connecticut Ave., N.W., Suite 408

Washington, D.C. 20008

202-237-2280 (*not a crisis hotline*)

Fax: 202-237-2282

American Foundation for Suicide Prevention (AFSP) (www.afsp.org)

"AFSP is the only national not-for-profit organization solely dedicated to funding suicide prevention research, initiating treatment and projects, and offering educational programs and conferences for survivors, mental health professionals, physicians and the public."

This excellent site has many links to domestic and international chapters of the AFSP. Like the AAS site, it includes book lists, warning signs, tips on how to help a suicidal thinker, and more. It also lists a national directory of survivor support groups (for families and friends of a suicide) and answers commonly asked suicide-related questions.

American Foundation for Suicide Prevention

120 Wall St., 22nd Floor

New York, N.Y. 10005

1-888-333-AFSP (*not a crisis hotline*)

212-363-3500, (*not a crisis hotline*)

Fax: 212-363-6237

E-mail: inquiry@afsp.org

American Psychological Association (APA) (www.helping.apa.org)

At this informative and user-friendly site, click "Site Map" and you'll get a listing of everything offered: access to free brochures published by the APA HelpCenter such as "Change Your Mind About Mental Health: A GetHelp Guide for Teens and Young Adults," information about the benefits of therapy and exercise, about the mind-body connection, and more. Click on "search" and you can access the HelpCenter for specific mental health information. For a referral to a psychologist in your area, call 1-800-964-2000 (not a crisis hotline).

Befrienders International (www.befrienders.org)

"Befrienders International has a network of 361 centers in 41 countries, providing a free, confidential, and nonjudgmental listening service to people who are lonely, despairing and suicidal. Its centers are run by 31,000 volunteers."

With services available in ten languages, Befrienders International befriends people by telephone, in face-to-face meetings, by letter, and by e-mail. It provide an excellent site for anyone who is depressed or suicidal, and for loved ones wanting to help. With links to international online support, crisis hotlines, and more, this site presents extensive, user-friendly information.

Center for Elderly Suicide Prevention (CESP) (www.gioa.org)

Part of the Goldman Institute on Aging (GIOA), the CESP provides a Friendship Line: "Seniors, family members, caregivers, and advocates can call and receive emotional support, crisis intervention, and information and referral. The 1-800 number is available to anyone calling within the United States, either at home or on a public pay phone."

For information about the CESP Friendship Line, you'll need to scroll down to the bottom of the homepage to access a listing of the various programs offered by GIOA.

> Center for Elderly Suicide Prevention
> 3330 Geary Blvd., 3 East
> San Francisco, Calif. 94118
> 415-750-4180, x232 (*not a crisis hotline*)
> Fax: 415-750-4136
> U.S. Friendship Line: 800-971-0016
> San Francisco Friendship Line: 415-752-3778

Center for Mental Health Services Knowledge Exchange Network (KEN) (www.mentalhealth.org)

"National information and referral center for mental health consumers, their families, professionals, and the general public. We offer referrals to mental health organizations and facilities on the local, state and national levels. Over 200 free publications on mental health."

This site provides a *huge* variety of mental health information that is highly organized and user-friendly (available in Spanish). The many offerings include: access to mental health agencies and advocacy organizations by state; selected mental health publications—fact sheets, pamphlets, newsletters, posters—for browsing, reading, and ordering; the Center for Mental Health Services Mental Health Services Locator.

> Center for Mental Health Services Knowledge Exchange Network
> P.O. Box 42490
> Washington, D.C. 20015
> Helpline: 800-789-2647 (*not a crisis hotline*)
> Fax: 301-984-8796
> E-mail: Ken@mentalhealth.org

Centers for Disease Control and Prevention (CDC) Division of Violence Prevention (www.cdc.gov)

"CDC's Division of Violence Prevention is working to raise awareness of suicide as a serious public health problem and is focusing on science-based prevention strategies to reduce injuries and deaths due to suicide."

This site is recommended for the media and mental healthcare professionals. It has links to suggestions that will "help guide the media to educate readers and viewers about the steps they can take to prevent suicide." It also links to "The Surgeon General's Call to Action to Prevent Suicide," "The National Suicide Prevention Strategy," the Suicide Prevention Research Center, SafeUSA, and more.

Centers for Disease Control and Prevention

4770 Buford Hwy., Mailstop K-60

Atlanta, Ga. 30341-3724

770-488-4362 (*not a crisis hotline*)

Fax: 770-488-4349

SafeUSA information line: 888-252-7751; 800-243-7012 (TTY) (*not a crisis line*)

*Covenant House (www.covenanthouse.org)

"Covenant House is the largest privately funded childcare agency in the United States, providing shelter and service to homeless and run-away youth in fourteen cities across the country. Founded in New York City, it also has established programs abroad. In addition to food, shelter, clothing, and crisis care, Covenant House provides a variety of services to homeless youth, including health care, education, vocational preparation, drug abuse treatment and prevention programs, legal services, recreation, mother/child programs, transitional living programs, street outreach, and aftercare." Please see Covenant House Nineline listing under "Hotlines."

The site is sort of wordy. When you get to the homepage, go to the far left of the screen and click on the bottom option, "Site Map," to get a listing of what's offered. If you are looking for a Covenant House center near you, scroll to the bottom of the next page for a listing of locations. For immediate assistance, I recommend calling the 1-800-999-9999 Nineline over the website.

Covenant House

346 W. 17th St.

New York, N.Y. 10011

Crisis hotline: 1-800-999-9999

212-727-4036 (*not a crisis hotline*)

Fax: 212-727-4992

*Focus Adolescent Services (www.focusas.com)

"Internet clearinghouse of resources for families with troubled teens. State directory of family help, hotlines, and helplines; information on teen and family issues, schools and programs."

This site offers a vast array of information related to teen suicide, including links to Web resources such as: the homosexuality factor in the youth suicide problem; family skills—recognizing your teen's cry for help; bipolar disorder; preventing teen suicide; and more.

Focus Adolescent Services

1113 Woodland Rd.

Salisbury, Md. 21801

877-362-8727 (*not a crisis hotline*)

Helpline (toll-free): 1-877-362-8287 (*not a crisis hotline*)

Fax: 410-341-7470

E-mail: help@focusas.com

*Girls and Boys Town (GBT) (www.girlsandboystown.org)

Girls and Boys Town National Hotline (hotline@boystown.org)

"Highly trained counselors provide free confidential services twenty-four hours a day, seven days a week. Calls range from relationship and parental discipline to depression and suicide. In crisis situations, counselor assists callers and provides community resources and emergency intervention."

I recommend this hotline for immediate assistance. On the website are links to GBT programs, services, and parenting assistance; if you are being hurt right now, they suggest calling the crisis hotline 1-800-448-3000.

Girls and Boys Town (national hotline)

14100 Crawford

Boys Town, Neb. 68010

Fax: 402-498-1875

Crisis hotline: 1-800-448-3000

*Kids Help Phone (kidshelp.sympatico.ca)

"Kids Help Phone is a national bilingual and anonymous phone counseling and referral service for children and youth [of Canada]. Their professional counselors answer an average of 1,000 calls every day. Kids call about a range of concerns, including relationships, substance abuse, violence and suicide. Any problem, big or small, they are here to help you through." Please note that this number works only in Canada. If you are in the United States, dial 1-800-SUICIDE (1-800-784-2433).

This is an excellent interactive and comprehensive site for youth, available in English and French. It provides links to a variety of websites on other topics: parenting tips, family, diversity, abuse, sexual abuse, violence, STDs, AIDS, friendship and love; online discussion groups on suicide, violence, family, eating disorders, drug abuse, sexuality, and more; interactive videos about bullying, dating violence, targeted violence, and gang issues; information on abuse in amateur sports. Highly recommended.

Kids Help Phone

439 University Ave., Suite 300

Toronto, Ont. M5G 1Y8

416-586-5437 (not a crisis hotline)

Fax: 416-586-0651

Crisis hotline (for Canada use only): 1-800-668-6868

Parents' hotline (for Canada use only): 1-888-603-9100

Kristin Brooks Hope Center/National Hopeline Network
(www.hopeline.com; www.livewithdepression.org)

"The National Hopeline Network links the caller to the certified crisis hotline nearest to them. You can expect to reach a trained crisis line worker who will do a lethality assessment, make appropriate referrals, and provide intervention if needed. You can also expect to reach a nonjudgmental empathetic listener."

In the year 2000, the National Hopeline Network routed over 250,000 calls. The website www.hopeline.com provides descriptions of and links to a variety of suicide prevention organizations, state prevention programs, and information on crisis centers and hotlines. The website www.livewithdepression.org "gives you a personal glimpse into depression, and how it affects you and those around you. In addition, you will find a clear, step-by-step path to follow out of the darkness."

Kristin Brooks Hope Center/National Hopeline Network
609 East Main St., #112
Purcellville, Va. 20132
1-800-422-HOPE (4673) (*not a crisis hotline*)
Fax: 540-338-5746
Crisis hotline: 1-800-SUICIDE (1-800-784-2433)

Lifekeeper Foundation (www.lifekeeper.org)

"The Lifekeeper mission is to raise awareness for the great need of suicide prevention in the United States. Efforts are directed toward providing resources for survivors of suicide, encouraging them to participate in their own healing process through involvement therapy, and affirming life through art with the Lifekeeper Memorial 'Faces of Suicide' National Memorial Quilt Project."

The website provides moving photos of the National Memorial Quilt Project, as well as guidelines and tips on how to make your own quilt and join it with other quilts statewide. Lifekeeper jewelry and poetry are available for sale; a portion of the proceeds is donated to various suicide prevention organizations.

Lifekeeper Foundation
3740 Crestcliff Ct.
Tucker, Ga. 30084
E-mail: Lifekeeper@aol.com

*Lite for Life Foundation—Yellow Ribbon Suicide Prevention Program (www.yellowribbon.org)

"Community-based prevention with curriculum and intervention tools. Yellow Ribbon [YR] cards are being used internationally to help save lives. The organization was started in 1994. The cards are a 'voice' for youth when they can't find the words to say 'I need help.' Teens who have attempted suicide tell that they were so over- whelmed at the time of their crisis that they did not know what to say to ask for help! The program is two-fold: Get cards to youth and inform adults what they are. This is very important so that adults can respond appropriately and immediately if they receive a card from a teen/youth. Learn how to start the program in your area so youth will be able to get cards locally. YR cards can also be customized to include local crisis information. This allows youth to find help in their home area."

It's a little hard to get around the site, but it's excellent for learn- ing about the Yellow Ribbon program. The site provides instructions on how to start a program in your school or community and lets you print free copies of Yellow Ribbon cards directly off the site, and more.

Yellow Ribbon Suicide Prevention Program
P.O. Box 644
Westminster, Colo. 80036-0644
303-429-3530 (*not a crisis hotline*)
Fax: 303-426-4496
E-mail: ask4help@yellowribbon.org

National Alliance for the Mentally Ill (NAMI) (www.nami.org)

"NAMI is a non-profit, grassroots, self-help, support and advocacy organization of consumers, families, and friends of people with severe mental illnesses, such as schizophrenia, major depression, bipolar disorder, obsessive-compulsive disorder, and anxiety disorders. . . . Working on national, state, and local levels, NAMI provides education about severe brain disorders, supports increased funding for research, and advocates for adequate health insurance, housing, rehabilitation, and jobs for people with serious psychiatric illnesses. . . . Consumers, family members, friends, and the public are encouraged to call the toll-free helpline for information and referral to the NAMI affiliate group in their area. The NAMI Helpline is staffed by trained volunteers, Monday through Friday, 10 A.M. to 5 P.M. (Eastern time), and has a 24-hour, 7-day-a-week message line."

The NAMI website is an excellent resource. Hold the cursor over the items listed down the left-hand side of the homepage and you'll see that the site offers information on illnesses and treatments (available in Spanish), education and training programs, book reviews, research news, and more.

National Alliance for the Mentally Ill
Three Colonial Place
2107 Wilson Blvd., Suite 300
Arlington, Va. 22201-3042
703-524-7600 (*not a crisis hotline*)
NAMI Helpline: 1-800-950-NAMI (6264) (*not a crisis hotline*)
Fax: 703-524-9094

National Center for Post-Traumatic Stress Disorder (www.ncptsd.org)

"Since its inception in 1989, the National Center for PTSD has been at the forefront of efforts to study the effects of psychological trauma.

National Center staff have been involved in over 500 research studies and 200 educational projects. The website services veterans and other survivors of traumatic experiences, clinicians, researchers, journalists, family members, students, policymakers, lawyers, librarians, and more."

This is a thorough, informative site offering a *huge* amount of information about PTSD—causes, treatment, research, and so on—in the form of articles, resources, and links.

National Depressive and Manic-Depressive Association (NDMDA) (www.ndmda.org)

"Patient-focused advocacy organization facilitates over 400 nationwide patient/family support groups and publishes numerous materials about depression, manic-depression, treatment and suicide prevention."

It's a little hard to read the homepage, which offers a support group directory, success stories, a bipolar disorder screening tool, and information on adolescent depression, manic-depression, depression, and suicide prevention. It also provides patient-consumer support, information on pharmaceutical company patient assistance programs, and more.

National Depressive and Manic-Depressive Association
730 N. Franklin St., Suite 501
Chicago, Ill. 60610-7204
800-826-3632 or 312-642-0049 (*not crisis hotlines*)
Fax: 312-642-7243
E-mail: letusknow@ndmda.org

National Institute of Mental Health (NIMH) (www.nimh.nih.gov)

"The mission of the NIMH is to reduce the burden of mental illness through research on mind, brain, and behavior. This public health mandate demands that NIMH harness powerful scientific tools to achieve better understanding, treatment, and eventually prevention and cure of mental illness. The NIMH Office of Communications and Public Liaison carries out educational activities and publishes and distributes research reports, press releases, fact sheets, and publications intended for researchers, health care providers, and the general public."

A publications list may be obtained by calling NIMH. The website is excellent, easy to use, and chock-full of valuable information on mental health for the public, practitioner, and researcher.

National Institute of Mental Health
Office of Communications and Public Liaison
6001 Executive Blvd., Room 8184, MSC 9663
Bethesda, Md. 20892-9663
301-443-8431 (*not a crisis hotline*)
TTY: 301-443-8431
Fax: 301-443-4279
E-mail: nimhinfo@nih.gov (*not a crisis address*)
For anxiety information: 1-888-ANXIETY (*not a crisis hotline*)
For depression information: 1-800-421-4211 (*not a crisis hotline*)

National Mental Health Association (NMHA) (www.nmha.org)
"The NMHA is the country's oldest and largest nonprofit organization addressing all aspects of mental health and mental illness. With more than 340 affiliates nationwide, NMHA works to improve the mental health of all Americans, especially the 54 million individuals with mental disorders, through advocacy, education, research and service." The twenty-four-hour information line has a lengthy recorded message available in English or Spanish. Through a series of prompts, the caller can gain access to any number of topics, including information on mental illness, local referrals, merchandise, and publications. To speak to a human being, try calling on Thursday or Friday.

This is a good resource. The site gives access to a confidential depression screening; message boards for people with mental illness and "compassionate friends" (those affected by someone else's mental illness); boards on advocacy, the media, stigma, children's mental health, and more.

> National Mental Health Association
> 1021 Prince St.
> Alexandria, Va. 22314
> 703-684-7722 (*not a crisis hotline*)
> E-mail: infoctr@nmha.org
> TYY: 1-800-433-5959
> Fax: 703-684-5968
> Information line: 1-800-969-6642 (*not a crisis hotline*)

National Organization for People of Color Against Suicide (NOPCAS) (www.nopcas.com)

The NOPCAS website is user friendly and offers suicide facts and statistics—some dealing specifically with the black community; a large number of crisis hotline numbers, a photo gallery of NOPCAS conferences, board member profiles. To access links, be sure to scroll to the far right, where you will find links to prevention organizations around the country, the Surgeon General's "Call to Action to Prevent Suicide," and more.

> National Organization for People of Color Against Suicide
> P.O. Box 125
> San Marcos, Tex. 78667
> 512-531-5067 ext. 2190 (*not a crisis hotline*)

National Resource Center for Suicide Prevention and Aftercare (www.thelink.org)

The National Resource Center was founded by the Link Counseling Center, a nonprofit family counseling center in Atlanta, Georgia. Services include information and referral, consultation, community education and awareness, speakers and training on suicide prevention, intervention and aftercare, support groups for survivors (both adult and children), group facilitator training, a survivor's journal called *The Journey*, management of a Survivors of Suicide Support Team providing home visits to the newly bereaved by trained survivors, and participation as a member of the National Council for Suicide Prevention.

The NRC is the only national organization providing regular Support Team Training in Atlanta and in other cities across the country.

The Link and the NRC maintain a website with links to major sources of help in the nation and Canada.

Not My Kid, Inc. (www.notmykid.org)

"Dedicated to promoting healthy families by empowering parents to make educated decisions about their children's behavioral health. This interactive website provides immediate, confidential recommendations, articles, and community resources. We believe that parents can make a difference in the quality of their kids' lives."

The site is excellent for parents looking for positive ways to relate to their children. Informative articles describe warning signs, treatment options, how you can help, anxiety and panic disorders, ADHD, bed-wetting, Internet addiction, eating disorders, children of divorce, substance abuse, PTSD, self-esteem issues, and more. Helpful books, videos, and other products are also suggested. Links are provided to other parenting sites.

Not My Kid, Inc.
3040 E. Cactus Rd.
Phoenix, Ariz. 85032
602-652-0163 (*not a crisis hotline*)
Fax: 602-494-3131

Organization for Attempters and Survivors of Suicide (OASSIS) (www.oassis.org)

"OASSIS' mission is to enrich the lives of those who have been and will be touched by suicide. It seeks to achieve this goal by working with six major systems: businesses, corporations, colleges and universities, health care delivery systems, law enforcement, military and religious communities."

OASSIS publishes the biannual "Enriching Lives" newsletter. The website discusses educational programs and training for professional caregivers, interfaith resources, and more.

Organization for Attempters and Survivors of Suicide
4541 Burlington Pl., N.W.
Washington, D.C. 20016
202-363-4224 (*not a crisis hotline*)
Fax: 202-363-1468

QPR Institute (www.qprinstitute.com)

Developed by psychologist Dr. Paul Quinnet, who has specialized in the treatment of suicidal people for thirty years, QPR stands for Question, Persuade, and Refer, "three simple steps," according to the institute, "that anyone can learn to help save a life from suicide. People trained in QPR learn how to recognize the warning signs of a suicide crisis and how to *question, persuade*, and *refer* someone to help. QPR Institute offers a full array of suicide prevention training for both private citizens and mental health professionals. QPR is both an awareness raising and a skill building program. It is theory-based and is supported by research on gatekeeper effectiveness."

The site provides a comprehensive presentation on QPR—theory, effectiveness, training programs, and much, much more. It's highly recommended for caregivers, schools, mental health professionals, health-care providers, and others.

QPR Institute

P.O. Box 2867

Spokane, Wash. 99220

1-888-726-7926 (*not a crisis hotline*)

509-536-5100 (*not a crisis hotline*)

Fax: 509-536-5400

Suicide Awareness Voices of Education (SAVE) (www.save.org)

"SAVE is a grassroots nonprofit organization founded by survivors. Its mission is to educate about suicide prevention and speak for survivors. Focusing on building public awareness and community education, SAVE teaches people the knowledge and skills they need to help prevent suicide. SAVE is a resource of information; community action ideas; speakers; and public awareness tools such as billboards, print ads, and radio public service announcements."

The site provides straight-talking explanations on common misconceptions of suicide; information on hospitalization; questions and answers about suicide; information on symptoms and danger signs; book lists; depression facts; access to a community action kit and public service announcement ad campaign, and more.

Suicide Awareness Voices of Education

7317 Cahill Rd., Suite 207

Minneapolis, Minn. 55439

1-888-511-SAVE (*not a crisis hotline*)

952-946-7998 (*not a crisis hotline*)

Fax: 952-829-0841

ORGANIZATIONS IN CANADA

Canadian Association for Suicide Prevention (CASP/ACPS) (www.suicideprevention.ca)

"CASP is a national association of professionals and volunteers who saw the need to provide information and resources to communities to reduce the suicide rate and minimize the harmful consequences of suicidal behavior. CASP facilitates, advocates, supports and advises."

This site is another source for facts, brochures, and information on crisis centers and how to help.

Canadian Association for Suicide Prevention
301 11456 Jasper Ave.
Edmonton, Alb. T5K OM1
780-482-0918 (*not a crisis hotline*)
Fax: 780-488-1495
E-mail: casp@suicideprevention.ca (*not a crisis address*)

Suicide Information and Education Center (SIEC) (www.suicideinfo.ca)

"SIEC [pronounced "seek"] is a library and database on suicidal behaviors, prevention, intervention, and postvention. The library of more than 27,000 print materials is also available for on-line access. Library provides literature searches, document delivery and a free publication, 'SIEC ALERT'."

The site has a wide focus, from information about suicide prevention training programs to multicultural training manuals, print resources, a youth suicide awareness package, information kits, and a library and resource center. (A membership fee is required to access the online database.) It also provides numerous links to mental health organizations. *SIEC Alert* is a free, quarterly quick-reference guide to some of the newest resources in the field of suicide prevention.

Suicide Information and Education Center

201-1615 Tenth Ave., S.W.

Calgary, Alb. T3C OJ7

403-245-3900 (*not a crisis hotline*)

Fax: 403-245-0299

Twelve Step Organizations

I include Twelve Step organizations as a suicide prevention resource because substance abuse or addiction is often associated with suicidal behavior and mental illness. Also, my own spiritual growth and understanding were profoundly influenced by Twelve Step philosophy and practice. Through exposure to the Twelve Steps, I found that I was no longer alone in my struggle, that there are many alternatives to self-harm, and that people—many people—do have the ability and willingness to listen.

Most Sunday newspapers have a help calendar that lists local meetings and contact numbers. If you need access to a newspaper, libraries have newspapers for the public to read. The phone book is another place find contact numbers.

One note of caution: Twelve Step meetings are very focused, centered on a particular topic such as alcoholism, overeating, or gambling. Some meetings discourage sharing about anything other than the topic at hand. I was lucky; I found places to vent all my feelings and thoughts. I've since learned that this is not always the case.

- Adult Children of Alcoholics (ACA) (www.adultchildren.org)

- Alcoholics Anonymous (AA) (www.alcoholics-anonymous.org)

- Al-Anon/Alateen Family Group Headquarters (www.al-anon.org)

- Co-dependents Anonymous (CODA) (www.codependents.org)

- Narcotics Anonymous (NA) (www.na.org)

- Overeaters Anonymous (OA) (www.overeatersanonymous.org)

- Survivors of Incest Anonymous (SIA) (www.siawso.org)

Book Lists

When caught in suicidal ideation, I searched high and low for self-help books on suicide prevention written from the point of view of a suicidal thinker. I found none. That was the primary reason I wrote this book.

I've divided this book list into six sections: titles that have been useful to me; a general list of readings on suicide prevention; youth-related readings; readings geared toward the elderly; books and other works for professionals; and resources for survivors (those left behind after a completed suicide).

Bibliography

BOOKS USEFUL TO ME

Courage to Change: One Day at a Time in Al-Anon (Al-Anon Family Group Headquarters, 1992). Daily affirmation book. Excellent spiritual insights and daily reinforcement based in the Twelve Steps and Twelve Traditions as adapted from AA. Can be adapted to any life situation.

Shakti Gawain, *Creative Visualization* (Bantam Starfire, 1983, distributed by New World Library). This book changed my life immeasurably. I highly recommend it to anyone of any age. It's fun, imaginative, and inspirational. Toll-free ordering 1-800-972-6657.

———, *Reflections in the Light: Daily Thoughts and Affirmations* (New World Library, 1988). Daily affirmation book based on creative visualization. Excellent.

Kahlil Gibran, *The Prophet* (1923). The Phone Media (Australia) edition is distributed in the United States by Seven Hill Book Distributors, Cincinnati, Ohio. A little treasure of insightful poetic prose about all aspects of life.

Thaddeus Golas, *The Lazy Man's Guide to Enlightenment* (Gibbs Smith Publisher, 1996). This simple, easy-to-read book got me started on meditation and mind expansion.

Louise L. Hay, *You Can Heal Your Life* (Hay House, 1999). One of the first books I read on the mind-body-spirit connection, it's about making new choices, following intuition, undoing the unproductive messages from the past, and learning how to love ourselves completely.

———, *Colors and Numbers: Your Personal Guide to Positive Vibrations in Daily Life* (Hay House, 1999). Interesting little book about numerology and the positive effect that color vibrations can have on our lives. I recommend it for people with curious and open minds. The exercises are fun and made a difference in my life.

James Jennings, *In God's Care: Daily Meditations on Spirituality in Recovery: As We Understand God*, illustrated by David Spohn (Hazelden Information Education, 1996). Basic yet profound thoughts and ideas to start each day; this book helped changed my life and enhance my spiritual understanding.

Ezra L. Marler, *Golden Nuggets of Thought*, vol. 1 (1946; rep. ed., Publishers Press, 1969). A yard-sale gem, chock-full of quotes, poems, and sayings. As Marler writes, "Mental vitamins, they are, which add zest to the joy of living." I found it helpful to read and reread certain inspirational passages to lift my spirits or refocus my thoughts.

A. A. Milne, *The World of Pooh: The Complete Winnie-the-Pooh and The House at Pooh Corner*, illustrated by Ernest Shepard (rep. ed., E. P. Dutton, 1988). See entry for E. B. White, *Stuart Little*.

David K. Reynolds, *Constructive Living* (University of Hawaii Press, 1984). I got this book in the psych ward. I was required to read it and practice the exercises. Doing so helped me to see that I had choices in how I reacted to situations and how I maintained my mental state.

Seung Sahn, *Only Don't Know: Selected Teaching Letters of Zen Master Seung Sahn* (rev. ed., Shambhala, 1999). This is a series of correspondence between a Zen master and people searching for answers. The basic concept I came away with was that not knowing is preferable to knowing. In not knowing—having a beginner's mind—there is limitless potential because our minds are open to possibility.

Evelyn Underhill, *The Fruits of the Spirit* (1942; rep. ed., Morehouse Publishing, 1982). Another yard-sale gem. This collection of spiritual writings touches on everyday events, with a Christian slant. It talks a lot about love and service to others. Reading a segment of this little book is like sitting through a great sermon at church, without the aggravation of a baby crying in the third row.

E. B. White, *Stuart Little*, illustrated by Garth Williams (rep. ed., Harper Trophy, 1999). Great light reading before bed, to reassure the inner child and spark playful imagination. I sometimes read *Stuart Little* (and *Winnie-the-Pooh*) aloud to my inner Sue, as if I were her parent, putting her to bed. It soothes her.

GENERAL WORKS

Harold Bloomfield and Peter McWilliams, "How to Heal Depression." National Hopeline Network recommendation. The entire text is available free on the website: www.hypericum.com/dep/deptoc.htm.

John Cook, *How to Help Someone Who Is Depressed or Suicidal: Practical Suggestions from a Survivor* (Rubison Press, 1993). American Foundation for Suicide Prevention recommendation.

Thomas E. Ellis and Cory F. Newman, *Choosing to Live: How to Defeat Suicide Through Cognitive Therapy* (New Harbinger Publications, 1996). "A well-written book for the general public. It is filled with practical advice but remains cautious of the limitations of a self-help approach to reducing suicide risk." American Association of Suicidology recommendation.

Gillian Ford, *Listening to Your Hormones* (Prima Publishing, 1997). NHN recommendation.

Richard A. Heckler, *Waking Up, Alive: The Descent, the Suicide Attempt, and the Return to Life* (Ballantine, 1994). "A powerfully told book that traces the path from courting death to embracing life, containing stories from scores of people who attempted suicide, but did not complete." AAS recommendation.

Cait Irwin, *Conquering the Beast Within: How I Fought Depression and Won . . . and How You Can Too!* (Times Books, 1999).

Kay Redfield Jamison, *Touched with Fire: Manic-Depressive Illness and the Artistic Temperament* (Free Press, 1996).

———, *An Unquiet Mind: A Memoir of Moods and Madness* (Knopf, 1997). AFSP recommendation.

Demitri Papolos and Janice Papolos, *Overcoming Depression* (Harper & Row, 1987). AFSP recommendation.

Dr. Alvin Poussaint and Amy Alexander, *Lay My Burdens Down: Unraveling Suicide and the Mental Health Crisis Among African-Americans* (Beacon Press, 2000).

Paul Quinnett, *Suicide: The Forever Decision . . . for Those Thinking About Suicide, and for Those Who Know, Love, and Counsel Them* (Crossroads, 1997). Available in several languages. Dr. Quinnett is the president and CEO of QPR Institute.

Edwin S. Shneidman, *Definition of Suicide* (Wiley, 1985).

Bernie S. Siegel, *Peace, Love, and Healing* (rep. ed., Harper/Perennial Library, 1990).

Bryan L. Tanney, Roger Tierney, and W. Lang, *The Suicide Intervention Handbook* (Living Works Education, 1994). Deals with the basics of suicide prevention for both professionals and the general public. AAS recommendation.

ON YOUTH

David G. Fassler and Lynne S. Dumas, *"Help Me, I'm Sad": Recognizing, Treating, and Preventing Childhood and Adolescent Depression* (Penguin, 1998).

Gary Remafedi, *Death by Denial: Studies of Suicide in Gay and Lesbian Teenagers* (Alyson Publications, 1994). Focus Adolescent Services recommendation.

Michael Riera and Joseph Di Prisco, *Field Guide to the American Teenager: A Parent's Companion: Appreciating the Teenager You Live With* (Perseus Books Group, 2000). FAS recommendation.

Andrew Slaby and Lili F. Garfinkel, *No One Saw My Pain: Why Teens Kill Themselves* (Norton, 1994). AFSP recommendation.

Kate Williams, *A Parent's Guide for Suicidal and Depressed Teens: Help for Recognizing If a Child Is in Crisis and What to Do About It* (Hazelden Information and Educational Services, 1995). FAS recommendation.

ON THE ELDERLY

Erik Erikson, Joan Erikson, and Helen Krinick, *Vital Involvement in Old Age* (Norton, 1989). Center for Elderly Suicide Prevention recommendation.

Betty Friedan, *The Fountain of Age* (Simon & Schuster, 1993). CESP recommendation.

Gary Kennedy, ed., *Suicide and Depression in Late Life: Critical Issues in Treatment, Research, and Public Policy* (Wiley, 1996). CESP recommendation.

Nancy J. Osgood, *Suicide in Later Life: Recognizing the Warning Signs* (Lexington Books, 1992). "Discusses reasons for elderly suicide, describes the symptoms and warning signs, and proposes risk reduction strategies. Written for older adults, family members and caregivers, and all those who provide services for older clients/patients." AAS and CESP recommendation.

FOR PROFESSIONALS

American Association of Suicidology, *Suicide Prevention/Crisis Intervention Directory*. Compiled and updated every fall by the AAS, "this directory lists more than 600 crisis agencies in the U.S. and Canada."

Alan L. Berman and David A. Jobes, *Adolescent Suicide: Assessment and Intervention* (American Psychological Association, 1991). "Provides information relevant to theory, research, practice, and intervention. Provides practical guidance for the clinician." AAS recommendation.

David C. Clark, ed., *Clergy Response to Suicidal Persons and Their Family Members* (Exploration Press, 1993). "Interfaith resource book for the clergy and congregations. Provides basic knowledge about: theology and suicide, recognizing suicidal risk, and referral to appropriate caregivers." AAS recommendation.

G. Jacobs Douglas, M.D., *Harvard Medical School Guide to Suicide Assessment and Intervention* (Jossey-Bass, 1999). AAS recommendation.

Kay Redfield Jamison, *Night Falls Fast: Understanding Suicide* (Knopf, 1999). "Recommended [by the AAS] for all medical doctors, psychologists, psychiatrists, school administrators, and students."

Antoon A. Leenaars, Ronald W. Maris, John L. McIntosh, and Joseph Richman, *Suicide and the Older Adult* (Guilford, 1992).

David Lester, *Suicide in African Americans* (Nova Science Publishers, 1998). For practitioners, researchers, teachers, and students in psychology, psychiatry, social work, sociology, public health, and epidemiology.

Scott Poland, *Suicide Intervention in Schools* (Guilford, 1989). "Provides step-by-step guidelines for setting up and maintaining a comprehensive crisis intervention program." AAS recommendation.

Paul Quinnett, *Counseling Suicidal People: A Therapy of Hope* (QPR Institute, 2000).

Joseph Richman, *Preventing Elderly Suicide: Overcoming Personal Despair, Professional Neglect, and Social Bias* (Springer, 1993). "Written for mental health professionals and others who work with the elderly." AAS recommendation.

Edwin S. Shneidman, *The Suicidal Mind* (Oxford University Press, 1996). "Groundbreaking work presents cases that reveal the inner workings of the suicidal mind, and offers practical, explicit steps to assist in treating a suicidal individual." AAS recommendation.

———, *Comprehending Suicide: Landmarks in Twentieth-Century Suicidology* (American Psychiatric Association Books, 2001).

FOR SURVIVORS

Victoria Alexander, *In the Wake of Suicide: Stories of the People Left Behind* (Jossey-Bass, 1998). AAS recommendation.

Iris Bolton and Curtis Mitchell, *My Son, My Son . . . A Guide to Healing After Death, Loss or Suicide* (17th printing, Bolton Press, 2001). AFSP and AAS recommendation.

Trudy Carlson, *Suicide Survivor's Handbook: A Guide for the Bereaved and Those Who Wish to Help Them* (Benline Press, 1995). AFSP recommendation.

Carla Fine, *No Time to Say Good-bye: Surviving the Suicide of a Loved One* (Doubleday, 1997). AFSP and AAS recommendation.

Susan Kuklin, *Surviving Suicide: Young People Speak Up* (Putnam, 1994). AFSP recommendation.

Rebecca Parkin and Karen Dunne-Maxim, *Child Survivors of Suicide: A Guidebook for Those Who Care for Them* (AFSP, 1995).

Notes

PART 1

1. Edwin S. Shneidman, *The Suicidal Mind* (New York: Oxford University Press, 1996), pp. 97, 98.

PART 2

1. Elaine N. Marieb, *Human Anatomy and Physiology*, 4th ed. (San Francisco, Calif.: Benjamin Cummings Science Publishing, 1998), p. 363.

2. Winn Kapit and Lawrence M. Elson, *The Anatomy Coloring Book*, 2nd ed. (Glenview, Ill.: Pearson Education, 1993), p. 132.

PART 3

1. From the SafeUSA website:www.cdc.gov/safeusa/suicide.htm.

2. The entire letter by Gillian Ford can be found on the Kristin Brooks Hope Center "Live with Depression" website: www.livewithdepression.org.

3. Marieb, *Human Anatomy and Physiology*, p. 391.

PART 5

1. Shneidman, *The Suicidal Mind*, p. 4. Dr. Shneidman is the former chief of the Center for Studies of Suicide Prevention at the National Institute of Mental Health and founder of the American Association of Suicidology (AAS).

2. Edwin S. Shneidman, *Definition of Suicide* (New York: John Wiley & Sons, 1985), pp. 124-127.

3. From the Befrienders International website: www.befrienders.org.

4. Ibid.

5. Centers for Disease Control, unpublished mortality data from National Center for Health Statistics, mortality data tapes.

6. U.S. Public Health Service, "The Surgeon General's Call to Action to Prevent Suicide" (Washington, D.C.: USPHS, 1999). The entire document can be found at www.surgeongeneral.gov/library/calltoaction. The source for this particular data is L. F. McCraig and B. J. Strussman, "National Hospital Ambulatory Care Survey: 1996," in *CDC Emergency Department Summary: Advance Data from Vital and Health Statistics* 293 (Hyattsville, Md.: National Center for Health Statistics, 1997).

7. From Befrienders International website: www.befrienders.org.

8. See part 7 for website addresses. Dr. McIntosh's report, "The Suicide of Older Men and Women: How You Can Help Prevent Tragedy," can be found on the AAS website or Dr. McIntosh's homepage: www.iusb.edu/~jmcintos/homepage.html. On "The Surgeon General's Call . . . ," see part 5, note 6.

9. John L. McIntosh, "U.S.A. Suicide: 1999 Official Final Data," prepared for the American Association of Suicidology, available at www.suicidology.org.

10. From the Centers for Disease Control and Prevention (CDCP) website: www.cdc.gov/ncipe/factsheets/suifacts.htm.

11. U.S. Department of Health and Human Services, "National Strategy for Suicide Prevention: Goals and Objectives for Action," 2001. This comprehensive resource is available free by calling 1-800-789-2647, reference document number SMA 3517; and on the web at www.mentalhealth.org/suicideprevention.

12. McIntosh, 1999.

13. John L. McIntosh, "The Suicide of Older Men and Women: How You Can Help Prevent Tragedy," available at the AAS website (www.suicidology.org) or Dr. McIntosh's home page: www.iusb.edu/~jmcintos/homepage.html.

14. McIntosh, 1999.

15. Ibid.

16. John L. McIntosh, "1999 Official Final Statistics USA Suicide," prepared for the American Association of Suicidology, available at www.suicidology.org.

17. The AAS, the American Foundation for Suicide Prevention, Focus Adolescent Services, Befrienders International, Parents Against Teen Suicide, and the Centers for Disease Control and Prevention; I've also used the reports of Dr. John L. McIntosh.

Permissions

The author and publisher gratefully acknowledge permission to use selections and information from the following copyrighted materials:

The Suicidal Mind by Dr. Edwin S. Shneidman. Oxford University Press, 1996. Reprinted with the permission of Regina Ryan Publishing Enterprises, Inc., 251 Central Park West, New York, NY 10024.

Definition of Suicide by Dr. Edwin S. Shneidman. Oxford University Press, 1985. Reprinted with the permission of Regina Ryan Publishing Enterprises, Inc., 251 Central Park West, New York, NY 10024.

In God's Care: Daily Meditations on Spirituality in Recovery: As We Understand God by James Jennings, illustrated by David Spohn. Hazelden Information Education, 1996. Various quotes reprinted with permission of the Hazelden Foundation, P.O. Box 11, CO3, Center City, MN 55012-0011.

Illustration on p. 39 from *The Anatomy Coloring Book,* 2nd ed., by Wynn Kapit and Lawrence M. Elson. Copyright © 1993 by Wynn Kapit and Lawrence M. Elson. Reprinted by permission of Pearson Education, Inc.

"Step Into Your Skin" by David Wilcox. © 2001 Midnight Ocean Bonfire Music (ASCAP) and Cindy Lou My Dear (ASCAP), a division of Soroka Music Ltd. Used by permission. All rights reserved. From the CD *What You Whispered* by David Wilcox. For more information about David Wilcox and his music please visit www.davidwilcox.com.

Excerpt from *Creative Visualization* by Shakti Gawain © 1995. Reprinted with permission of New World Library, Novato, CA 94949, *www.newworldlibrary.com.* Toll-free ordering 1-800-972-6657, Ext. 52.

Merriam-Webster's Collegiate Dictionary, 10th ed. © 2001 by Merriam-Webster, Incorporated.

"Destiny" by Jeff Schwartz © 1999 New Groove Records (BMI) Used by permission. All rights reserved. From the CD *Loving Earth* by Jeff Schwartz. For more information about *Loving Earth,* visit *www.newgroove.com.*

Human Anatomy and Physiology by Elaine N. Marieb. Benjamin Cummings Science Publishing, 4th ed., 1998.

"Feelings Chart" reprinted and adapted with the permission of Judith Redding.

Index